Being Chris Hani's Daughter

Much love
Xhehela

Lindiwe Hani
& Melinda Ferguson

MF BOOKS
JOBURG

First published by MFBooks Joburg,
an imprint of Jacana Media (Pty) Ltd, in 2017

10 Orange Street
Sunnyside
Auckland Park 2092
South Africa
+2711 628 3200
www.jacana.co.za

ISBN 978-1-920601-81-2

Cover design by Shawn Paikin
Set in Sabon 11/15pt
Printed by Creda Communications
Job no. 002961

See a complete list of Jacana titles at www.jacana.co.za

*To the ultimate soldier and gentleman,
Martin Thembisile Hani, my father*

Authors' notes

"Every phrase and every sentence is an end and a beginning,
Every poem an epitaph. And any action
Is a step to the block, to the fire, down the sea's throat
Or to an illegible stone: and that is where we start.
We die with the dying:
See, they depart, and we go with them.
We are born with the dead:
See, they return, and bring us with them."

– T.S. Eliot

I was in Europe on 10 April 1993 when news of Communist Party leader, Chris Hani's bloody murder swept across international airwaves. In fact, I was in Germany. First time out of the confines of a pre-democratic South Africa, on a three-week emancipatory trip to show a film, my boyfriend at the time, Alex and I had made, at an international film festival.

I recall trying to cling to foreboding words in a language I could not understand, spewed from television screens and newspaper headlines. The pictures we watched showed the great struggle icon felled in pitiless pools of blood in his Dawn Park driveway. Many of the images we pored over were taken by *The Star*'s chief photographer Debbie Yazbek. She was the sister of my then boyfriend, Alex, who, pale-faced and anxious, sat beside me trying to establish what had happened.

I turned to strangers for help to decipher the words; we floundered, lost in translation. It seemed somehow wrong that we were on foreign soil when back home our struggle-shattered land was bleeding.

We had left South Africa so close to transition. Now this news threatened to cast the precarious negotiations into yet more bloodshed. But our land had been bleeding for years. Would this be the tipping point? Would we return to a South Africa pushed over the precipice of peace, thrown now into a devastating civil war that had been looming in the wings for what felt like a 1000 years?

We flew back home a few days later, to a country steeped in chaos.

I first met Lindiwe Hani, daughter to Chris in April 2013, almost twenty years to the day after her father's passing. I was writing a "Children of the Struggle" cover story for *True Love* magazine where I'd been working as a journalist and features editor for the last decade.

Lindiwe and I met in a restaurant in Oxford Road Rosebank, close to Thrupps where old and new money meet to buy foie gras.

I am ashamed to admit I hardly saw Lindiwe the person that day; I was far too taken with the idea that I was meeting *the* Chris Hani's daughter. The first thing I did was tell her where I was when her father was assassinated.

But I do recall how bubbly and animated she was – I was expecting to find an angry, bitter woman.

At the end of our interview, we briefly spoke about the idea of collaborating on a book on being Chris Hani's daughter, growing up in the shadow of tragedy. However, I could sense that Lindi was torn and keeping a part of herself back.

It was only much later that I discovered that back then, Lindi was deep in the midst of fighting her own demons with addiction. Being in recovery myself, at the time 14 years clean of a dark addiction to heroin, crack cocaine, dope, alcohol and any other substance that had happened to cross my path, it made total sense that, back in 2013, she was simply not ready to come clean about herself.

In October 2015 I reconnected with Lindi. Timing in telling stories, especially no-holds-barred memoirs, is everything. This time Lindi was much readier and soon the work began. It has not been an easy book to collaborate on, but then I guess nothing worthwhile is ever straightforward. In writing the book I have not only learned about Lindi and the Hani family, but hard truths about myself. As last year unfolded and the project took shape, I had a growing sense that Lindi's father was giving the book his blessing.

– Melinda Ferguson

For the longest time I dreamed of writing a book. I have a great love for reading and, after Daddy died, I would often immerse myself in amazing stories that would transport me far from my reality. The book I had in mind to write was never about my life or even that of my father's; the story that fascinated me most was the one about my mother and her sisters.

When Mel interviewed me for her *True Love* cover story back in 2013, she mentioned that perhaps I should write a book on being my father's daughter. But at that stage, deep in the clutches of addiction, I was reluctant. My biggest concern was that if I was to write this book, there would be a huge chunk of my story missing and some people would know that I was lying about my drug-fueled life.

A year into my sobriety, in late 2015, I happened to hear Mel on the radio talking about her then latest book *Crashed*. Almost immediately I reached out to her and so the book came into being. One of my character defects is that I am quite possessive, which proved to be the biggest challenge in the writing of a book about myself with another person. It was at times incredibly difficult to share certain aspects of my life. It was particularly hard to go through the journey of meeting my father's killer with Mel. There were days I simply didn't want to communicate – which must have been hell for her. Writing this book challenged me to my core. It's a book based on my memories, which were often painful. I have learned how to stand up for myself, set boundaries, but most importantly, I've learned to be kind and forgive myself.

As much as this book is about my life, it's also about family, human tragedy and, as corny as it may sound, triumph of the human spirit.

– Lindiwe Hani

Dead

"Your father's been shot."

I had woken up on Saturday, 10 April 1993, with a joyous song in my 12-year-old heart. The previous day, my mother and I had driven to the mountain kingdom of Lesotho for the Easter weekend.

My older sister Khwezi had a school social on Saturday night so Daddy had offered to stay with her at our family home in Dawn Park, Boksburg, so that he could take her to the hair salon and play taxi in his old Corolla. Khwezi was usually such a bookworm, but she had been really excited about the party.

Although I would miss being with Daddy over Easter, going to Maseru meant a sleepover with my best friend Nomathemba, whom I hadn't seen for months. From the day we set eyes on each other as energetic five-year-olds on the first day of prep school, we'd been two mischief-makers joined at the hip. We did everything together; I would either cycle to her home or she to mine where we'd play 'house-house', go to the movies or just roam the streets of Maseru. We got a huge kick out of telling strangers we were twins. It was totally believable to us as we were both high yella.

Saturdays meant we could go and watch a movie in town. I never really minded what was showing, I just loved getting lost in the dark of the cinema, transfixed as the pictures flickered up on the screen. They would transport me far away from my tightly tucked-away unruliness that came from constantly having to say goodbye to my beloved Daddy, whom we hardly ever saw for more than a few weeks a year. My father always in hiding, and my mother checking our car for bombs every morning, were simply regular events in my childhood.

Double features were my best because as the reels were changed we'd run across to Maseru Café and buy Chappies and Simba chips to eat during the next show.

My father didn't have time for movies. In fact, I hardly ever saw him switch off or relax. There was always something to do: meetings, phone calls, reading, writing – he was always busy. When we all moved to South Africa at the end of 1990, we'd go to the local video store in Boksburg, but he always waited in the car. When it came to films, he only had time for the serious stuff, like the news and documentaries. Sometimes he was even on TV, on *Agenda*, a current-affairs show presented by a man with black hair called Freek Robinson.

The morning was already warm in Maseru, despite the fact that winter was on its way. As we were getting ready to catch the mid-morning feature – along with Teboho, Nomathemba's older brother, who'd decided to invite himself along – my sister Khwezi's best friend, Palesa, and her father Ntate Maieane appeared at the door. Mr Maieane looked frantic; he immediately asked where my mother was. No one had a cellphone back in '93 so you could sometimes search the entire town before finding who you were looking for. I offered to pass on a message, but Mr Maieane insisted he needed to speak urgently to my mom, face to face. Not wanting to appear rude, I suggested he try the hair salon. But time was ticking on and we still needed to finish dressing.

I hated missing the beginning of a show, that swelling in my heart that something extraordinary was about to happen, as the lights dimmed just before the titles came up. And at this rate we would be lucky to make it in time for the end credits!

But my irritation was forgotten as we cracked jokes, finally weaving our way through the dusty streets of Polo Ground, kicking stones, taking short cuts through the houses. Then Teboho suggested we go past the Maieane household, which was right along the way, to ask Mako, his best friend, to join us.

As we approached the house, I immediately noticed my mother's Opel Rekord parked in front. I should have told Mr Maieane to try looking for her at his own house! I vaguely remember Teboho saying, "See, your mum is here! If you're so worried about us being late, maybe she can give us a lift." Knowing my mother, I responded, "Yeah right."

As I opened the gate, my cousin Pali rushed out to us, her eyes streaming with tears.

Other people began to emerge from the house. Confused, I searched desperately for my mother's face in the small crowd. The moment I saw her eyes, I knew something bad had happened. As she made her way unsteadily towards me, pale and bewildered, she did not look herself. For a moment my heart stopped.

And then those words: "Your father's been shot."

In the long echoey silence that followed, my mother's words had no meaning.

"Which hospital is he in?" My voice was small. My thoughts racing. How bad was it? Where was he shot? How?

"No," my mother made herself clear, "Daddy has been shot dead."

More words. Echoing across the silent, empty sky.

Dead?

Nothing made sense as I was bundled into the back seat of our car. Malome Jaoane, my mother's brother, was behind the wheel, my mother in the passenger seat in front. It was deathly still.

Dead. My father was dead?

I vaguely recall driving past a series of houses to collect our belongings before we left for home. Everything was a blur, moving in slow motion. Inside I was completely still.

Dead. The word kept circling through my mind, holding my thoughts hostage. I knew what dead was but surely not Daddy? Not Daddy.

He had survived so many attempts on his life. Like the car bomb from which he escaped in Maseru in 1980, the year I was born, and all the others that followed. He was stronger than anyone else in the world. He was a giant. There must have been some mistake. How could this be true? My head wrestled with itself, refusing to believe the power of that four-letter word. Dead.

The silence almost swallowed us as the car ate the tar on the long drive back to Joburg. My mother's absolute stillness was unbearable. I wanted to scream, shout, cry. But I said nothing. Perhaps it was a mistake? All we had to do was get back to Dawn Park and my strong, beautiful daddy would be there to greet us.

On the drive I vacillated between wanting desperately to get back home and choking with dread by what we may discover on our arrival. Perhaps if we didn't return to our Dawn Park home none of this would be true. My mind kept thinking of my 15-year-old sister, Khwezi, at home all by herself. How had it happened? Where exactly? I had so many questions, but my voice failed me. I couldn't talk. Just that word ... Dead. Whirling round and round in my head.

I thought of my sister discovering my dad, sitting alone with his body. All I wanted to do was see her. If I could just talk to her, I would know that there had been a mistake. That none of this was true.

But the kilometres through the darkening mountains stretched endlessly ahead.

Still no one spoke. Just the gospel tape that played our favourite soundtrack:

'Just another talk with Jesus, tell him all about your troubles.'

To this day what sticks out most for me on that drive is that song.

○

Cold reality hit when we pulled into the cul-de-sac in Dawn Park; the car could hardly weave its way through the street lined with people. They stood shoulder to shoulder, sombre sirens, their voices stretching across the dying sky of that Saturday afternoon.

Hamba kahle, Umkhonto weSizwe

Thina bant' abamnyama siz' misele ukuwabulala wona lama bhulu.

(Rest in peace, Spear of the Nation / We, black people, have dedicated ourselves to killing the Boers.)

Years later, when I recall that day, I clearly remember those shell-shocked crowds of ordinary people, standing stiff like soldiers, bidding farewell to their commander as they shouldered both sides of the street with stoic dignity and military precision.

As we made our way towards the driveway I saw the yellow police van. The dread inside my heart grew deeper.

The noise, the chaos, overwhelmed me as I was helped out of the car like an old cripple. I saw the blood as I struggled through the throngs of people, searching for my sister Khwezi. When I eventually found her, no words were needed. I could see it in her eyes: Daddy was dead.

The tears I had stifled all this time finally burst free. They were tears that would crash from my heart and that of the nation's for many years to come – bereft of our father and leader.

That night Khwezi and I huddled together in the bedroom. She kept repeating that it was all her fault, that if she hadn't been on the phone, Daddy wouldn't be dead. I tried to comfort her, saying, "Well, you would be dead too … He wouldn't have hesitated in shooting you too."

That night 'he', my father's killer, was still the unknown, the dark shadow, the Bogeyman. It would be many days later before I would comprehend that it was a mere mortal who had slain my father, my giant.

One hears about how a day can change a life completely. The day Daddy died was to change mine forever.

PART 1

The Early Years
(1980–1995)

CHAPTER 1

My name is Lindiwe Hani

I guess the best place to start a story is at the beginning. My name is Lindiwe Hani. I was born on 27 December 1980 to Limpho and Thembisile Hani. My father was also known as Chris. My parents named me Lindiwe, which in isiXhosa means 'the daughter we have waited for'. In that year – a leap year – the world's population sat at 4 434 682 000, the *Voyager 1* space probe confirmed the existence of a moon of Saturn that was to be named Janus (or Janusz) – how's that for prophetic – and Robert Mugabe was elected president of Zimbabwe.

I made my grand entrance into this world in the small village of Roma in Lesotho, at around 6pm. Apparently I slipped out of my mother's womb after a mere two hours of labour. I grew up hearing my mother tell of how my birth was by far the easiest of all her three girls. By all accounts, from those who knew me, this easy birth set the stage for me to shine as a sweet, lovable toddler.

I was the last-born Hani daughter, after my eldest sister, Neo Phakama, who was nine years older than me, and my middle sister, Nomakhwezi Lerato, who was two years older. Nomakhwezi would come to be known simply as Khwezi. According to my mother, the births of her first- and second-born were excruciatingly long in labour. She would often tell us that Khwezi was a mother's nightmare and cried for the smallest of things. So by the time I appeared, Mama was well and truly exhausted. Luckily, I rewarded her by being one of those contented babies who hardly ever cried and slept a lot. I was often told that as a baby I didn't even mind lying in my own faeces. (Anyone who didn't know my usually highly attentive mother could easily have put it down to child neglect!) The story goes that Daddy, who lived with us until I was almost two, came home one day and enquired, "How is the baby?" Startled, my mother – who was clearly exhausted, pushed to the limits from having three young children to tend to – jumped up in fright and went to check. She had forgotten all about me. I was happily playing in my crib at the back of the house in my thoroughly soiled nappy. That day my cot was moved permanently into the kitchen.

Daddy met Mama in 1973, seven years before I arrived. I loved hearing the story of how Uncle Jaoane, Mama's older brother, played matchmaker. He had met my future dad at a political meeting in Botswana, and when he heard Daddy was off to Zambia, Uncle Jaoane asked him to take a handwritten note to his sister Limpho, who was attending a tourist conference there.

The story goes that for my parents it was love at first sight. They began dating, even though Daddy was on the move a lot, and within a year they were married. They didn't have a big wedding; they simply went to a court in Zambia and tied the knot. My parents soon moved to Lesotho along with baby Neo, and Khwezi came along in 1978.

While my oldest sister Ausi Neo – or Momo, as she was affectionately known in the family – was my protector, Khwezi and I were like two she-cats at war. Due to the big age gap, Momo was often tasked with babysitting the two of us. It was more like having to play referee. Khwezi was the proverbial pain in my young behind. Because she was older than me, she often teased me about not being able to read like she could. When it came to having an argument, Khwezi was superior on every level, winning every debate and dishing out words like blows. She would often mock me by calling me 'test-tube baby' – of course, I had no idea what a test-tube baby was, I just knew it must be bad. Her teasing would send me into a flurry of tears, wailing my little head off, asking Mama, "What is a test-tube baby? Am I a test-tube baby?"

I remember one particular day when Momo was watching over us; I must have been about six. I was enthralled by cartoons on TV when Khwezi came in and snatched the remote. One of her outstanding traits was being a prolific TV-remote bully. Naturally, chaos ensued, with me screeching my little head off. Momo had had enough. She purposefully walked towards Khwezi, grabbed her skinny arm, marched her to the balcony and proceeded to hang her upside down from her feet, all the while telling her that if she didn't stop bullying me, she would be dropped from the second floor. I stood in shocked awe and, of course, glee that my nemesis might finally be silenced.

As so many addicts seem to experience, I think I was born with a feeling of being lesser than. I often felt that Khwezi was Mama's favourite and Momo Daddy's. I envied Momo because she had lived longer with my father than any of us and he had taught her many exciting skills, like being able to swim. I was never overlooked or neglected, but I definitely had this feeling of being less loved, a complex I would carry with me into adulthood and often use as an excuse to get drunk and high.

While our mother loved and took great pride in us, she was also very strict; she was notorious for her temper and, like most mothers in those days, didn't hesitate to dish out smacks. As a weapon of choice, she would grab whatever was in range, be it a dishcloth, a wooden spoon, or even a skaftini. My absolute worst punishment was when she instructed us to "go pick a stick so I can beat you". This entailed a long, fear-filled walk to the garden to find the right stick. One could not be complacent in one's own punishment; you had to make sure you didn't pick some flimsy twig, or Mama would get her own weapon, which would invariably be twice as big and lethal as the pathetic one you'd chosen. But you also didn't want to make the mistake of choosing the biggest one either, in case she settled for something smaller.

From the outset, Daddy was totally against smacking. I remember sitting with him one evening, when he asked me how I was doing and, without thinking twice, I told him I'd received a thrashing from Mama. He immediately left the room to speak to her. All I know is that after that conversation we never got another hiding again. Much later my mother told me that Daddy had warned her, "If you ever touch my children again, I will kill you." The threat from a soldier trained by uMkhonto we Sizwe (MK) clearly worked.

While Daddy did not believe in corporal punishment at all, in a lot of ways his form of discipline was far worse. He would sit you down, sternly tell you how unacceptable your behaviour was and how extremely disappointed he was in you. His strong words had the ability to cut right to the heart and invariably produced the intended results.

Although Mama's whippings stopped, she was also extremely gifted in the area of verbal discipline. We got yelled at a lot. Her go-to admonishment was always how ungrateful we kids were and how hard it was raising us on her own. I learned to backchat pretty early on and so my stroppy self would answer back: "Well, we didn't ask to be born!" I'm sure those were the times she really wished she could have given me a mighty backhand.

I was a mischievous child and went through a stage where I loved to play with matches. I'm not sure if I could have been labelled a full-blown pyromaniac but I was clearly fascinated by fire. I could spend hours watching as the orange flame devoured the stick until it almost singed my little fingers. At the very last second, as I felt the heat on my skin, I would unceremoniously drop the match.

And so the inevitable came to pass ... Mama had just installed brand-new wall-to-wall carpets in the bedrooms and, as usual, I was playing with matches in our room when one singed my stubby little fingers. When I dropped it, the flame burned a deep hole in the new carpet. Instead of stopping, however, I thought it a great idea to continue my game in Mama's room. Shock and horror – it happened again. Now what was a six-year-old girl to do? Well,

I did what probably any other little girl would and kept dead quiet. Mama came home from work to find these burned holes in not one, but two of her new carpets. Naturally, my perfectionist mother went ballistic. She called all of us into the room and asked who had done it. Of course, Momo and Khwezi denied it – and I was so terrified that I denied it too. Well, somebody must have done it, said Mama. Still, no one said a word. To my sisters' credit, they didn't rat me out. So Mama punished all three of us and we had a good hour, if not more, of tongue-lashing.

Later, I would grow to understand the stresses our mother must have been under, which helped explain her notorious temper. She wore many caps, from being a single mother – even before Daddy was killed because he was away in exile for so much of our lives – to dodging bombs and bullets, all the while trying to raise three energetic, opinionated girls. She also had the added pressure of having to be a dutiful daughter to both sides of the family. Growing up, I was caught up in my own world, unaware of the burdens she shouldered. As I grew older, I would come to appreciate how extremely fortunate I was in my upbringing because my mother was an excellent homemaker – lawd, she could cook and bake! My favourite day was Sunday when Mama would begin baking treats for the week. There'd be scones, cakes, mince pies and, my favourite, apple pie.

Birthdays and Christmas were a huge deal in our family. On your birthday you'd be woken up with the whole family singing, treating the birthday girl to breakfast in bed, surrounded by a pile of presents to be opened in front of everyone. To top it off, there was always a big party to which all your friends would be invited. Mama, the gifted homemaker, would of course do everything herself, including baking the birthday cake and making treats like jelly in orange casings.

Christmas was the same, a huge affair with detailed planning and thorough execution. On Christmas Day we would wake up and run to the lounge to find presents delivered by Father Christmas under the Christmas tree. I remember asking her one Christmas, "How does Father Christmas come because we have

7

no chimney?" Without missing a beat, she responded, "Via the TV antenna." I was sold.

Funnily enough, even though our father was away so much, and although I missed the physical everydayness of him intensely, he was always there. He would phone almost daily, and we'd all have a chance to talk to him. I would breathlessly narrate my day, filled with "and then, and then" to which he would listen lovingly and patiently. Wherever he happened to be, be it Russia, Mozambique or Zambia, there were phone calls for birthdays, Father's Day and Christmas Day. And of course our report cards were always sent to him. Heaven help you if you didn't do well. Stern 'talking-to's could go on for what felt like hours. He was such a huge presence in our lives that even when we misbehaved, as soon as Mama said "I'm going to tell your father" there would be instant about-turn in our behaviour. For at least an hour.

The only thing we could never ask him was where he was at any given time; we learned that from the start.

Although we lived in a few different places in Maseru, the one I most clearly remember is Devcourt, where we stayed from 1983 to 1990.

Devcourt comprised two blocks of white-painted flats on one property. We were very close to the city centre and within walking distance from school. Behind the block of flats was rugged terrain, while on one side a huge garden spread out, with the most majestic willow tree.

Devcourt felt like living among an extended family. We were a very tight-knit community where neighbours knew each other by name and looked out for each other. There were so many kids living in the flats that during holidays and weekends I would leave home immediately after breakfast to join my gang of friends. The extent of our little tribe was when we all decided that we would orchestrate a mock wedding; Khwezi was betrothed to a neighbour Tau Tlabere. All the adults pitched in and the happy couple was even bought a suit and a white dress, plus there was food and ululations throughout that day.

My mother's only rule was that you always had to be back for all meals and get your butt into the house before the streetlights came on. Most days I would come back purple-streaked from pilfering the blueberries next door, which we managed to steal by scaling the wall and returning with laps full of our sweet, sticky treasures. I remember one year one of our neighbours requesting some blueberries; in exchange she would make us a pie. This mission was incredibly tricky as we had to make sure that we were not caught by the owner or our curmudgeon of a caretaker, Ntate Baxtin. The grief we gave that poor man will probably come back to haunt me one day, but at that time tormenting Ntate was what gave meaning to our lives. We loved hiding in the stairwell and screaming our lungs off, waiting for him to hear us. As soon as we heard him coming, we'd scamper off as he angrily gave chase.

When not driving Ntate Baxtin crazy, we would play house-house. Sadly for me, being the youngest, I was always given the rather unenviable role of being 'child' when all I wanted to do was to graduate to being 'wife' and 'mother'.

We would sneak food from the house and combine it with leaves, mix them up and arrange the mush in little silver tins, make a fire and cook it. It was paradise to play kick-the-can or hide-and-seek, or flatten cardboard boxes and slide down the hill. I was always filthy on my return home and most of the time my Goddess-of-Clean mother would make me strip at the door so as not to track my nastiness through the house.

Once there was a huge fire in the adjacent block of flats, forcing us to evacuate in the middle of the night. I remember watching from across the street, transfixed by the giant orange flames as they engulfed one entire section of the block, but really thankful that all of us had made it out okay.

Summer was my favourite time in Maseru. Mama would go to the Gatti's factory and buy boxes of sticky-sweet ice cream and ice lollies, which cooled us down in the boiling 30-plus-degree temperatures in the capital.

We would walk or ride our BMXs to the Maseru club and swim the entire day, eating hot chips for lunch while lying on the steaming concrete paving around the pool. These were the milk-

and-honey days of my childhood. Then there were the long drives out to Molimo-Nthuse, a small town in western Lesotho, which in English means "God help us". The harrowing drive up the steep, endlessly winding mountain pass, where the roads were so narrow that it felt that we would fall off the edge of the world, still remains clearly carved in my memory today. The final destination always took my breath away: the hotel's main building in the shape of a Basotho hat perched on stilts, surrounded by rivers and trees around which we would laze and enjoy picnics with our family and friends. As a child, I harboured ideas of buying that place and living there one day when I grew up. I still get pangs of longing to do that today.

I was an exuberant, busy child, not to mention helluva talkative. I remember my first day of nursery school vividly. I was placed into Mrs Da Silva's class at the Montessori school, the same one Khwezi had attended. Within minutes, as Mrs Da Silva greeted with "Good morning, children", I was in trouble. For some reason, I thought it would be hilarious to mimic her and repeated, "Good morning, children" in a mock teacher's voice. Needless to say, she did not find me very amusing and called my mother to take me home immediately.

After a year with the overly serious Mrs Da Silva, I was enrolled at Maseru English Medium Preparatory School (MEMPS), or 'Prep', as we called it. Once again I was following the Great Khwezi legacy, floundering in her huge shadow. My clever and talented sister was a model student and the teachers were not shy at expressing their hope that I would prove to be as exemplary as she was. *Ha!* I was definitely not as studious and way more talkative, but I like to believe that what I lacked in scholastic discipline I more than made up for in cuteness and my fun-loving demeanour. On my first day in Class 1 at Prep, I was put in Mrs Lee's class. She was a slim Irish woman with short brown hair; I loved her kindness and was especially mesmerised by her lilting accent. Within the first few hours, I made fast friends with Nomathemba Mhlanga, who would be my best friend throughout my entire school career.

On Saturdays, I loved getting ten Maluti from Mama and

meeting my group of friends in town. Much to my horror, Khwezi often tagged along. We would buy tickets for the double feature, and during the reel change, before the second feature began, we'd walk across to the Maseru Café for snacks. After movies, Khwezi and I loved to go to the local mall, the LNDC centre, where we'd wander round the CNA, picking up comics for the week. Once we'd each had our fill, we'd swap them, so she'd buy *Archie* and I'd get *Betty & Veronica*.

Prep was a multiracial international school and from day one I was totally colour blind – I never felt any prejudice and didn't even know at this stage what racism was or that we were geographically positioned in the middle of the bastion of segregation, South Africa. Until I actually saw it on a map, I thought that South Africa was some dangerous, faraway country 'Overseas', a place that we as a family were forbidden to enter, but this had no direct bearing on my young life. In fact, in my world, South Africa, Zambia or Russia – any place that wasn't Lesotho – were all conveniently labelled 'Overseas'.

Oblivious to the real dynamics at play in the country of my father's birth, I attended school in my green-and-white checked tunic and went about my days in Maseru with the innocence of an ordinary child.

In retrospect, there were clues that maybe all was not as it appeared to be. Each morning, before driving us to school, Mama would make us stand a few metres away from our green Toyota Corolla, while she systematically opened the bonnet and then checked underneath before finally turning the ignition. It only dawned on me years later that she was checking for bombs, that our lives were under constant threat.

At the time, I believed that this was how all families began their days. I was completely confused one day when I tried to open a package of books that had been sent to me after I joined a book club in some magazine. Before I could get to my precious stash, my mother grabbed it out of my hands and tossed it off the second-floor balcony. I watched in complete disbelief, horrified by her sabotage of my treasure. Little did I know that she was expecting an explosion, a *Boom!* as it hit the ground. Thank the mother of all dragons, it simply hit the pavement below with a thud. I shot her as angry a look as my eight-year-old self could muster, then stalked downstairs to retrieve my books.

Years later I would understand that these were the consequences of being connected to one of South Africa's most wanted 'terrorists'.

Before Daddy was killed in 1993, he had had a number of death threats and lived through many attempts on his life. I would only really get to discover these things about him in the years after he was no longer with us, when I was obsessed with discovering everything I could about my father.

In 1981, in the year after I was born, a bomb was planted in Daddy's car in Maseru, but for some reason it failed to go off. A few months later Daddy's trusted driver, a man by the name of Sizwe Kondile, was abducted by the South African security police while driving my father's car just outside Bloemfontein. Always loyal to Daddy, he refused to divulge any information about my father's whereabouts despite being badly tortured. When they realised they could get nothing out of him, he was drugged and shot dead close to the Mozambican border.

A year later, on 2 August 1982, there was another car-bomb attempt on Daddy's life, but this time the bomb exploded in the hands of the would-be assassin, a man by the name of Ernest Ramatolo, before he could get to Daddy. Less than four months later, in December 1982, the Lesotho Raids would target our entire family. After the Raids, Daddy was forced to relocate to Lusaka.

Over the following years, from the end of 1982 right until 1990, Daddy was not a permanent fixture in our lives because, over those eight-or-so years, he was based 'Overseas'. Most of the time we would only see him once a year during our July holidays. I accepted this as normal as this was all I'd ever known. I would only come to terms with the sense of loss and abandonment much later in my life. As a child, you adapt to what is given to you and we simply got used to my father not being around.

Despite Daddy not being there physically, I had what seemed like a pretty idyllic childhood. There were times in the early years after the Lesotho Raid that my parents discussed relocating us to Zambia to be closer to my father. They finally decided that it was best that we were raised in Maseru because that was where Mama had been born; her entire family still lived there, providing us stability and support as we grew up.

As a result, we were very close to Mama's family. One of my favourite places to visit was the home of our maternal grandfather, Ntatemoholo Sekamane. His garden was something out of a picture book, with a mini vineyard bursting full of plump grapes and the most amazing orange and peach trees. But heaven help you if you didn't ask permission before picking the fruit. He was tall with very short hair and startling blue eyes. From the time I could remember, he walked with a cane due to the arthritis in his knee. Every time I asked him why he had such blue eyes he would glare at me and hiss 'Voetsek!', vehemently reluctant to discuss his lineage. Only later, through the family grapevine, I came to learn that his father was Scottish and his mother a Mosotho woman. In those early years, I resented the fact that I hadn't inherited my mother's green or his blue eyes. The home of my aunt Maseme – whom we affectionately called Sammy – was also a place of refuge for me; she too had a large luscious garden where I could lose myself for hours in a world of make believe.

I was always a child with a vivid imagination who loved to play dress up in my older cousin Pali's sophisticated clothes. I was obsessed with her high heels. I loved getting lost in a fantasy world where I was either a princess or a lawyer. The scenario would invariably entail me meeting the love of my life, getting married and having a whole batch of children.

But my perfect world was rudely interrupted when Pali gave birth to a little boy, Tsitso. He was the first baby in the family after me, which really put my nose out of joint. Suddenly I was no longer 'the baby', the focus of the family. My princess life changed dramatically when little Tsitso came to live with us because suddenly everything belonged to this imposter. "Don't make a noise, the baby is sleeping", "Don't eat that Purity, it's for the baby". Dethroned, I went out of my way to eat all the blasted

Purity with a vengeance.

At the age of nine, long past my terrible twos, I suddenly became a tantrum thrower of note – in direct competition with Tsitso, who had graduated to toddler status. I was convinced that he was trying to take me out when one afternoon, this dangerous one-year-old intruder bashed me on the head with the end of a heavily weighted curtain rail. Somehow, he had managed to grasp it in his chubby hands, draw his arms back and bring it down with incredible force against the side of my head. Naturally, I took full dramatic advantage of my injury, wailing at the top of my voice – only to be told by the adults that he was "just a baby" and that it was "only an accident". Sure! All I could see was his demonic smirk.

And yet, despite my run-ins with the toddler and Khwezi, when I recall my otherwise sheltered childhood, the best decision my parents ever made was having us grow up in Lesotho.

CHAPTER 2

Less idyllic

S elective memory has a way of whitewashing details. There were naturally less-idyllic experiences in my childhood, like those times when we had to steal out of our home in the middle of the night, cruelly woken out of deep sleep in the middle of a dream, and hastily bustled off to my aunt Sammy or Ntatemoholo Sekamane's houses. Our exodus would usually start with Mama, having heard whispers that we were the target of a possible SADF raid, shaking us awake and telling us that we needed to pack our things quickly. Without fail, each time it happened, it was a huge disruption of our safe, cosy world.

These panicked pack-ups happened quite regularly until one day Khwezi simply put her foot down and refused to leave the house. There was no drama, no shouting; she just dug her heels in and said, "No." There was nothing Mama could do to convince my sister otherwise. The rest of the night was spent lying in bed, eyes fixed to the ceiling in terror, waiting for an attack in the dark, until morning dawned only to discover we were all still alive. After Khwezi's night of resistance, we didn't leave as often as before, unless Mama really insisted.

Although I tried to erase them from my thoughts, preferring to live in the rose-tinted land of my fantasy world, in the back of my mind my mother's fears played havoc, for I knew they were based on real evidence of how seriously the SADF wanted to see the destruction of Chris Hani's family.

Only a few years earlier, we had survived a very real attack. I was too young to have known what sinister forces were really at play, but the incident had a traumatic effect on our mother. Although I have hardly any real memories of that night, it would become one of the strongest story threads in my life, told over and over throughout the years to come.

Two weeks before I turned two, on 9 December 1982, the Lesotho Raids took place between 00:30am and 05:30am in Maseru. At the time, we were staying in Letsei flats, in the centre of the capital. In the dead of night, while the rest of the world slept, special forces from the South African Defence Force used helicopters to drop off a load of guns, grenades and explosives in Maseru. They were on a deadly mission to look for ANC comrades, or so-called 'terrorists'. Our family was one of the main targets.

At the time of the attack, we were all fast asleep, unaware of the bloodshed that was raging outside. When the SADF came for us they approached the old guard who was on night duty downstairs, demanding information on the whereabouts of the Hani family.

The guard had been an ANC cadre who had fallen ill and, when nobody would take him in, Mama had brought him into our home and nursed him back to health. That fateful night, terrified but steadfastly loyal to our family, he saved all our lives when he told the group of soldiers that we lived in number 303, instead of our actual flat, number 302. By this point the terrible sounds of the attack erupting had woken us all. Petrified, we huddled together, Mama, my two sisters and me, cowering under the bed. The chaos outside reverberated as though the killers were right there inside our flat. We lay in terror as they stormed flat 303, bashing down the neighbour's door. Then we heard the desperate screams of the woman as she was shot dead. My little mind back then could not process the horror she must have gone through.

When I was older I was told how, the following night, Pik Botha went on South African national TV to state that the SADF had killed Chris Hani's wife. It was clear that the South African government would have loved to have seen Mama and us, the wife and children of one of South Africa's most hated terrorists, dead. Although I could hardly comprehend the complexities, my almost two-year-old self subconsciously understood something about the closeness of death that night.

The details of the attack soon spread throughout the usually vibrant streets of Maseru, which had now fallen deathly quiet, like a cemetery. During the raid the SADF had massacred 12 local civilians, killing 30 South Africans, and leaving hundreds of homes bombed and gutted. The massacre would also become known as Operation Blanket because, during the attack, some people were wrapped in blankets by SADF officials and set on fire. The idea of people burning to death, wrapped in the very thing that was normally used as protection and comfort, haunted me for years.

As soon as light broke, Mama, grey-faced and shaken, gathered us together and, along with a few suitcases containing some of our belongings, we took the first flight out of Lesotho to Zambia via Mozambique. Mama soon returned to Lesotho to be with Momo who was at school there and left Khwezi and me in Lusaka where we stayed with our Aunty Margaret, an ANC family friend. I remember crying a little as Mama said goodbye, but we were soon distracted by being loved and spoilt by Aunty Margaret. When our mother eventually returned a whole year later, apparently I did not recognise her! By that stage we were speaking fluent Nyanja.

CHAPTER 3

My fantasy Huxtable world

Reality was not a street I liked to play on much. So when *The Cosby Show* came to Lesotho via the SABC I found my alter ego in Rudy Huxtable. I truly believed that Rudy was the girl I was meant to be – so much so that I emulated everything about her, especially the way she spoke. First prize of course would have been having her hair. She had this amazing full head of hair, which she often wore bunched up in two cute little plaits. Since mine grew like tufts of pubic hair, I was forced to watch hers on the little television screen in envy. It didn't help that Mama had decided to shave my hair when I was three to punish me for not combing it. For years I carried a deep resentment.

I was constantly mimicking Rudy, so I decided that it would be a grand idea to answer the phone just like her, "Cosby residence, hello," but I substituted it with, "Hani residence, hello." Well, that happened only once before my mother snatched the receiver out of my hand, slammed down the phone and told me in no uncertain terms to *never* tell people whose house this was. She proceeded to lecture me that if people ever asked, "Who am I speaking to?" I was to respond with, "Who would you like to speak to?" You would think I would have asked her why, right? Nope, not me;

once again I just went with it and again chalked it up to "this is how all families are".

I was told by my parents that the reason we didn't live together as a family was because my father was working 'Overseas'. I'm sure they probably explained to me what my father actually did because my older sisters knew, but I just could not get it. As a result, when asked at school what my dad did for a living, depending on the day, my father would either be a lawyer or a doctor, obviously like Dr Cliff Huxtable – I mean, the similarities were obvious: Daddy even wore those wildly patterned jerseys.

Prep, the school I attended, followed the American system, which saw us breaking for the 'summer' holidays, except with us being in the southern hemisphere, these holidays fell over winter in Lesotho.

It was during these months that we usually travelled to visit Daddy wherever he was working at that particular time. I loved most things about travelling, from the waking up early, to the drive to the airport, to boarding the plane, excited for the moment that the plane would start slowly down the runway, then gather speed as it took off. It was the flying part that I dreaded because most of the planes we flew in weren't sleek jets or 747s. We would depart from Moshoeshoe II airport in some rickety metal contraption that shuddered and shook as it slowly lifted into the sky. I felt that at any moment it would either fall apart or we'd crash into the mountains we flew so perilously close to. We would usually stop in Botswana for a layover and then board for Lusaka where we'd be reunited with Daddy.

Flying Zambian Airways was always much more exciting as these were bigger planes with proper air hostesses in snazzy uniforms. Plus, on these flights we always got a meal. For a long time I felt like there were no more glamorous women in the world than air hostesses and for years I fostered the idea of becoming one. What better profession could there be than a job that entailed looking outrageously glamorous while spending most of your life on a plane, flying to exotic places?

I remember the anticipation and relief in the moments just

before the plane landed, then waiting for it to park before we were allowed to disembark. By this stage I could hardly contain myself. Once we'd collected our bags off the conveyor belt, and we were through the Arrivals door, my eyes would be on super high alert, darting around like some firefly, trying to find Daddy's face in the waiting crowd. As soon as I spotted my target, I would sprint like hell and literally take off like a little plane into his arms.

I was a Daddy's girl through and through. He was so tall and strong that when I was with him I felt the absolute definition of pure safety, like nothing bad could ever happen to any of us. My admiration for Daddy was so intense when I was young that whatever he did I would be right there copying him. When he'd lie on the bed and read the newspaper, there I'd be, mimicking his every action, reading my own paper – except mine was invariably upside down.

When we visited Daddy in Zambia, we didn't always go to the same house because Daddy moved around a lot, but there are two houses that stand out in my memory. The first was a small one in Lusaka's version of a township; it had only two bedrooms, one communal area and a kitchen. He never lived alone but when we arrived to visit, the comrades would move out so we could stay together as a family. The second house was in a much smarter suburb in Lusaka called Woodlands. I loved this house; it had a huge garden and in my little eyes it was the biggest space I'd ever lived in. It had a tall wall with glass shards jutting out on top, clearly to deter criminals or intruders. But what I remember most are the vicious dogs that made our lives hell by eating anything we left lying around, from books to food to shoes. When we complained to Daddy, his standard response was, "Well, don't leave your things lying around." It was that simple to him.

From as early as I can remember, Daddy was a fitness fanatic. No matter where he was, he would wake up early every morning to work out. When I managed to wake up early enough, I would attempt to do all the exercises with him, while wearing his huge gown – overcompensating much? Then, once a year during the school holidays, there were the rare times we spent as a real family, where the father kisses the family goodbye in the morning to go off to work while we stayed home, or went to the market, visited friends and then all congregated in the evening to eat supper together. I loved these precious times, when we were just the normal Hanis. It felt just like we were the Huxtables.

But sometimes something would happen to jolt me out of my *Cosby Show* la-la land, like the time that Daddy, clearly without thinking, asked one of us to fetch his gun. You know, normal stuff, just as all fathers do. Khwezi and I both went barrelling out of the room to fetch it, vying with each other as to who would get it first. As we grabbed it simultaneously, Mama walked in to find us wrestling back and forth, tugging at a dangerous weapon, screaming at the top of our lungs, "No, I'll give it to him! I will!"

After picking her jaw up from the floor, she grabbed the weapon, smacked us both on our heads, and severely berated my father for his carelessness. Needless to say, that was one errand we were never asked to do again.

During our big mid-year holiday we would go off on mini holidays as a family. I particularly loved the road trips where we'd travel together to the Victoria Falls. There's a photograph of me and Daddy standing close to the thundering falls, him wearing a blue sweatshirt and me in my multicoloured checked shirt. I remember the roaring sound of the water, me clinging to my father, both terrified and excited, while nursing a cut on my hand, which stung like crazy as the powerful spray from the falls drenched us.

One Christmas, I was probably five or six years old, my mother – sorry, Father Christmas – gave me a black baby doll similar to what we know today as Baby Borns. I fell completely in love with this doll, who for some odd reason I christened George. George had to be constantly changed and fed, and I annoyed just about everybody around me, insisting that they babysit. I told Daddy all about George every time he called and, naturally, the next holiday that we saw Daddy, George was taken along to meet Grandpa. Upon arrival in Lusaka, I immediately hoisted George up to Daddy and, to his credit, he acted elated to meet his first grandchild.

There was a day during that week that we had to go out for the whole day and I insisted Daddy look after George while we were out. He tried to explain to me that he had meetings all day and he wasn't sure whether he could give George his full attention. I promptly insisted that he should take his grandchild along with him. So that's exactly what my sweet father did. As he got ready to leave the house, he carried George in his arms, much to my delight. Up to this day I'm not sure whether George was left in the car when he met with the comrades – all I know is that George left the house in his grandfather's arms. What a guy, my dad.

$$\bigcirc$$

I was around six or seven years old when we went overseas with Daddy for the first time, really *over the seas*, I mean. Flying to East Germany, part of Soviet Russia, was by far the longest trip I had ever been on.

Daddy's ties with the Soviets were strong. He had gone into exile to the Soviet Union in 1963, long before I was born. Along with 30 MK cadres, he initially went for six months' military training but that was extended to a year when many of his comrades were arrested on Liliesleaf Farm back in South Africa. In 1974 Daddy went back to that part of the world, to East Germany, for three months' military training.

Taking off from the little airport in Maseru on a rickety old plane, then flying to Zambia to meet Daddy, who was waiting for us, to head off in a huge plane, all together as a family over the huge continent of Africa to East Europe, took what felt like forever! What I remember most was the sweet fragrance of summer in Eastern Europe.

On another trip, we went to the seaside on the Baltic, with my parents and Uncle Thabo and Aunt Zanele. I absolutely loved staying in that hotel, which had a glass elevator. My sister Neo and Aunty Zanele really hit it off that holiday, spending hours together doing keep-fit exercises to Jane Fonda videos.

I can still smell the freshly baked bread that seemed to waft from every part of the hotel. I adored spending time with my father, playing in the water alongside him as he swam, and mischievously pressing all the buttons of the elevator just because I could. I can't remember being quite as carefree and happy as on that holiday.

Then there was the holiday with Daddy when we flew all the way to Russia, where my love affair with collecting teddy bears began, and the rides in Gorky Park spun in my memory long after the holiday ended.

But the highlight of that trip was viewing Lenin's body displayed in Moscow. We queued in Red Square among hundreds of tourists for what felt like an eternity. I had no idea what we were waiting for, but when I stood in front of the glass coffin I remember that sense of utter amazement. Lenin had died in 1924 at the age of 53, but almost 70 years later his body was still perfectly preserved. It was such a powerful sensation; I just knew that I was witnessing something great. Who would have known that fewer than six years later, I would be standing in front of my own father's coffin lying in state.

It was such an anti-climax going back home to Lesotho, leaving behind all the exoticism, the new tastes and landscapes of Russia. Home and Maseru meant returning to school, which was a depressing thought on its own. But much more than the onset of school, after spending six whole weeks with Daddy, watching him leave us again left me totally bereft. I had learned to accept that greetings and partings were just the way of our existence and somehow I knew life would carry on regardless.

The year that I turned nine Daddy came to visit us at home in Maseru. I waited at the entrance of Devcourt for what seemed like hours, scanning every vehicle that happened to drive past or stop to see if I could spot his car. When his dark sedan eventually drove through the entrance I began screaming like a banshee while sprinting behind it. The next day was school, and the thrill that my father was going to take me to school for the first time in my life was more than I could bear. I wanted to show him everything, but more importantly I wanted to show him off to all my peers and teachers. In fact, I was hoping that the entire school would notice Daddy by my side – that's how proud I was of him. All the other kids at school had fathers and mothers who lived together, and now it was my turn to have my perfect little Huxtable family.

That Saturday Prep was holding its inter-house school cross-country races and thereafter the parents were expected to participate. I ran my race as fast as my little legs could carry me, managing to come either first or second. But the price that I paid for my blind enthusiasm was not pacing myself, so I stood for a good 15 minutes after the race, panting like a wild dog, trying to catch my breath. But seeing Daddy bursting with pride made every rasping breath worth it.

Naturally, being the fitness fiend that he was, when Daddy ran the parents' race, he came in first. As I watched him take the lead, I screamed myself hoarse, "*Go, Daddy!*" from the sides. I don't think I had ever experienced a prouder moment.

All too soon, the precious time with Daddy flew by and, without warning, the dreaded moment arrived to say goodbye. Somehow this time felt different, because this time I was not saying goodbye to him in some foreign land. For the first time in my life, since the Lesotho Raids, when I was barely two years old, he had entered the very centre of our existence. Briefly, I had felt the unguarded joy of having him live with us and how it felt to have a father as part of our daily lives. And now he was leaving.

CHAPTER 4

Daddy

Over the years many people have asked me what it was like having Chris Hani as my father.

I believe every little girl, if she is lucky, considers her father her hero. I was no exception. I didn't realise that my father was *the* Chris Hani until after he died. To me, he was just Daddy. Yes, I acknowledge he didn't live with us like so many of my friends' fathers did with them, but that made no difference to me. This was our lived existence. I knew no other way.

Most people find it absurd that, as a child, I didn't know that my father was an exceptional freedom fighter. That's because my parents succeeded in making sure that I had the most normal childhood I could possibly have. My father made sure to phone us and speak to each one of his daughters while he was in exile. The conversations were never about world affairs. Instead, I would tell him that I came first in a race or that there was a girl at school who was bullying me. Not matter what I chose to tell my father, he would listen intently and give me advice as though I was discussing the freedom of Nelson Mandela. I now realise that that's one of the reasons he is one of the most beloved leaders of the struggle – his capacity to listen to every problem as though his life depended on it.

I often wish I had asked Daddy more about his experiences as a boy, when he was growing up in South Africa. If I'd known I would not have him around for much longer, I would have grabbed every hour we had together, to find out about his childhood home and family, what inspired him as a boy growing up in a small village, and what he dreamed about when he went to sleep at night under the huge black sky.

What I do know is that my father arrived on this earth on 28 June 1942 in the tiny rural Eastern Cape village of Sabalele in Cofimvaba, about 200 kilometres from East London. It was the same year that the first *Archie* comics were published, there were race riots in Harlem, New York, and Jews in European Nazi-occupied territories were ordered to wear a yellow Star of David.

Daddy was christened Martin Thembisile Hani, but later decided to give himself the name Chris, which was actually the name of his younger brother. His father, my paternal grandfather, Gilbert Hani, was, according to Daddy, a man who would love to have been educated but was instead a semi-literate migrant worker on the mines in the old Transvaal. My grandfather later found low-paying work as an unskilled worker in the building industry, as well as trying to eke out a living as a hawker. Daddy hardly ever saw his father, who was away from home most of the year, struggling to make a pittance.

While Daddy's family – his brothers Uncle Victor and Uncle Chris and his mother, Nomayisa Hani – continued to live in Cofimvaba, my grandfather, whom I grew up knowing as Tamkhulu, moved to Mafeteng, about 76 kilometres south of Maseru. Mafeteng literally means 'The Place of the Passers-by'.

Occasionally, Mama would take us to visit him but I always dreaded it because I truly disliked the woman he lived with, the one who turned out not to be my grandmother, as I had thought – a fact I only found out a few years after I had met her. I found her very harsh and abrasive, not warm and loving, the way I imagined a grandmother should be. This, I believed, was a bone of contention between father and son.

So when it was announced it was time to take a trip to Mafeteng, I went into total whinge and protest mode. Weirdly, Tamkhulu – much like my maternal grandfather Ntatemoholo Sekamane, who had blue eyes – had green eyes and was light skinned. He always wore thick, square black-rimmed glasses and, even though he intimidated me, now and again he showed signs of kindness by giving us chips and cooldrinks. His paramour, on the other hand, could be needlessly cruel and this was exacerbated by the fact that she was an alcoholic. One night when our mother had left us there the woman threw a terrible scene and was so verbally abusive that Momo took us down the road to a family friend Me' Mphu Mofolo until Mama returned to pick us up.

Daddy's mother, my grandmother Nomayise – Makhulu, as we got to call her – never left the village of Cofimvaba. My father was the fifth of six children, three of whom died shortly after birth. "Because," said my dad in an interview with historian Luli Callinicos just weeks before he was assassinated in 1993, "in the rural areas, in those days there were literally no health facilities. A family was lucky to have the whole offspring surviving. If 50 per cent survived, that was an achievement."

From the stories I've been told, life was extremely harsh for the Hani family. My Makhulu, who was completely illiterate, was basically a single parent while her husband was away working. She did her best to raise her three surviving sons on her own, working herself to the bone to make ends meet from subsistence farming.

Up to the age of seven, I had never laid eyes on my Makhulu, nor my uncles Victor and Chris.

Sometime in 1988, it was decided that it was worth the risk to smuggle Momo, Khwezi and me into South Africa to meet Daddy's family. This was a direct request from Daddy – I guess he was concerned that time was passing and that it was imperative that we meet his family, especially my Makhulu, who was getting older. I have a vivid memory of driving towards the South African border, all excited and bright-eyed to travel 'Overseas', into the big unknown. As we got closer to the border post, we were bundled into the boot of the car. Instead of feeling fearful in the cramped, dark space, all I felt was great excitement to be going on this big adventure. We crossed over the border without incident and once we'd travelled some distance, we were let out the boot. As we made our way to Cofimvaba, it was like exploring some new, exciting foreign land. On the way, we stopped over in Queenstown and stayed with the Baduzas, who were relatives of our mother. I was completely in awe of their huge mansion-like property, just as I imagined Daddy's Warbucks house looked. That night we slept in a double bed with blue satin linen. There were little silver salt and pepper cellars as well as a bell on the table to summon 'the help'. Apart from the hotel on the Baltic Sea in Russia, this was the most luxurious night I'd ever experienced.

The next day we got up at the crack of dawn and drove for the next 2.5 hours to the very rural village of Cofimvaba, off to see my grandmother and my uncles. It was something of a culture shock to travel on untarred red dirt roads, to see rondavels and the villagers of the outlying areas. Knowing that this was where Daddy had been born brought my little heart enormous pleasure. This was the place where, as a boy not even old enough to go to school, Daddy had woken up each morning to look after the family's small herd of livestock.

As the car pulled up in front of a tiny house, my Makhulu appeared. This tall, dark and stately woman hurried towards us and simply pulled us into her arms, babbling away in a string of isiXhosa that I did not understand even if she had spoken slower. For me, it was love at first sight. Makhulu was kind and open-hearted; she just kept touching and kissing us as though we had appeared in a dream and were now standing in front of her.

As per tradition, a goat was slaughtered in front of us to welcome us home. I was horrified, watching the meat being cooked and knowing that we would be expected to eat it. Yho! I was one of these wussie kids who, although I loved meat, I refused to eat the meat of an animal that was killed in front of me. I was about to refuse to eat the goat that Makhulu proudly placed in front of me when I felt Momo glaring daggers at me, so reluctantly I started nibbling on a tiny piece.

On seeing Daddy's two brothers, Uncle Victor and his baby brother Uncle Chris, I was transfixed by the miracle of genetics; it was astonishing to see how much they looked like my father. But it was not only their looks that had me staring; on hearing their voices and watching their mannerisms, it felt like I was seeing Daddy's doubles. Time flew by far too quickly and soon the moment arrived for us to return home to Maseru. Back in the boot, as we neared the South African/Lesotho border, my heart and mind were filled with such joy, having finally met another part of our family. It made me feel even closer to Daddy, especially meeting and bonding with my Makhulu. Out of the boot back in Lesotho, I could not wait to see Mama to tell her of our big adventure.

○

Although I never heard Daddy speak about his aunt, his father's sister, in Daddy's interview with Luli Callinicos he mentioned her as having a huge influence over him as a child.

"I remember as a small boy I used to have a fascination of books, I would read those books although I understood very little. [My aunt] encouraged me and taught me a few necessary rhymes and began to open up a new world even before I got to school. A world of knowing how to write the alphabet, how to count, in other words not only literacy but numeracy."

So by the time Daddy was seven years old, when he was enrolled in the Roman Catholic school nearby, he was already able to read. "When I went to school I was in a better position than most boys in the village, and I remember the principal of the school got encouraged, how I would read a story and actually memorise that story – without looking at the book, I would actually recite it word by word."

I grew up often hearing what a mission getting to school was for Daddy. He had to walk over 20 kilometres to and back from school every day, five days a week, and then on Sundays another 20 kilometres to get to church and back. I cannot imagine me or my sisters ever showing that kind of commitment for school, let alone church! All that exercise probably helped to make him the fitness fanatic he would later become. By the time he turned eight, he was an altar boy, feeding into his dream to become a priest. "I was under the spell and influence of the priests, the monks and the nuns," he told Luli. "There was something one admired in them – a sense of hard work, selflessness. These people would go on horseback to the most rural parts of the village, taking the gospel to the people, encouraging kids to go to school, praying for the sick and offering all sorts of advice. In other words, they were not only priests, but they were nurses, they were teachers, they were social workers. I must submit that had a very, very strong impression on me and in the formation of my character."

But my Tamkhulu was completely against the idea of priesthood as a vocation; he desperately wanted Daddy to be educated and to live a better life, a life that had never been available to him. So Daddy had to give up his dream of entering the priesthood.

It was during this time – Daddy must have been eight or nine – when some of his teachers joined the Campaign against Bantu Education. Their commitment to protesting against the introduction of inferior Bantu Education lit a fire for justice in Daddy at a very early age.

In 1954, at the age of 12, he enrolled in Matanzima Secondary School in Cala, Transkei, which was named after the head of the Transkei, Chief Matanzima. This was the year that the apartheid regime forced Bantu Education into black schools, a system described by Daddy as "designed to indoctrinate black pupils to accept and recognise the supremacy of the white man over the blacks in all spheres". It upset him deeply and was another fire that inspired him to become involved in the struggle for equality and freedom in South Africa.

Daddy did very well at school, especially in English literature and languages. He landed up writing his Standard 5 and Standard 6 examinations in the same year and was promoted to high school. He was awarded a Bhunga scholarship that allowed him to leave the small village school and enrol for high school at Lovedale College in Alice in 1957.

It was here that Daddy's activist spirit would really be awakened. He soon got involved in student politics, first joining the Unity Movement's Society of Young Africa, then six months later he was recruited by Simon Kekana, head prefect at Lovedale and chair of the African National Congress Youth League, to join the League. Getting involved in politics at school was illegal, so everything Daddy did at the time was in secret and underground. My father was deeply affected by the events surrounding those who were arrested and charged during the Treason Trial of 1956. By the time he was 15, he had been heavily influenced by the writings of Govan Mbeki on the problems and struggles in the Eastern Cape. When I think of what I was up to at that age – dressing up for socials and reading Danielle Steele – I am in total awe of my dad.

By 1957, Daddy had already started reading journals and newspapers such as *The New Age*, *Torch* and *Fighting Talk* by Ruth First, which added to his political awakening and introduced him to Marxist concepts.

"There was a page in *New Age* which dealt with the struggle of the working class throughout the world," he told Luli Callinicos in their interview. "What was happening in the Soviet Union, Czechoslovakia, the GDR, China – the life that people were building there. And that had an appeal in my own impassionate young mind. Given my background, I was attracted by ideas and the philosophy which had a bias towards the working class, which had as its stated objective, the upliftment of the people on the ground."

Daddy matriculated in 1958, achieving really high marks in all his subjects – English, Xhosa, Latin, History, Mathematics and a subject called 'Hygiene'.

When news arrived that he had gained admission to Fort Hare University, a relatively liberal campus considering the apartheid regime's iron grip over South Africa and its neighbours at the time, the entire Hani family, especially my Tamkhulu, was elated.

"I got a bursary and a scholarship to go to university because I was performing rather above average," he downplayed his achievements in his interview with Luli. "When I went over to Fort Hare, I won a government loan to go to university. I think basically that is what helped me to go. It was extremely hard. One would have only one pair of shoes, one jacket and it was not easy because other students from families which were more comfortable than mine, the kids would be better clothed than myself. But I had accepted the fact that this was not important for me. It was through this spirit of self-sacrifice and accepting that the priority was to get my education. There were a number of us coming from rural areas who got their pocket money because parents sold hides and wool whenever it was the sheep-shearing season. We had some sheep and some cattle and goats at home. So my father bought a sewing machine for my mother. Now and again through that I could get a bit of pocket money whilst I was at Fort Hare."

Daddy had a never-ending thirst for knowledge. From the moment he became a student at Fort Hare he embraced his new intellectual environment and he read and read and read – English, Latin and Greek literature, modern and classical; he literally gobbled up all this new information. I think his early fascination with Catholicism inspired him to be particularly drawn to Latin studies and English literature.

I remember my father often sitting with a book, reading for hours, when we lived in Dawn Park – he took his deep thirst for knowledge everywhere he went. There were even stories that he had copies of Shakespeare and Virgil in his backpack when he was on the run from the apartheid forces during the exile years.

At Fort Hare, he was soon devouring Marx and any literature that criticised South Africa's racist capitalist system. By the age of 19, Daddy joined the South African Communist Party, and quickly converted to being a full on Marxist.

"In 1961, at Fort Hare, I was doing my third year, studying for a BA degree and majoring in Latin and English," he told Luli Callinicos. "I am approached by some comrades who apparently had been moulded or welded into a Communist Party unit by Comrade Mbeki. So, in 1961, I joined the Party and I began seriously studying Marxism, the basic works of Marxist authors like Emily [Burns] *What is Marxism?*, *The Communist Manifesto*, *The World Marxist Review* and a number of other publications. I began to read the history of our Party by people like Edward Roux for instance, *Time Longer than Rope*, giving the earlier history of the Communist Party."

In the same year, uMkhonto we Sizwe (MK), the military wing of the ANC, was established. He was clear in his interview with Luli about why he was drawn to the SACP.

"I belonged to a world, in terms of my background, which suffered I think the worst extremes of apartheid. A poor rural area where the majority of working people spent their times in the compounds, in the hostels, away from their families. A rural area where there were no clinics and probably the nearest hospital was 50 kilometres – generally a life of poverty with the basic things unavailable. Where our mothers and our sisters would walk 3 kilometres and even 6 kilometres whenever there was a drought to fetch water. Where the only fuel available was going 5, 6 kilometres away to cut wood and bring it back. This was the sort of life. Now I had seen the lot of black workers, extreme forms of exploitation, slave wages, no trade union rights. Where it was said that workers create wealth but in the final analysis they get nothing. They get peanuts in order to survive and continue working for the capitalists. For me the appeal of socialism was extremely great. But I didn't get involved with the workers' struggle out of theory alone. It was a combination of theory and my own class background. I never faltered in my belief in socialism. For me that belief is strong because that is still the life of the majority of the people with whom I share a common background."

The following year, in 1962, Daddy became one of the first volunteers for MK, which marked the beginning of his long journey into the armed struggle, a cause and approach he passionately believed in. Halfway through his studies, my father decided to leave Fort Hare to complete his BA at Rhodes University, which he believed was a better university.

During holidays he would return home to the village.

"I used to go and be with my mother, help her in the fields, growing maize and harvesting," he told Luli. "Because, if you harvested probably 20 bags of maize, the rest would be sold to the white shopkeeper, because that was the only market available in the rural areas. It was the white shopkeeper who would buy at prices determined by him. In other words, I contributed even to the slender financial resources of the family by working very hard during holidays in the fields and also looking after the stock."

In that same year, 1962, Daddy graduated with a BA degree in Latin and English and decided to pursue law. The following year he moved south to do his articles at the law firm Schaeffer & Schaeffer in Cape Town. He soon got caught up with his new life there, spending long hours with ANC icon Govan Mbeki, who became a mentor and father figure to him, as well doing volunteer work in trade unions. In the same year, at the age of 20, he was elected to MK's highly secretive seven-man regional committee, dubbed the 'Committee of Seven', in the Western Cape.

"I became a member of the Committee of Seven, in overall charge of the underground of the ANC in the Western Cape," he told Luli. "It [was] in the course of my activities within that Committee of Seven that I [was] recruited to become part of the MK set up. I [was] recruited into a unit and I began to operate in small ways, throwing Molotov cocktails, cutting telephone cables and all that."

Towards the end of that year, Daddy had his first real run-in with the law when he was arrested, along with his friend and comrade Archie Sibeko, at a roadblock on their way to Nyanga East to distribute leaflets against the 90-day Detention law. After spending the weekend at Philippi Police Station, they were both charged under the Suppression of Communism Act for "furthering the aims of a banned organisation" and being in the possession of banned material. They spent the following 30 days in isolation cells before the trial began. I am sure Daddy was tortured during this time.

My father was found guilty and sentenced to 18 months in prison with hard labour. The exorbitantly high bail was set at £125. While out on bail, waiting to hear whether his lawyers would consider appealing the sentence, Daddy left the country to attend an ANC conference in Lobatse, Bechuanaland, known today as Botswana.

When news reached my dad, in February 1963, that his sentence had not been overturned, he and Archie decided to go into hiding. Daddy secretively travelled to Soweto, where he stayed underground with a family sympathetic to the struggle. In

May 1963, along with a small group of exiles, my father set off for Bechuanaland and then on to Northern Rhodesia, today known as Zambia. This was to mark the beginning of Daddy's time in exile. It would be almost three decades before he could return to South Africa.

As the small group of revolutionaries arrived in Lusaka, Zambia's capital, they were all arrested. However, unlike his humiliating experience in South Africa, this time the court procedure was brief and soon they were free to travel across the Zambian border to Tanganyika, now Tanzania.

Within six months of arriving, along with 30 other MK cadres, Daddy flew from Dar es Salaam to Moscow, in Russia, which was then known as the USSR, to undergo military training. Out of Africa for the first time in his life, this experience must have been mindblowing and would influence my father deeply, both as a human being and a military man.

In his interview with Luli Callinicos, he explained what a mind shift landing in the USSR was. "I came from a very racial society and therefore the first time most of us as blacks are received as human beings, as equal human beings, we are received by people from the Central Committee who are based in a secret house, and at this time we have these white ladies actually cooking for us and looking after this place. So for us this is a new world. A new world of equality, of people where our colour seems to be of no consequence, where our humanity is recognised. We had not been exposed, we had not been to Britain. We had no comparative experience. So for us this strengthened our feelings, our strong feelings in socialism."

Meanwhile, back in South Africa, on 11 July 1963 the core of MK, including Daddy's mentor Walter Sisulu, Govan Mbeki, Raymond Mhlaba, Ahmed Kathrada, Lionel (Rusty) Bernstein and Bob Hepple were arrested at Liliesleaf Farm in Rivonia, the underground headquarters of the ANC. On hearing the fate of the South Africans back home, it was decided that Daddy and the newly exiled cadres in Russia should intensify their training. So they extended their stay from six months to more than a year.

The time spent in Moscow drastically changed Daddy. Not only was he exposed to military training, the theories of guerrilla warfare and the politics of socialism, but also to the cultural richness of Russia. "We visit(ed) museums ... concerts, the Bolshoi theatre ... For the first time I actually watched ballet dancing. I mean a new world for us. We never saw it in our country. We begin to appreciate classical music. We moved around in Moscow in buses. Of course these were guided tours, and we don't see starving people, we don't see beggars. We'd go to factories and watch the Russian workers. Now of course I know that we were not exposed to everything that was happening, but that partial opening of the window into this new society served to strengthen our strong socialist convictions. I want to say, without reservations, that shaped my outlook, strengthened my politics ... For me that was an unforgettable experience."

Not only was he experiencing a cultural awakening, in Russia Daddy also learned invaluable military skills and his fitness levels peaked.

"Every morning we had to go out ... on marches, tactical marches," he told Luli Callinicos. "We had to go out into the Russian villages, set up camps there in the forests and the marshes around Moscow, and stay there and look at maps, orientate ourselves. We learnt topography, firearms, engineering skills, the manufacture of explosives and the use of standard explosives. So I was fit physically, I was in very good shape."

In 1964, at the age of 22, along with 30 newly trained cadres, Daddy travelled back from the Soviet Union to Tanzania where they were offered a piece of land at Kongwa, 400 kilometres south of Dar. Daddy was put in charge of the team to set up a military training camp.

As the South African government tightened its grip on anyone who resisted the apartheid government, within a year many exiles had fled South Africa and soon the Kongwa camp grew to more than 500 strong. Daddy's love for literature and education meant that he was much loved by the new exiles, as he spent many hours teaching adult basic education to counter the high level of illiteracy among the cadres who had all been exposed to the inferior Bantu Education system back home.

In 1966 Daddy was on the move again, this time back to Zambia. His Soviet training had prepared him well and he was put in charge of setting up a joint training programme with the Zimbabwe African People's Union (ZAPU), preparing soldiers for a covert operation into Rhodesia. This would later become known as the Wankie Campaign.

But again Daddy came head to head with the law as he was arrested trying to re-enter Botswana. Fortunately, he was detained for only two weeks before being sent back to Lusaka.

On 2 August 1967, less than a week after my father turned 25, he led a group of soldiers across the Zambian border into Rhodesia. They entered the Wankie Game Reserve on their first covert mission and, on 13 August, after a heavy battle with the Rhodesian army, they successfully forced the army to retreat. And then, just 12 days later, they experienced another victory against the Rhodesian Army. Their spirits were high as they marched towards the Botswana border.

But their luck was not to last long. Within a week they were arrested by the Botswana security forces and, after an appearance in court, were each sentenced to six years' imprisonment for possession of illegal arms. Again my father found himself behind bars.

Daddy eventually had his jail time reduced to two years and, on his release, returned to Zambia in 1969 to live with intellectual and struggle exile Livingstone Mqotsi in Lusaka.

But two years is a long time. Despondent and feeling let down by certain members of the leadership of the ANC who had done little to help them during their time behind bars, my dad and six of the soldiers who had fought in the Wankie Campaign drafted a letter, which become known as the Hani Memorandum. In this document they made explosive allegations against many members of the ANC's leadership in exile.

We, as genuine revolutionaries, are moved by the frightening depths reached by the rot in the ANC and the disintegration of M.K. accompanying this rot and manifesting itself in the following way: The ANC Leadership in Exile has created machinery which has become an end in itself. It is completely divorced from the situation in South Africa ...

We are disturbed by the careerism of the ANC Leadership Abroad who have, in every sense, become professional politicians rather than professional revolutionaries. We have been forced to draw the conclusion that the payment of salaries to people working in offices is very detrimental to the revolutionary outlook of those who receive such monies.

It was a very controversial and highly risky move, which was typical of Daddy's outspokenness and fearlessness – action that saw him and the six other signatories expelled by the ANC NEC in exile. It would not be the first time my father would be disciplined by those within his organisation. The document furthermore criticised Joe Modise, then Commander-in-Chief of MK. As a result, seeds of bad blood were sown between Daddy and Joe Modise, who was so enraged by the Memorandum that he called for my dad to be executed for treason.

Oliver Tambo, then president of the ANC and supreme commander of MK, was also extremely upset by the Memo, afraid that the sentiments expressed would cause huge distrust in the structures of the ANC in exile. As a result, an urgent gathering was called to discuss the allegations, and the Morogoro Conference took place in Tanzania between 25 April and 1 May 1969. It was a watershed moment, resulting in wide-ranging changes to the political and military structures of the ANC.

At the Morogoro Conference it was recommended that Daddy and the other signatories of the Hani Memorandum be pardoned and reinstated as full members of the ANC and MK. A year later, in 1970, as a result of his uncompromising commitment, Daddy's influence had substantially grown. He was 28 years old when he was elected to the Central Committee of the SACP.

Over the following four years Daddy would travel a lot overseas, but not the 'Overseas' of my childhood imagination; he visited Europe, spreading the ideals of the ANC and SACP while receiving further military training in East Germany. In 1973 he was one of the ANC delegates to the Southern Africa Conference of the United Nations' Organisation of African Unity (OAU) in Oslo, Sweden. It was the same year he met Mama.

In 1974, along with Thabo Mbeki, Daddy was elected to the ANC's National Executive Council, the two of them becoming the youngest members ever. Thabo, who was also a June 1942 baby, was just 10 days older than Daddy.

Daddy briefly returned to South Africa that year to help build the ANC underground. It was a top-secret visit, of course, as he was regarded as a dangerous terrorist by the apartheid government. After his stay, he left for Lesotho to carry on his work strengthening the ANC in South Africa from across the border, leading the MK units responsible for guerrilla ops in South Africa.

In that same year, Daddy and Mama – who were now married – relocated to Lesotho, Maseru, where they would live together as a family for the next seven years, welcoming all three of us girls into their lives.

After the shattering night of the Lesotho Raids in December 1982, it became clear that all of our lives, but especially Daddy's, were in great danger. He was redeployed to Mozambique and for the following eight years he remained in exile, spending most of his time in Zambia.

While in exile, Daddy's influence within the organisation and back home in South Africa grew enormously. Between 1983 and 1984 he was appointed second in command of MK and frequently travelled between Mozambique and Angola, where he helped address concerns among dissatisfied MK cadres who were threatening mutiny in the organisation's military camps.

Daddy was forced to leave Mozambique when the Nkomati Accord was signed in March 1984 between the governments of Mozambique under Samora Machel, the leader of FRELIMO, and the then president of South Africa, PW Botha. Under the Accord, the two neighbouring countries agreed not to allow their countries to be used as launching pads for attacks on one another – in other words, not harbour 'terrorists' and enemies of the South African regime, such as my dad. As a result, Mozambique, a war-torn country economically dependent on South Africa, was forced to expel the ANC from their country. In turn, the South African government agreed to cease supporting RENAMO, an anti-government guerrilla organisation in Mozambique. Not surprisingly, the agreement was soon broken by the South Africans, who continued to clandestinely support the activities of RENAMO.

Just 10 months later, in January 1985, Daddy received the highest number of votes for a seat on the Politburo, at the SACP's sixth conference. It was the same year that the first State of Emergency was declared in South Africa. The townships had become ungovernable as the power of the MK structures and NGOs grew among South Africans at home, resisting the apartheid regime.

Broadcast from various neighbouring African countries, Daddy often spoke on Radio Freedom, the ANC underground radio station, urging people to derail the apartheid military machine.

"If you are working in a factory which produces weapons, vehicles, trucks which are used by the army and police against us," he advised listeners, "… you must ensure that there are frequent breakdowns in those machines you operate. You can clog some of them by using sugar and sand."

By mid-1987 my dad had been appointed MK Chief of Staff. Over the next few years, under his leadership, campaigns to sabotage and destabilise South Africa intensified. He was always clear that the only way that white South Africa would ever wake up to the reality of the viciousness of apartheid was when they experienced terror themselves.

In an interview with *The Christian Science Monitor*, an international publication, he famously said: "When we began to attack targets in the white areas, for the first time white South Africans began to sit up and say: 'This thing is coming.' … When they actually began to hear explosions in the centre of Johannesburg, Cape Town, and Durban, they began to realise that what they saw happening in other countries … was beginning to take place in South Africa."

Over the years, especially in the mid- and late-1980s, due to his uncompromising military approach, Daddy's reputation grew to near-mythical status among young exiles and the oppressed in the country of his birth, especially among the militant black youth in the townships.

In 1989 Daddy moved to the big house in Woodlands, Lusaka. As one of the South African government's most wanted men, he now had two permanent teams of bodyguards accompanying him around the clock – and, of course, the guard dogs in the garden I remember so well from my time there.

A few months after his move to Woodlands, in February 1990, the ANC and SACP were unbanned in South Africa.

CHAPTER 5

Unbanned

On Friday, 2 February 1990, news broke that the ANC had been unbanned and Nelson Mandela was to be released. This could only mean one thing for our family … As I walked down the passage towards our flat on the second floor after school that Friday afternoon I heard a huge commotion. Sounds of jubilation could be heard all the way down the stairs. I rushed inside to find Mama screaming, "Daddy is coming home, Daddy is coming home!"

I could not contain my excitement. Stumbling over my words, my first question was, of course, "When?" Face gleaming with joy, Mama didn't yet have any details. All she knew was that the ANC had been unbanned, Mandela was to walk free and my father's freedom would soon follow. That day will forever be etched in our psyches. Just as the Americans have their "Where were you when Kennedy was shot?" or "What were you doing on 9/11?", we have our "Where were you when Mandela was released?" Little did we know at the time that within just three years, "What were you doing when Chris Hani was assassinated?" would become the refrain.

Nine days after the ANC's unbanning, on 11 February, we watched on TV as Madiba walked out of prison, which we recorded for prosperity on our old VHS machine. I remember the palpable joy radiating from all the grown-ups in the room, glued to the events unfolding on the small screen. Up until that moment, I don't think I quite realised the enormity of the occasion.

For impatient me, now almost 10 years old, change did not come half as quickly as I had hoped it would. Although the laws had changed in February, in real time we only moved back to South Africa with Daddy at the end of the year, in December 1990. During this time I finished Class 5 in Maseru in July and began Class 6 in September. I was livid with my mother, who insisted that instead of following all my friends into Mrs Bean's class, I was forced to follow in Khwezi's footsteps and go to Mr Ramsey's class. He was a tall, balding, intimidating man who still referred to Zimbabwe as 'Rhodesia' – need I say more? Mama's reason for what seemed to me a highly unjust decision was that my friends were a distraction because, in her eyes, all we ever did was talk. Mr Ramsey's favourite instrument was a wooden metre ruler, which he used to smack the shit out of you. Alternatively, he would make you stand on the table and force you to sing. I felt isolated and extremely lonely during that period, away from all my friends whom I had been with since Class 1. Once again, due to our circumstances, I was separated from that which others considered 'normal and safe', something I would have to deal with a lot in years to come.

During our year of uncertainty, Mama and I made several trips to South Africa to find ourselves a new home and school for me. They were exciting times, tinged with a breath of hope. There was no longer any need to hide, no squeezing into the boot of a car to get over the border undetected. We could literally smell the sweet scent of freedom in the air.

My parents decided to settle in Dawn Park, near Boksburg, in what had previously been a white suburb, mainly inhabited by conservative Afrikaners. I didn't notice any of that. The first time we drove into Dawn Park I was blown away by the beauty of the place: neat houses, green grass, a picket-fence paradise, all safe and suburban – not unlike my fantasy of the Huxtable home.

The first time I saw the house we were to move into I immediately fell in love with the facebrick perimeter walls. The fact that it was nestled into the tail end of a cul de sac made me feel all safe and cosy. Walking through the security gate into the house, huge open spaces with arched doorways welcomed us. When through the sliding glass I spotted a swimming pool in the back yard, I literally yelped with joy. But the deal was sealed for both Mama and me when we encountered the kitchen. It was like one you might see today on a cooking show on TV. It was certainly the biggest kitchen I had ever seen, with white cupboard doors with tan wooden handles, plus an island-type butcher's block in the middle of the L-shaped room. It seemed to ooze with master-chef potential. Of course, to me, having grown up within the confines of a flat, everything looked enormous in that house. Without hesitation, my mother and I agreed that this would be our new home. The fact that it wasn't even up for sale did nothing to deter Mama, who quickly convinced the owners to accept her offer.

I realised I had very little choice about where I was to attend school: it was either Saheti, a Greek school, or King David Linksfield, both in Linksfield, near Bedfordview. But at the last minute we were informed that King David was a no-go because I was not Jewish. I had suspicions, though, that it had more to do with my surname being attached to the man who until recently had been one of South Africa's most wanted terrorists. Suddenly the choice had been narrowed to no choice at all, so Saheti it was.

Driving through the school gates, to meet the principal, my nerves were on edge. The school seemed enormous, much bigger then Prep and even bigger then Machabeng High School in Lesotho, which was the biggest school I had ever seen. Both my parents and I walked into Mr Armstrong's mahogany-wooded office. The three of them discussed me as though I wasn't there – especially my academic history at Prep. Then the headmaster's piercing eyes framed by little spectacles finally settled on me. Quite out of the blue, he said, "So, young lady, what is 7x7?"

For a moment that stretched into eternity, I went completely blank and froze. I began to furiously calculate the numbers on my fingers under the table – a method I still use today! I finally blurted out, "49!" The entire room sighed with relief but not as loudly as I. Mr Armstrong promptly said: "Welcome to Saheti." That was it. Two numbers timed by each other – my entrance exam to my new academic life.

Once all the excitement of a new school, new country, new home settled down, it suddenly became real that I would have to leave Maseru and all my friends. I was well and truly devastated. There was some small part of me that believed that we would continue living in Lesotho, except that Daddy would join us. Now we were moving to South Africa – actually, to be clear, I was the only child moving to South Africa. Momo was already studying in Cape Town and Khwezi, as usual, dug in her heels and insisted that she stay at Machabeng High, where she would become a boarder. I was devastated that I hadn't been afforded a choice like my older sister had. I mean, what fuckery was this?

CHAPTER 6

Dawn Park

We drove out of my beloved Maseru as a family in early December 1990.

My heart felt like thunder as I watched forlornly, from the back of Mama's car, my familiar childhood streets fade into the distance behind us. Gone was all the hype and excitement I had initially felt when we were looking for a new house in South Africa. All I felt now was an enormous sense of loss. But after the four-hour journey, once we entered Dawn Park, drove down Hakea Crescent, and got closer to our facebrick dream house, I began to feel the first stirrings of excitement. As Daddy parked the car in the driveway, I found myself dashing out, through the front rooms and arches, into the back yard, stopping at the edge of the huge blue swimming pool, and taking the wonder of it all in.

Not only did our new house have a pool and the best kitchen on the planet, it finally dawned on me that for the first time in my life I would have my very own bedroom. Mama had told me I could choose any colour for my walls. (I think this was mainly to drum up some excitement to change my despondent mood.) Well, it worked – I chose cornflower blue for my bedroom and it wasn't long before the 'leaving Maseru sulks' were a thing of the past.

For the first few weeks we had no furniture because deliveries – we had bought all new furniture – would only resume in January.

To tide us over Mama went to the Hyperama and bought garden furniture, which we used inside the house. Although it looked quite hillbilly, I loved every new piece of it. Mama also bought a Nintendo so all we did that December was play Mario Brothers. In fact, the incessant noise blasting from the console irritated Daddy so much that he banned us from playing it with the volume up. When we weren't playing Mario B, we swam in our pool and lazed around in our fantastic plastic chairs. I also made my first friend in the neighbourhood, a vivacious blonde Afrikaans-speaking girl, Sonya, who lived next door. From the moment we laid eyes on each other, we were inseparable and spent most days running in and out of each other's houses.

At this time, about to turn 10 years old, I was still entirely oblivious to racism. I had grown up in the multicultural mixing pot of Maseru and even during those first few months in South Africa I was unaware of any racial undercurrents. The irony that my first real friend in South Africa was a white Afrikaner girl from Boksburg totally escaped me. It was only during the holidays, when Khwezi and I ventured out to Boksburg's East Rand Mall, that I was suddenly confronted by the irrational ugliness of racism when we overheard someone call us 'kaffirs'. We looked at each other, completely bewildered. I don't think either of us even really knew what 'kaffir' meant, but we instinctively sensed that it was derogatory. We went home and immediately told our parents. Daddy and Mama simply told us that such people were ignorant and we were not to pay them any attention.

With Daddy at home, we were now a 'real' family. Initially, however, it was quite an adjustment because we had all kind of got used to having a dad we only saw a couple of times a year. As thrilled as I was to have him home, I now faced many challenges accepting my dad as the new head of the family. I had lived many years with just having Mama as the be-all-and-end-all, so I found myself challenging him on a number of issues. One of the areas of contention was my bedtime: I was used to going to bed after watching TV shows such as *Dynasty* or *Dallas*, which I simply adored, but he wanted to set my bedtime at 8pm! I vehemently resisted, shouting that "Mama always lets me go to bed later". We finally struck a compromise in which some days I went to bed earlier, while on others I enjoyed some leniency.

Very soon the TV remote also became a battleground. My dad immediately laid claimed to it but all he ever seemed to want to watch was the news or serious documentaries. He was a news man to the bone, and even slept with the radio on. Numerous times I'd get out of bed in the middle of the night to go to the toilet and hear, "This is the BBC" coming from my parents' bedroom. That particular conflict was finally resolved by getting another television set, which was placed in their bedroom.

That December was also the first time I met Judy and Tokyo Sexwale. We had just arrived back from the shops one day when the Sexwales appeared at the house. Uncle Tokyo introduced us to Judy and I remember staring at her for much longer than was polite. In his usual Tokyo style, he bellowed: "Have you never seen a white woman before?" Horribly embarrassed, I scurried away, humiliated. Of course I had seen white women – mixed couples were nothing new to me, growing up in colour-blind Maseru – I had just never seen a pregnant woman whose tummy was so enormous.

The Sexwales lived down the road from us and I loved going to visit Judy. She was so warm and lovely; she always welcomed me and never seemed to find it annoying that I was often underfoot. The first time I tasted prawns was courtesy of Judy – they were unforgettable.

'Judes', as I liked to call her, drove an old blue Fiat that she'd brought up with her from Cape Town. Sometimes she'd let me sit on her lap to take control of the steering wheel as we drove. She was simply the coolest adult I had ever met. I loved listening to her stories about life in Cape Town and the way that she, as a paralegal, had met Uncle Tokyo when he was a prisoner on Robben Island – it all seemed incredibly romantic to me.

I became besotted with Baby Gabriella when she finally came along, and was soon a firm fixture in the Sexwale household. Finally, I had my own gorgeous real deal baby George. I was obsessed with carrying her and bathing her at every opportunity.

By the time the school term started on my first day at Saheti in the new year of 1991, I was a ball of anxiety. I had never been 'the new girl' before and I was petrified. Fortunately, I was only to find out much later that, due to Daddy's politics, certain parents really did not want me at the school. They even wrote letters of complaint, horrified that Saheti had opened its doors to the daughter of South Africa's most dangerous terrorist. But, oblivious to these undercurrents, my social nature soon shone through and I quickly bonded with my classmates.

I soon developed my first crush on a boy named Savva, one of the most popular boys in my grade, but made the mistake of telling Momo, who was in Cape Town. That titbit of news soon made its way back to Daddy; as a result, I was playfully teased by the rest of my family with 'Ooohh, Savva'. But there was a good reason I liked Savva. I had been invited to my first boy-and-girl party and I felt incredibly nervous about the evening. Then came that moment when the slow jams began playing, and everybody seemed to pair off – except me. I felt like a real little loser sitting on the couch all alone, when Savva suddenly appeared in front of me and asked me to dance. I will always be grateful to him for that gesture; it really made me feel accepted.

It wasn't long before I began to enjoy an active social life and often found myself invited to at least one party per weekend. The upside to this was that my mother, who always wanted me to look impeccable, would get me a new outfit lest I be seen wearing the same thing twice – much to Daddy's irritation. He would shake his head at us as we walked into the house with shopping bags. I'd run off to my room with the blue cornflower walls, get changed into a new outfit and then model for him. Of course his frowns would invariably break into smiles of approval.

During those first few months in Dawn Park, I basked in the limelight of being an only child as neither of my sisters was living at home. Then one night, in early 1991, we received a distressed call from Khwezi, telling us she wanted to leave Machabeng in Maseru, that something had happened and she couldn't bear being there another day. Less than an hour later, Daddy had us all in the car, driving straight through the night to arrive in Lesotho well after midnight. First thing the following morning my parents went to the school and promptly took Khwezi out. I never did get to hear exactly what went down to make her so unhappy, but the next thing I knew she was sitting beside me in the back seat as we drove back to Johannesburg.

I suddenly had my big sister with me, which made me deeply annoyed because I had become accustomed to my only-child lifestyle. Luckily, my cornflower blue palace remained my own, and Khwezi moved into the study, which was converted into a bedroom. Before long, however, we were at each other's throat. For the smallest gap I had experienced the wonderful feeling of being able to just be me at school and at home. But now there was Khwezi.

For all the years I'd been at Prep, I'd faced the constrictions of living in her shadow. Although we were less than two years apart in age, it always felt like Khwezi was the talented older sister who could do no wrong; the shining example of the perfect pupil, the one to whom I was always compared. The last thing that I needed was for her to join me at Saheti and to dim my shine. So I was much relieved when my parents decided to enrol her in St Dominic's in Boksburg – in fact, I was thrilled. But at home our 'not getting along well' soon escalated into full-on warfare, which quickly deteriorated to physical blows. To this day I maintain that the scars left from scratches to my face are due to Khwezi's catlike fighting tendencies.

But Khwezi or no Khwezi, the truth of the matter was I was finding myself struggling academically at Saheti. According to Mama, I wasn't applying myself properly – maybe she had a point. I was the type to study for tests on the 45-minute drive to school. At the end of my first term I had done atrociously, barely scraping through.

My mother, sternness personified as she perused my dismal report, berated me. In my ten-year-old cheekiness I challenged her with, "What's the problem? At least I passed!" I kept spelling it out and repeating. "P-A-S-S. That's all that matters – P-A-S-S."

She looked at me, her eyes stone cold, and said: "Well, let's see what your father thinks."

Oh my, I had completely forgotten about Daddy. I knew I had a few hours until he came home but was unsure what time he would actually walk through the front door. I made a desperate plan to avoid him and an inevitable scolding, so before the sun had even thought of setting, I hit the sack at 5pm.

Next morning I lay in bed for a few hours hoping that by the time I emerged he would have left the house. Seeing nobody as I tentatively opened the bedroom door, I marched confidently into the lounge – only to run smack into Daddy. His first words were, "We need to talk about your report."

Gone was all my previous day's bravado. "Yes, Daddy," I replied meekly.

My eyes were glued to the carpet as we sat down together in the lounge. His eyes didn't leave me as he quietly spoke.

"I am disappointed in your results, Lindiwe. I expect more from you. Now, is this the best you can do?"

"No, Daddy."

"Well, I expect better marks next time, Lindiwe."

Eyes still downcast. "Yes, Daddy, I promise."

I felt like a failure, that I had really disappointed and let him down.

That was the thing about my father; he would say very few words, but each one – carefully chosen – had the power to make me want to crawl into a hole and change everything about myself. Mama's nagging and screeching, however, had absolutely no impact on me whatsoever. Sitting beside him on the couch, eyes boring holes in the carpet, feeling like my world was about to come to an end, he suddenly smiled at me and said, "What about some breakfast?"

Besides the few battles over bedtime and the television remote, I adored having Daddy permanently back in our lives. I was especially drawn to his passion for exercise. I loved nothing more than swimming with him in our beautiful blue pool. He taught me how to dive and how to master all the different strokes –

backstroke, breast stroke, butterfly, crawl. I mainly joined him in the pool in the early summer evenings, though he often swam at dawn as well. We soon bought him a stationary exercise bike and a treadmill so even in bad weather the man wouldn't be deprived of his endorphin and adrenalin fix. When he jogged out on the suburban streets, I would be right behind him on my bike, keeping up with him as much as my wheels would allow.

The one thing Daddy was totally hopeless at was handyman stuff. The man who could put an AK-47 together in under two minutes had no idea how to wire a plug or change a light bulb. A few months after we moved into Dawn Park, the swimming pool began to go a little off colour. Before my mother could call the pool man, Daddy insisted that he would sort it out. Under my father's guidance, from being slightly off-blue, the pool deteriorated into a mess of the deepest swamp green. The minute Daddy had to leave town for a few days, my mom called the pool guy to sort things out. When my father returned home, the pool was back to sparkling blue – we all told Daddy his methods had worked.

My father constantly attracted people to him. Our new home always seemed full of visitors and activity. There was hardly a time that you didn't walk in to find comrades either in the lounge or outside around the pool, engrossed in robust discussions. Mama would invariably be in her dream kitchen preparing food for the men. It seemed like I was forever being summoned to make coffee or bring drinks out for Uncle So-and-so.

My main gripe with so many people in the house was that I was often not allowed to watch TV, because the noise from the television would drown out the conversation. I, on the other hand, saw it very differently – all these loud voices were interrupting my favourite shows. How could I lose myself in the world of *Beverly Hills 90210* or *Dallas* with all this crazy noise going on in the lounge? The one show Daddy insisted on not missing, besides the news, was *Going Up* with Joe Mafela. I loved watching it with him, giggling as my dad roared with laughter. If he wasn't there to watch it, we would have to tape it on our big VHS video machine.

The other TV show Daddy never missed was his favourite news

show, *Agenda* – unless, of course, he was being interviewed for the show by Freek Robinson. I would sit glued to the screen, watching every second, literally shaking with pride for my father, knowing that the whole country was watching him talk about politics like an expert. After the show I would wait up for him, as he made his way home from the SABC. The moment I heard the door open, I'd be sitting at the dinner table, knowing that he didn't like eating by himself. While he was chewing on a meal that my mother had lovingly prepared for him – shepherd's pie, roast chicken or lamb chops – I would take out my carefully prepared notes and go through what he had mispronounced in all my 11-year-old wisdom. "Daddy, it's *Vic-tree*, not *Vic-tawry*." He would sit there all serious, nodding at my crit, listening to every word and pretending to take it all on board.

The one thing the whole Hani family had in common was a love for meat. So when Daddy was diagnosed with gout not long after we moved to Dawn Park, he really suffered on the strict no-red-meat diet of fish and chicken that Mama now insisted on. But that didn't mean a thing when it came to lamb chops, his favourite meal. One morning Khwezi woke up to discover that her carefully stashed-away leftover chops were missing. Khwezi immediately freaked out and went to interrogate Daddy, who very casually responded: "What leftovers? Oh, you mean the lamb chops left in *my* fridge?" Gout or no gout, as far as my dad was concerned, all leftovers were considered communal property.

○

On 28 June 1992 Daddy turned 50 and Mama decided that it was cause for a big celebration.

Since his birthday fell on a Sunday, we had a huge party at home the following Saturday. I could hardly squeeze through the throngs of friends and family. Later that night I went to the bathroom to change but when I opened the laundry hamper to look for my pyjamas, much to my horror I discovered a human turd. My first instinct was to scream – it felt as if I'd discovered a dead body.

Everyone came running in and, when they saw the turd, Sammy took the entire basket to the bottom of the garden and immediately proceeded to burn it. According to Sammy, this was a very bad omen, signifying an imminent death in the household. We never did find out who had left the offensive offering in the bathroom.

A few weeks later, in July, on arriving home from school one afternoon, I heard from my pale-faced mom that there had been an attempt on Daddy's life in broad daylight in the centre of Joburg's CBD. I managed to gather bits of details that a young man had followed my dad, who was walking to the SACP office. Apparently, the man had slipped into a hair salon and begun fiddling with something hidden in his windbreaker. The ladies working in the shop had found his behaviour suspicious and, as he quickly left the shop, they followed him. When they saw my dad, they immediately recognised him as Chris Hani and ran to warn him that a man was following him. The would-be assassin bolted across the road, dodging traffic until he managed to scramble into a car carrying two white men that had been parked across the street. The car then sped away.

Luckily, Daddy was okay, but I was terrified. I couldn't shake the feeling that something disastrous was about to happen, and kept thinking about the turd and the bad omen it symbolised. It was around this time that I began to have vivid nightmares almost nightly. Initially my dreams began with a stranger coming into our house looking for Daddy. In the dream we all panicked and scurried around the house, trying to find places to hide. The man who had come to hunt my father down would search and search but never seemed to find him. I'd wake up terrified, heart beating like I'd just run a marathon, and rush to my parents' room. They'd sleepily soothe me while I crept into bed with them. Then my dreams began to change. This time the man looking for Daddy would find him and kill him. By this stage I was a permanent fixture in my parents' bed.

Less than a year later, on Thursday, 8 April 1993, Daddy had an interview on *Agenda* and came home late. As usual, I watched the show and was awake when he arrived. I was also super excited because it was the start of the long Easter weekend and Mama and I were travelling to Lesotho the next day. Mama remembered that she had left washing hanging on the line. Daddy volunteered to go and get it and, being my dad's shadow, I chimed in that I would accompany him. On the way through the kitchen I pulled open a drawer and took out a huge butcher's knife. Perplexed and even slightly amused, Daddy asked what it was for. I looked at him in all earnestness and told him it was for his protection.

On Friday, 9 April 1993, we woke up at the crack of dawn and set off early on our four-hour drive to Maseru. As usual, Khwezi had her own agenda. She'd decided to stay at home in Dawn Park to attend a social on the Saturday evening. Daddy had reluctantly agreed to take her to the hair salon. Before we left, he came to the car to say goodbye. As we drove away, something urged me to look back. The last image I saw before turning the corner was Daddy standing at the garage with his hand up, waving goodbye. For a moment I was overcome with a deep pang of sadness at my father standing there alone in the driveway.

CHAPTER 7

That day ...
10 April 1993

I t was almost dark by the time we pulled into Hakea Crescent in Dawn Park. The car could hardly move through the crush of people lined up on both sides of the cul de sac. Slowly, like Moses parting the Red Sea, they shifted to make way for us to inch towards the house. Their mournful voices grew louder as we got closer. Then I spotted a yellow police van. I was helped out of the car by who-knows-who. As soon as I stepped onto the concrete driveway, I saw the blood.

I needed to see Khwezi. Despite hearing the people on the street singing and seeing the darkening blood on the paving, I knew that once I looked into my sister's eyes I would know whether any of this was really happening or whether there had just been some terrible misunderstanding.

I knew the answer as soon as I saw Khwezi's shattered face. We collapsed, weeping in each other's arms. It felt like our tears would never end.

With the house heaving with so many people, we managed to slip away into the bedroom where, between our uncontrollable sobs, she choked out the details of what had happened. Despite Daddy telling her, as he left the house to buy the newspaper, not to "talk forever" on the phone, as usual she'd laughed and chatted with a friend from the moment he left. When she heard Daddy ring the doorbell, she'd shouted she was coming, telling her friend that she had to go. At that moment there was the deafening crack of a gunshot. She'd run to open the garage but that's when she heard more gunshots. As she rushed through the side door leading into the garage, a bullet whizzed past her. By the time she got to the driveway, Daddy was on the ground in a pool of blood. That's when she started screaming.

The unbearable pain of hearing Khwezi sob out the details of what had happened to our father, her inconsolable guilt for not being quick enough to open the gate, haunt me to this day. That night it felt like our hearts had been shattered, that the hole of grief would never be mended. Today that empty chasm of loss remains. Time froze as we sat in a blur of aching helplessness that night, waiting for our older sister Momo to arrive from Cape Town. There was nothing more to say, but hold onto each other as we simply waited to be told what to do.

Years later I would read that the day after Daddy died over 20 000 ANC and SACP supporters gathered close to our Dawn Park home to pay their respects and express their inconsolable grief.

But in my broken little world, the outside was far away. Everything was hazy on that Sunday. I must have eaten at some point and I am sure I must have slept, but I have no memory of walking through the very basics of existence. I vaguely recall wandering from room to room, moving through the throngs of people, strangers, neighbours, family – lost – moving like a thread of invisible air through the passageways. I remember staring at our mother who now, according to tradition, had taken to the mattress. Tears everywhere. Men wept like little children. I remember sometime during the day a doctor prescribing pills to help all of us sleep. Sunday blurred into Monday. I think I went to the Sexwales' for a few hours, just to escape the tearful chaos that threatened to swallow our house.

Later that day a delegation from my school came to find me at Tokyo and Judy's house. I vaguely remember Kpia Soula, the head of Greek at Saheti, embracing me, holding me tightly, trying to comfort me. I ached from emotional exhaustion when I returned home a few hours later. Without telling anyone – me being the addict that I would later discover myself to be – instead of one sleeping pill, I took two of the tablets the doctor had left for the family, which of course was not recommended. As I walked into the kitchen, the last thing I remember was collapsing to the floor. I had fainted. It was clear that I was not coping at home. Nobody was. So on Monday, two days after Daddy was killed, it was decided that I should stay at my friend from Saheti, Demetra Constantinides. The family took me into their home like I was one of their own.

I received so much love and comfort from them over the following days, it was like balm to my shattered self. Nothing was expected of me; Demetra was just there, beside me, in the background. There was no pressure to talk about anything, so we landed up watching a lot of TV. Sometimes hours would pass in which I could just forget about what had happened, managing to lose myself in moments of normality.

Outside of my little world, in the days that followed Daddy's death, protests, violence and looting erupted all over South Africa. Mass stayaways were called for. Security forces swarmed the townships. Over 500 people were injured in sporadic violence across the country. Memorial rallies sprang up everywhere. Police responded with brutal force against grieving protestors.

On the Tuesday morning I woke up to hear that I was to be collected by relatives to view Daddy's body in the morgue downtown. I remember how freezing it was when I walked into the cold, bare-cement room lined wall to wall with coffins. I was led to a closed, rectangular mahogany wooden box in the middle of the room. We all stood around in silence, my mother, my two sisters, our relatives, and some of Daddy's comrades. A man opened the coffin and there he was – my Daddy, still in his blue tracksuit, the one he loved to wear when we went jogging. But this man lying there, so still and frozen, didn't look like my beloved Daddy at all. He seemed all puffed up and swollen, unreal, even slightly grotesque. Like some alien moulded from clay. They had applied heavy make-up but I could still see where the bullet had penetrated the side of his face. I stepped forward to touch him. I needed to touch him, to feel whether it was him, to feel whether he was real. When I looked up, the first person I saw was his bodyguard, Mazda. This big man, standing there, huge and imposing, just couldn't hold back his emotion. He caught my eye, and quickly looked up at the ceiling, blinking furiously, fighting back fierce tears that now ran down his cheeks.

For the first time, I saw with my own two eyes that my father was dead. Gone was my vibrant, loud and loving Daddy. There'd be no more morning runs, no long conversations, no watching *Agenda* together, swimming lessons, hugs and jokes. In that morgue, I knew he was never coming back.

When I got back to the Constantinides' home, I was numb. I remember listening over and over to Boyz II Men's, 'It's so hard to say goodbye to yesterday', which was a big hit at the time. It felt as if it was speaking directly to me.

It was only then that I let myself cry properly. The tears seemed to have no end, like I would drown in my tunnel of sadness and never come back.

Over the next few days, each time I played that song, I cried and cried and cried. I think I must have driven poor Demetra and her family mad.

Dem had a younger sister, Eva, who must have been about four years old, a little shadow who loved following us around. I remember sitting in the TV room with Dem one afternoon when little Eva came running in to try to find us when she suddenly slipped on her bum. We looked at each other and just burst out laughing. That was the first time I had laughed since Daddy had died.

Although I left our family home, Khwezi had insisted on staying with our mom in Dawn Park. Later I found out that she had got to meet Muhammad Ali. I was totally jealous. Throughout my life I have had intense crushes on military types like Lenin, Che, Malcolm X. And then, of course, Muhammad Ali – he was one of my heroes. Even today, I still find myself saying that the man I would love to land up with must be a gentlemen and a soldier, which kind of describes my father perfectly. Talk about daddy issues ...

When I wasn't feeling numb or listening to Boyz II Men and weeping, I was filled with deep rage. Watching people riot and burn things on TV, I could feel their deep anger singe a hole right through my heart. I felt at one with each and every one of them.

Their rage was my rage. Inside I was like, "Burn this fucking place down, burn it!" For now it was clear that this country had brought us nothing but pain. Fewer than three years after we had Daddy permanently back in our lives, just as I'd got used to the Promised Land, my very own Huxtable family, that dream had been destroyed.

I remember seeing Nelson Mandela on national TV, four days after Daddy had died, trying to calm the shattered people of South Africa. As I watched him address the nation, sitting on the couch in the Constantinides' home, it was hard to process the mixture of pain, anger and sadness I felt that night.

At the end of his speech all I could feel was the huge emptiness, the black hole of senseless loss. My father was dead. I hated Nelson Mandela that night, I hated him for being alive – it should have been him who had taken the bullet, not Daddy, because more than anything, I wanted the pain that felt like it was killing me to be avenged.

CHAPTER 8

'It's hard to say goodbye to yesterday'

I finally went back to my family home on the Saturday, just six days after Daddy died. According to custom, the departed must be returned to the family before the day of burial so that the body can leave from home. But because Daddy had died a violent death, his body couldn't, so on the day of the funeral his body was driven past the house but the coffin never entered.

I have so little recall of what happened over the following two days. I know there was a memorial for Daddy on Sunday, 18 April, when his body lay in state so that mourners could have a chance to see him before the big funeral service at FNB Stadium on Monday. I have a single snapshot memory of Khwezi standing next to Daddy's coffin the entire time, refusing to sit down, as a stream of people walked past to view his body. Years earlier I had stood beside our father in Moscow, holding onto his big warm hand, staring at the body of Lenin. Now it was he who was in the coffin.

☽

I woke up on Monday, the day of the funeral, with our house in chaos. People were moving in and out of rooms, all trying to get dressed at the same time. I wore a black-and-white dress with long sleeves and a checked black-and-white, flared skirt. That was the first time in my life that I had worn black. Growing up, Mama had always insisted that we never wear it; we didn't even own black T-shirts because she believed the colour looked miserable on children. She had never been so right. As I looked at my reflection in the mirror, I could not have felt sadder. Or older.

Once we were ready, we made our way outside to a huge cream limousine waiting in the driveway. In the midst of all this horrendous tragedy I felt a weird tinge of excitement at the thought that I was to be chauffeured in such a spectacular car. For a moment, sliding across the plush, creamy leather seats I almost managed to forget the reason for my being there. But once the huge fleet of police sirens began wailing, with their blue lights flashing, as the limo lurched forward to drive us across town to the FNB Stadium in Soweto, the sad sickness in my stomach returned.

The air was icy. The sky, a huge achy blue, loomed above us.

I have never, to this day, seen so many people in my life as when we pulled into the stadium that day. Tens upon tens of thousands of people had gathered to say farewell to Daddy. Reports later estimated that over 100 000 had crammed into the stadium that early Monday morning, designed to usually accommodate no more than 80 000. Making our way across the field, which seemed to go on forever, clutching Mama's hand as though my life depended on it, the crowd roared, a thunderous cheer erupting from the stands. Their voices boomeranged in my ears for years to come. It seemed like the whole country, the whole world, the whole universe had come to say goodbye to Daddy.

I hardly remember who spoke or what was said. In my 12-year-old mind there were millions of words, words that seemed to go on for far too long, bouncing off my aching heart, as one by one people endlessly took to the podium to speak about Chris Hani the leader, comrade, soldier and friend.

I remember Nelson Mandela speaking for what felt like forever. I hardly managed to listen to his speech except for the last part ...

I would also like to address a final word to Chris himself – comrade, friend and confidant.

We worked together in the National Executive Committee of the ANC. We had vigorous debates and an intense exchange of ideas. You were completely unafraid. No task was too small for you to perform. Your ready smile and warm friendship was a source of strength and companionship. You lived in my home, and I loved you like the true son you were.

In our heart, as in the heart of all our people, you are irreplaceable. We have been struck a blow that wounds so deeply that the scars will remain forever. You laid down your life so that we may know freedom. No greater sacrifice is possible.

We lay you to rest with the pledge that the day of freedom you lived and died for will dawn. We all owe you a debt that can only be repaid through the achievement of the liberation of our people, which was the passion of your life.

Fighter, revolutionary, soldier for peace, we mourn deeply for you. You will remain in our hearts forever.

Amandla!

Over the course of the morning many speakers followed Nelson Mandela, but in my 12-year-old separated self, most of that Sunday whirred past me in a blurr. There were moments when it felt as though people were speaking about a stranger, not my father. What struck me most on that day of death was, for the first time, I really realised just how huge my father had been in the hearts and lives of South Africans. How relevant his life's work was to so many people.

After the service, at around noon, we climbed back into the limo; this time I felt no trace of excitement, travelling in this maudlin hearse. I knew we were on the last stage of our journey, the burial of Daddy, to say our final goodbye.

Inside what is now the Thomas Titus Nkobi Memorial Park in Boksburg, the sides of the white tent flapped, a sad shelter set up around a deep gash in the ground, a mound of earth piled up on one side. I remember grasping both my sisters' hands, struggling to breathe, pushed and squashed between people. But the part I remember most was when I was ushered forward and a white dove was squished into my hand. I was told to hold on tightly until I got the signal to release it. I was terrified of this feathered creature, its heart quaking in my hands. I don't know who was trembling more, the bird or me, as it struggled to break free. To this day birds and I have a mutual understanding to stay away from each other.

Finally, the 21-gun salute shattered the silent sadness, and my voice softly joined the mourners as they lowered the wooden coffin, holding Daddy's body, deep into the dark brown earth.

Hamba, hamba kahle mkhonto
We mkhonto, mkhonto we sizwe
Thina, thina bathmkhuntu sizmisele
Wafuna bulala
Thina wa mabunu

I don't remember where I went after that, what I ate or who I spoke to.

CHAPTER 9

The silence after

After the chaos of the week before, everything fell dead silent. Our house was now a tomb, a prison of pain. We wandered through rooms, dumbstruck. I even found myself longing for all the noise and the people I had hastily escaped when I went to stay at Demetra's house.

For the next few weeks there wasn't a day that went by when I didn't long for Daddy to walk in, fill the house with his larger-than-life presence, his booming laughter. My aching for him found its way into my dreams where he'd sometimes come to me and tell me that he was in hiding for his safety, that he had faked his own death.

I couldn't bear the gaping hole of sadness at home so I went back to school the following week. What a relief it was to be out of the house. It seemed everyone knew of my loss; there was no need for explanations. On my first day back, my close friends rallied around me like my own personal protection service; I don't think that I even went to the bathroom alone. As I made my way between classes I could feel eyes on me and looks of pity, but in a strange way all this attention made me feel a whole lot better than I would have been amid all that powerless sorrow at home.

On 24 April, just five days after Daddy was buried, Oliver Reginald Tambo died. I was devastated; having just lost Daddy and now

OR – it felt as though heartbreaking loss kept taunting me. OR had been such an integral part of my childhood, the name I heard over and over again while living in exile. Our whole family simply adored this man. In my mind Oliver Tambo *was* the ANC. There was no one like him. Every time I'd see him, he would greet me with a huge smile and a hug. I remember asking Mama how it was that OR knew all our names and she would respond, "That's Tata for you." During that week I heard many times, over and over again, that Daddy's death was too much for him to handle and that "the same bullet that killed Chris Hani killed OR Tambo".

Two days later FW de Klerk announced that South Africa's first democratic election would take place on 27 April 1994.

○

Initially, Mama didn't want me to attend the trial that followed Daddy's death, but I begged her so much that she finally relented, agreeing that I could go for just one day. I wanted to see the men responsible for killing Daddy, but most especially I wanted to see the man who pulled the trigger, Janusz Waluś, in person.

It was an icy winter's day in May, the day I went to court. As I stood, pale and wide eyed, in the old elevator taking us up to the courtroom, Uncle Tokyo, who stood beside me, looked at me and told me that I should be strong, that I should not show any emotion and especially not cry as the whole country was watching. To this day I loathe being told to be strong. But on that day I did as I was told. I kept my tears tight fisted inside and didn't crack.

I remember craning my neck as Waluś entered the courtroom. The first thing that struck me was how tall he was. I wasn't sitting close enough to see those cold, blue eyes that had stared at me from every single newspaper over the past few weeks. But I did notice his extraordinary white-blond hair. At the time, I was completely obsessed with Wesley Snipes and had recently seen the movie *Passenger 57*. Every time I saw a picture of Daddy's killer I was reminded of the terrorist played by Bruce Payne in that movie. By the end of that day in court I was filled with almost unbearable anger and an even deeper sense of complete desolation. I watched the rest of the trial on TV and read daily the headline stories in the newspapers.

While the trial unfolded, life creaked on as it invariably does after death. But as a broken family we were merely shells of ourselves, barely coping with the very basic motions of waking, eating, going to school and sleeping. At night, Uncle Tokyo's bodyguard, Smanga, slept on the couch in the lounge to protect us from the continuing right-wing threats against our family, which came by way of phone calls and letters. On one occasion, I picked up the ringing telephone to hear a woman's voice demanding to speak to my mother. When I told her Mama wasn't in, the woman claimed to be Gaye Derby-Lewis, insisting that her husband Clive Derby-Lewis – the man behind my father's murder – was innocent.

As comforting as it was to have Smanga in the house, there were occasions when it almost backfired, as Khwezi discovered one night, on her way into the kitchen for a midnight snack. The passage from our bedrooms to the kitchen was carpeted, making it impossible to hear footsteps. As she opened the family door to get to the kitchen, she was suddenly confronted by Smanga and his gun. After that incident, he told us to always announce ourselves, especially if we were wandering around the house at night.

On 15 October 1993, Janusz Waluś and Clive Derby-Lewis were sentenced to death for my father's assassination by Judge CF Eloff in the Rand Supreme Court. The ANC would later place a moratorium on the death penalty when they came to power, so ironically the lives of the men who killed my father were saved by their enemy when their sentences were commuted to life in prison.

Back at home, our house in Dawn Park heaved with pain and too many reminders of our loss, so we were all relieved when Mama announced that we were moving to a new house in Bramley.

A complete change of scenery was what we needed. Once we were in our beautiful, white split-level home with its luscious garden and tennis court, I finally found myself no longer constantly waiting for Daddy to come home. Slowly it began to feel like we had left the ghosts and the blood on the driveway behind. The year

1993 ended in the new house and at last it felt like our lives were starting to creep back to some kind of normality.

In the new year, Mama threw herself into canvassing for the upcoming first democratic election to take place on 27 April. On any given day we would come home from school to find our living room full of domestic workers as our mother passionately conducted voter education. Within months, Nelson Mandela became South Africa's new president and Mama, who'd been nominated as a member of parliament, now began travelling between Joburg and Cape Town to serve as an MP. During this time my Aunt Fozie really stepped up, helping to shuttle us to school when Mama was away. I loved when she stepped in because it brought about a sense of family with my cousins Luigi and Alessia. We would often travel between their home in Saxonwold or our home in Bramley.

At this point we moved out of Bramley into the house my mother had built in Morningside. With Mama now travelling so much, the house became a magnet for Khwezi's friends, some of whom would drop by armed with alcohol.

Initially, I took responsibility for the house, terrified that someone would get out of control and mess up the place. I was petrified that our mother would unexpectedly come home from Cape Town and freak out. It felt like I was forever telling Khwezi, who had a much more laid-back approach, "Don't do this ... Don't do that."

Although we had our nanny, Ausi Tsoana, looking after us, as well as friends and family who weighed in, I really struggled not having Mama there full time. In many ways, it felt as though, in one short year, we had lost both our parents. Without her watchful eyes, my schoolwork went down the tubes. With Khwezi more and more caught up with her friends and partying, I was feeling utterly isolated and lonely.

Seeing me so lost and forlorn was probably the reason Mama gave in and agreed that we could have a dog. This soon proved to be a huge mistake all round. I think we liked the *idea* of the dog rather than actually having one. Our neighbours presented us with the gift of a poodle, which I promptly named Sandy after the dog in my favourite movie, *Annie*. I thought Sandy would arrive clean, cute and already trained. Instead we got an annoying, messy dog that literally shat everywhere. As a result, she was banned from coming inside the house. But what else could I expect from my black, pet-unfriendly mother?

As the year dragged on, I became increasingly unhappy at Saheti, which reflected in my shoddy schoolwork. When people asked me how I was, I would reply robotically with, "Fine". Years later I would discover that 'fine' is an acronym for Fucking Insane Neurotic and Emotional, but I hung onto 'fine' no matter what.

One evening in 1994, alone in my bedroom, drowning in a pit of utter hopelessness and despair, I called my cousin Kobina in Lesotho, telling him that this life was just not for me. I missed Daddy too much. As hard as he tried to cheer me up and reassure me that he loved me and everything would be 'fine', I simply couldn't believe him. As soon as I hung up the phone I lay on my bed for a while, then walked into the bathroom, grabbed a box of Panados and decided to end it all. I took more than 10 tablets and lay there, waiting for death to take me from the hell I was living. I soon fell asleep, but woke up hours later in disbelief and despondency to the fact that I was still alive. The next thing I found myself hugging the toilet, throwing up a ghastly combination of Panados and bile.

Tearfully, I told Ausi Tsoana that I was 'fine', that I was just feeling a little sick, and proceeded to spend the entire day in bed. I decided to not tell anyone about what I had done, but at the same time I deeply resented my family for not noticing how desperately unhappy I was. My unheard cry for help was deafening.

CHAPTER 10

St Cyps

M idway through 1994 I told Mama that I no longer wanted to go to Saheti, that what I really needed was a change. Khwezi had also decided to leave St Dominic's so I was given a choice: either join Khwezi at Damelin in Joburg, or move to boarding school in Cape Town. And so the fight-or-flight instinct was ignited in me, a syndrome I would experience many more times in my life. I opted to flee because at this point I simply had no strength to fight.

Mama and I thus flew down to Cape Town to choose between two schools: St Cyprian's, a private all-girls school in Tamboerskloof, or Herschel, a private all-girls school in Claremont.

The minute I walked into St Cyps, I got a really good feeling. I immediately felt drawn to the headmistress, Mrs Fairbairn, a warm, earth-mother type with long brown hair and loose-fitting, brightly coloured clothing. She really touched the dormant hippie in me. The meeting was poles apart from my first interaction with Mr Armstrong at Saheti – and, best of all, there were no 7x7-type entry questions. Mrs Fairbairn was very attentive during the interview, genuinely interested in my interests and favourite subjects. Afterwards we took a tour of the school. The girls we encountered were really friendly, and I immediately felt at home.

Then it was off to Herschel. As we entered the school grounds, we passed a few girls who barely glanced up. Before we even got to the main reception I stopped abruptly, filled with panic, and told Mama and my Aunty Faz, "I don't want to go in." I instinctively knew that I wanted to go to St Cyprian's. Without further questions, they agreed. My decision was made: I was going to be a powder-blue-tunic-wearing St Cyps girl.

For the first time in over a year, I felt a glimmer of hope and a lightness in my heart. I managed to drag myself through the last few months at Saheti. Because my marks had been dismal the year in which Daddy died, it was decided, after writing an entrance exam for St Cyps, that I should repeat Standard 7. I had started school a year earlier back in Lesotho so I would still be within my age group when I enrolled in my new school.

As 1994 drew to a close, my mind was set on my new life in Cape Town, but there were still tinges of sadness, knowing I would soon be leaving my friends behind at Saheti. One Saturday my friend Nicky invited me to the movies; we were to meet at her house before we left. Mama kept fussing about what I was going to wear, which really irritated me as I was "only going to the movies". When we pulled into Nicky's driveway, the garage opened and most of the kids from Standard 7 at Saheti were there, yelling at the top of their voices "*Surprise!*", holding a huge banner with FAREWELL LINDI in big letters. I was so deeply touched I nearly wept.

I arrived at St Cyprian's in early January 1995, the Sunday before school began. As a huge fan of the *Malory Towers* and *St Clare's* books by Enid Blyton, all my fantasies about boarding-school adventures had been ignited. My head was bursting with images of midnight picnics and general shenanigans.

Reality hit hard, however, as I walked into the Standard 7 boarding-house open-plan dorm, partitioned into impersonal cubicles with curtains rather than doors. I was overcome with a rush of anxiety until Vuyo, a girl with a beaming smile, talking a hundred miles per hour, burst into my space, saying how happy she was that I had finally arrived and how she'd been expecting me. I immediately bonded with her.

After Mama and Aunty Faz helped me unpack and make my

bed, I bid them farewell. Then I met the rest of the girls. There was Zani from the Eastern Cape, Lindiwe from Johannesburg, Grace from Durban and Charlotte from Cape Town – although that night it was more like an assault of faces and names.

At supper in the dining room I was intimidated as all hell by the table of matrics who seemed to be super sophisticated, grown-up women to me. I soon discovered there was a strict hierarchy at my new school. If you happened to walk near a matric student, you had to stand aside and let them walk through a doorway first. At mealtimes the youngest pupil had to sit right at the end of the table and clear the plates once everyone had eaten. But far from offending me, I loved the orderliness of things. My first night in the boarding house was thrilling, especially when it came to lights-out. The sound of stifled whispers and giggles soon lulled me into a dreamy sleep. I hadn't felt this happy and safe for the longest time.

○

I initially enrolled as a weekly border and would spend my weekends at Aunty Faz and Uncle Sam's home in Bishopscourt. This proved to be a perfect setup for the broken child in me. I had a totally different relationship with Aunty Faz to the one I had with Mama. I found it incredibly easy to talk to her about just about anything happening in my life. I loved waking up in the morning, walking onto the balcony, knowing she would be there. Then there were the night-time chats when she'd summon me with, "Darling, come talk me to sleep" – and that is exactly what she meant: literally chat until she fell asleep. And only then could I leave the room.

My life in Cape Town also meant that I had suddenly scaled the sibling ladder, as I was older than both of Aunty Faz's sons, Tsepo and Arif. Being the eldest had wonderful benefits, including front-seat privileges in the car, TV remote access and babysitting. I looked forward to every weekend – until it dawned on me that becoming a full-time boarder might have its own privileges.

I discovered this after spending time in the room of the Head of Boarders. Compared to my tiny cubicle, Zenaida's huge private room was a palace – all this because she carried the HB badge. I made a vow to get that badge when I reached matric. The first step would be to change my status from weekly to full-time boarding, which I did the following year in Standard 8.

The year at St Cyps passed quickly and towards the end of 1995 I was given the opportunity to apply for a six-month exchange programme to the Deerfield Academy in Massachusetts, USA, for the following year. To my astonishment, I was accepted. My good friend Vuyo was also accepted – at an all-girls school in Connecticut – so it was decided that we would travel together. Khwezi, along with the rest of the family, was meant to escort me to the airport. She had also promised to loan me her bag. However, my party-animal sister had gone out for New Year's Eve with her friends and by the time we were ready to leave she hadn't pitched yet. I was deeply angry and hurt that she'd placed her friends ahead of me. Naturally, I swore to never speak to my sister again. For the rest of my life.

It was the middle of the northern hemisphere's blistering winter when we landed at JFK in New York on 2 January 1996 – to discover that my host family had gone off on a family holiday. So, after leaving Vuyo with her family in NYC, I was dropped off in the quaint little town of Deerfield about 280 kilometres from New York, where my first day in the USA was spent with a temporary family. It snowed that night, and the following day the entire town was covered in a white blanket. The family took me ice-skating, which had me wobbling around like a loony on the frozen lake.

Along with the jet lag of an 18-hour flight, I felt especially disorientated when I was dropped off on the Deerfield campus the following evening. It felt more like a university setup than a school, plus I soon discovered that Deerfield was co-ed. Seeing all these males around me was intimidating on a whole other level. I was placed in a cute little house near the edge of the campus, but soon discovered that the girl I had exchanged with had left me nothing: no linen or blankets. The thought of freezing my ass off in a strange new country almost had me in tears. Luckily, the family I'd stayed with helped me out with some basics. But I ached so from the cold those first few days that I called home, crying my heart out to Mama. Always the super organiser, she called family friends in Washington DC and the next thing I was being FedExed thermal linen.

After initially feeling so overwhelmed, I was soon marvelling at my new surroundings. Each room had its own telephone – no St Cyps tickey box for all to share.

I finally met my host family over the Easter holidays, but that meant catching a bus to New York. My host mother, a short chubby Puerto Rican woman with a cigarette-induced raspy voice, met me at the bus stop after which we caught a train together to the Bronx.

I spent the next few days with the family, which included a six- and seven-year-old, and a cat! Being highly allergic, I spent much of the time staying out of the feline's way. We did the usual, family-type things like watching the kids' school play and attending church where I heard my first black American preacher and, after the sermon, sampled my first fried chicken. New York was exactly like I'd seen on TV: yellow cabs, Times Square and high-rise skyscrapers. I was meant to spend time with Ambassador Jele and his family in Manhattan, and when, after a few days in the Bronx, my host mother asked me for money for cigarettes, I decided right there and then it was definitely time to get the hell out of Dodge.

Walking into the ambassador's high-rise apartment building in Manhattan couldn't have been more different from my experience in the Bronx. From the doorman to the shiny elevators and the wooden double doors, I'm ashamed to say the snob in me thought, "This is more like it".

Everything about the apartment exuded warmth, especially the welcome from the ambassador's wife, Aunty Catherine, and their daughter Khanya, who made me feel like a sister. I was transfixed by the view from my room, overlooking the New York skyline. But all too soon it was over and I found myself back at Deerfield.

With the icy weather changing, so the snow and my unease at all this strangeness began to thaw. I soon found my groove at school, and even landed my first job ever at the campus burger joint, The Greer. I joined the black students' club and began to make friends. To this day I still regret declining a date to the prom, but in the moment my debilitating fear of the opposite sex had overwhelmed me.

Six months flew by. Time away from South Africa, from my pain-wrecked family, had done wonders for me. Instead of flying straight home when the exchange programme came to an end, it was decided that I would visit family friends in New York and DC. The New York family lived in Manhattan, in the same building as Gladys Knight, who I ran into one evening in the laundry room! I tried hard not to appear too star struck, so I casually asked her what it was like working with young stars Brandy and Tamia on the song 'Missing you', but of course my gleaming eyes must have betrayed me.

I loved walking around the Big Apple, taking the subway and shopping at Express, which was heaven because they had pants that fitted my less-than-five-foot frame. So I was less than impressed when Mama called to say that she and Khwezi would be joining me for the last leg in DC. I was still pissed at Khwezi for not coming to say goodbye to me at the airport and now her bad behaviour was being rewarded with a family holiday. I said as much to Mama. I hadn't spoken a single word to my sister since I'd landed in Deerfield. Every time she had tried to call to apologise I would hang up as soon as I heard her voice. I know, I know … Grudge much, Lindi?

And so it was that I finally returned home to South Africa, with a delicious feeling that I was now a worldly wise, sophisticated tourist of the world. Perhaps it was cloaked in the notion that "nothing can touch me" – a feeling I would come to know all too well when I later plunged into my love affair with alcohol and drugs.

PART 2

Meeting my substances

CHAPTER 11

The seeds are sown

The first time I had a drink I was probably about five or six. We were living in Maseru, Lesotho, while Daddy lived in exile in a place called 'Overseas', otherwise known as Zambia. During that time my mom would often take us out to a Maseru club where we would meet up with family friends to go swimming and afterwards to a friend's home for a get-together. I was one of those kids forever crawling, in stealthy James Bond mode, along the floor and under chairs, taking secretive sips of the adults' drinks.

When we were in Zambia visiting Daddy, he often asked me to pour his favourite drink, a brandy and Coke, which made me feel very special, like I was the Chosen One. But before I delivered it, I would make sure I had taken a secret sip.

I vividly recall the first time I got drunk. I was probably six or seven. It was over a July school holiday on the annual trek to see my father in Zambia. One night my mom and dad went out to a party so the comrades were elected to babysit. As soon as we heard our parents drive off, my sister Khwezi and I made a beeline for our babysitters, sitting around in the lounge watching TV and drinking beer. We begged them to allow us to try some.

Before the night was over – I don't know how much I drank – I was finished. All I remember was struggling to breathe, my little boep about to burst right out of my skin. While Harry Belafonte crooned in the background, singing '*Day-O, Day-O, Daylight come and me wanna go home*', I lay flat on my back, spread-eagled, burning up inside, like I was fermenting. That song became the soundtrack for our holiday. I've never been able to listen to it without recalling that swollen, woozy feeling in my tummy.

A lot of people who become alcoholics recall with fondness the first time they got drunk, but I really hated my first blotto episode with the bottle. I remember my parents coming home and freaking out at our beer-dealer comrade babysitters. I probably didn't even drink that much that night, probably less than a bottle, but it felt like I'd consumed a six-pack.

I started drinking to fit in when I was about 14, two years after Daddy died. During that time, both Khwezi and I went through a total personality turnaround. She had always been quiet and studious, her nose invariably in some or other book. Look, books were always very important in our home, especially to Daddy, but Khwezi was the one who we relentlessly teased for being a 'bookworm'. In fact, she spent so much time reading at home that when her friends came over and we told her she had visitors, she'd become irritated and say: "I didn't invite them – tell them to go back."

Then, after Daddy died, something was unleashed in Khwezi and she became quite the wild-child party animal. I, on the other hand, who'd always been the little actress, an extrovert, the mischievous, happy little joker who clowned around, entertaining everyone in the room, felt a terrible silence descend on me. Try as I might, I could not find that carefree little girl I had once been. Almost overnight and without warning, I'd lost my voice. I now had my guard up; there was no laughter in my heart. It felt like I hadn't just lost Daddy, I had lost me.

And so my love affair with alcohol and drugs began.

○

I was about 14 when I next experienced the all-consuming power of losing oneself in alcohol.

It was during this time that 'bashes' were really popular. My cousins had come down from Lesotho to visit and everyone wanted to go to a 'bash' in Mmabatho. So the older kids approached me and my younger cousin Kobina, egging us on to ask permission from my mom and uncle to attend, knowing full well that the adults hardly ever refused us anything.

Naturally, when we two little mutts went all big-eyed and innocent to ask our parents, "Can we please go to a bash in Mmabatho?", we got the nod. We didn't even know what a 'bash' was!

Soon we were all off on our exuberant way. Those were the heady days of cider. I remember drinking Bernini – standing on top of a cooler box, whooping and dancing, the centre of attention, as Trompies and Boom Shaka rocked the place. For a few wonderful hours I could forget the pain and sadness and loss; I was joyous and free. At that stage I don't think I was drinking to get drunk; it was more of a case of tagging along with the older kids, feeling important, accepted, and fitting right in.

Then weed came to join the party.

I was probably 14 or 15 when I smoked my first joint at St Cyprian's before I left for the USA. One afternoon, after school, we all walked to Rhodes Park and someone pulled out a pre-rolled joint, and the next thing we had collapsed into a total cadenza of laggies! If I thought alcohol boosted my confidence, dagga took me to a place of freedom and joy I'd never experienced before. I just felt like this was it, that this was how all human beings should feel. We laughed like a pack of hyenas all the way back to school. It felt as though, in a matter of a few hours, my eyes had been opened to seeing the world in a whole new way, like I had tumbled through the magical doors of altered perception. Now dope really became my go-to drug.

The few times I got wasted on alcohol always ended with me severely hungover. As boarders, we always returned to school for the new term a day early. In the final year of school, my friend Cherie had organised a fashion show. The wine had been donated, and there were quite a few bottles left over. The night before school started, we attacked this wine like there was no tomorrow, despite me now being Head of Boarders. We didn't even have bottle openers, so we just pushed the corks down with knives, and proceeded to get totally smashed. I was so sick, I remember throwing up everywhere. Next day I was so green around the gills that I couldn't go to school; my excuse was that I was 'ill', but I'm sure the matron knew the truth because my room reeked like a brewery.

Combining booze and weed spelt an even graver disaster for my constitution. One night when I was back in Joburg during the school holidays, I got as sick as a dog after a night of drinking and smoking with Khwezi. I remember crawling on my hands across the bathroom tiles to the toilet, my aching head hot and sweating as I heaved my insides out and hugged my porcelain god. This is how I die, I thought. The only relief were the cool tiles. Of course I couldn't go to my mom to say that I was ill.

I remember Khwezi laughing, "You've got the greenies!" All I could think was, what are 'the greenies' and can you die from them? But of course this didn't stop me from over indulging.

Back at school in Cape Town my grades were okay, much better than at Saheti. Except for Maths. Even today I still use my fingers to count. I really loved my weed and was of the firm belief that weed elevated my studying abilities. But the truth was that by matric my weed smoking had started to escalate.

The teachers clearly seemed to like and trust me as Head of Boarders and, as a result, I managed to stay under the radar. There was one incident when I seriously thought my good-girl cover had been blown. A group of close friends, who were all boarders, decided to go clubbing one Saturday night, so we all bunked out, dressed up to the nines and had raucous fun. But, come Monday, one by one all the bunkers were called out of class. This went on throughout the day until I was the only girl not summoned.

Finally, my name was called.

I thought, okay, this was it, I was bust. I even considered calling my mom to tell her that they were about to strip me of my badge.

The headmistress called me in, but all she said was: "My

girl, what are we going to do about the bunking problem in the boarding house?" She never confronted me on it. Not a word. Personally, I think she gave me a free pass. She must have known I had been right in the middle of it all.

But, even then, it never occurred to me that I may have a problem. It just felt so good to escape. I was at my happiest when I was stoned; it felt like the only time that I could be myself. It was only years later that I would connect those early stages of my using with a desperate attempt to escape the aching loss that had descended on our family just a few years earlier.

But if I thought I was done with pain, I was about to be discover that pain and loss were not yet done with me. Not by a long shot.

CHAPTER 12

Falling in love

A fter I matriculated from St Cyps in 1998, I was accepted at the University of Cape Town to study a Bachelor of Arts in English and Communications. My mom, an MP, was still living and working in Cape Town. I was expected to go into res, but I convinced her that I would share digs with my best friend from school, Mathahle. Once we started studying, I finally felt free of all authority and I was determined to leap at any chance to get loaded.

My mom gave me a car to get around in and this became a passport to go wild at every opportunity. We were Long-Streeting it up like no one's business. The parties would start on Wednesday, and carry right on through to the end of the weekend. We would drink before we left for the club. Then, before we started dancing, we'd throw back five shooters; we'd dance all night and carry on drinking right through to the following day, before crashing – only to 'fix' our hangovers with the next wild session. Studying was the last thing on my mind.

Somehow, we managed to keep our partying pretty much under wraps from our parents. If they wanted to drop by, they had to give us the heads up, and we'd rush around like lunatics making sure the place was spotless.

Although boys were obviously scarce commodities at my all-girls boarding school, in Standard 8 I developed a serious crush on the boy of my dreams, Mathahle's big brother, Sikhulule. I met him one weekend when Mathahle invited me to her family home, a big sprawling flat in Rondebosch. I remember it as clear as yesterday, my insecure 16-year-old self on the couch in the living room when this 20-year-old walked in. Without looking at me, he started rattling off in isXhosa. When he turned around, he literally jumped in surprise. He thought he had been speaking to his younger sister, Sibe, who had a similar yellow-bone complexion to me.

That night we all went to a party and I found myself unashamedly drawn to him. There was something about Sikhulule; he was totally magnetic, oozing buckets of charm and confidence. On top of that, he was so kind and sweet to me. For the first time in my life it felt like a boy had really noticed me. When he looked at me and spoke to me I felt like the only girl in the room. By the end of the weekend I was head over heels in love.

Books had always been my escape. I'd been devouring Sydney Sheldon for a while, but when I met Sikhulule I'd recently discovered Danielle Steel romance novels. So I was ripe and ready for a huge paperback-inspired romance, violin strings and all.

He had a girlfriend at the time, but I didn't care. It felt like, in one short weekend, I had met my intended.

There is no more fruitful time for a crush than when you are a teenage girl. I am the world's greatest daydreamer, so every waking hour was consumed by thoughts of him. In class I would doodle his name with hearts, and before I slept I would dream of us being together one day, getting married and living a perfect life. My crush on Sikhulule grew like a wildflower.

On weekends I would convince Mathahle to find out where her big brother was going and, naturally, I'd always try to be wherever he was. How's that for stalker alert!

When he agreed to be my date for our end-of-year Standard 8 dance I experienced pure, teenage bliss. Before long, I was kissing him whenever any opportunity arose. Before I met him, I'd been consumed by my awkwardness – I didn't think I was pretty, I was totally tongue-tied around boys – but with Sikhulule everything felt so natural. With him there was this familiarity, this meant-to-be-ness about us.

On the flipside, he was quite the player and, in reality, a really lousy boyfriend. I knew there were other girls, but his erratic availability only fuelled my crush. When we were together nothing and no one else mattered.

We started seeing each other more frequently on weekends. I would stay over at Mathahle's and we'd go to parties, where of course there was alcohol and as soon as I'd consumed one drink, I would flower, unfold from my shy shell. We made out often – stopping short of having actual sex – and he was my entire world.

There were no cellphones at boarding school back then, just these two much-in-demand tickey boxes. The minute I'd hear, "Lindi! Phone call!", I'd be running like a mad woman, praying it was him. Usually, it turned out to be my mother.

In July of Standard 9, Mathahle and I went to the National Arts Festival in Grahamstown, which happened to be close to Mathahle's parents' home in King William's Town. All I could think of was finding ways to bump into Sikhulule somewhere. Being hormonal and moody, when I did finally see him, I decided to give him the cold shoulder and punish him for all the times he'd made me think of him. He worked really hard on getting my attention and, of course, I couldn't hold out for too long.

One night, under a beautiful black umbrella night sky punctured by a million stars, he suddenly stopped the car. We both got out and stared at the perfection above. Then, just like in a movie, he turned to me, told me how much he loved me and that he wanted to marry me. He then took his gold ring and gave it to me. That is when our crush turned into true, deep love.

Of course, when we got back to Cape Town, the brother went incognito again, but that's how it was with Sikhulule. That night under the stars, ring and all, gave me all the material for my happily-ever-after, convinced now that one day we would be together.

By the time I got to first-year varsity in 1999, Sikhulule and I simply picked up where we'd left off and became a proper item. I think I lost my virginity to him almost immediately. It was one of those things that had to happen; it had been on the cards for so long. In all honesty, it wasn't mind-blowing for me – I'm not sure if losing one's virginity ever is – but he was really so sweet and considerate. From then on, we saw each other almost daily and we just gelled. I know people say there is no such thing as the perfect man, but he was the one for me.

Sikhulule was a lot like Khwezi; the life and soul of any party, magnetic, popular and outgoing. He was really strong, bordering on bloody stubborn sometimes, but he could handle me and wouldn't take my shit. On top of it, he was gorgeous and really good at making me forget my pain. He'd often play pranks on me and make me collapse with laughter; he just brought me incredible joy.

I'd been so guarded with men after Daddy died, but now for the first time I could be myself with a member of the opposite sex. Sikhulule's father and mine had been good friends during the struggle, both in exile, away from home a lot. It was a reference point between us that needed no explanation.

On the flip side, in the land called Reality, there was the hard stuff. The relationship was pretty haphazard at times. He wasn't an angel, and I knew as much from early on. One horrible day I found out he'd been seeing someone else when I came across a scratch on the door of my car, with a note attached to my windscreen wiper that read, "Fucking home wrecker". I confronted him in a dramatic showdown on the street outside. I remember running into our flat, collapsing on a futon, listening to Babyface and bawling my eyes out. He managed to convince me he'd broken up with the note-leaving bunny boiler.

When Khwezi and her friends came down from Joburg to visit, naturally I told them all about this other woman and they were like: "Show us this bitch." And, one day on the Jameson Steps at UCT, they stayed true to their word. Next thing, this gang of girls marched up to her and told her in no uncertain terms to stay away. It felt pretty awesome that they had my back. Terrified of my sister, Sikhulule of course kept a very low profile during her visit.

A few weeks later I discovered that I was pregnant. It was early

1999 and although abortion had become legal in South Africa, oh my word, the news was a terrible blow to both Sikhulule and me. We tortured ourselves over what to do: were we going to keep it or were we going to terminate? I'd just turned 18, barely out of school, and we agreed we didn't want a child that would invariably be raised by our parents. I was terrified to tell my mother. Ironically, a few years earlier, when I was in high school, my mother had been in parliament where the ANC was trying to push the Legalise Abortion bill. She had said at the time she had no problem with abortion being legalised, but she wanted girls under the age of 18 to get consent from their parents. Although I was now 18, I was still too terrified to confide in her.

I told Khwezi and Mathahle, Sikhulule told his friends and the debate went on and on: what were we going to do?

We finally decided to go for the abortion. Sikhulule reassured me, explaining that there would be plenty of time for us to have kids one day, when we were ready. Despite feeling torn and traumatised, that idea soothed me. We were young and in love – we would be together forever.

The day for my abortion dawned, so we made our way to the Marie Stopes clinic in the Cape Town CBD. I remember sitting on what seemed like a dentist's chair, in a lot of pain and feeling very uncomfortable. I prayed to God, promising Him that if He got me through this okay, that I would never have another abortion again.

No one told me how much bleeding there would be afterwards. It went on for days, intense pain and constant haemorrhaging.

The abortion left me very angry. The loss touched a deep soreness inside that reminded me of Daddy's death, an issue that remained unresolved. But instead of screaming and dealing with it, venting my anger, as usual I chose the passive-aggressive route. For about two weeks afterwards I shut down, clammed up, all silence and hostility. I needed to lash out against someone, so I blamed Sikhulule. I didn't talk to him; I just closed down. I hadn't realise how sad it would make me feel.

Finally Mathahle said, "Lindi, you have to start speaking to my brother." Eventually, slowly, I came round and Sikhulule and I had a real heart to heart where I cried and told him how I was really feeling. I told him how disappointed I was in myself that I'd let this happen, to have taken a life with my own hands. The intense loss reminded me of losing my dad, that I had killed something precious, and the whole experience had made me miss Daddy terribly. Instead of just acting like this crazy bitchy from hell, I allowed myself to be vulnerable with him. The pain and anger I'd been suppressing since 1993, maybe even earlier, finally started to ebb.

☽

After the abortion, my love and I became inseparable.

My life slowly started to get back to normal. I landed a part-time job as a waitress at Kennedy Cigar Bar in Long Street in between studying. At the end of a busy day I would come home to our flat and collapse into the arms of my man. Life was sweet again.

Then one night in May, exhausted from a long day at work, I told Sikhulule that I wanted to take a shower and rest. He asked me if he could borrow my car to go and buy cigarettes. Once out of the shower, relaxed and dry, I lay on my bed and fell asleep waiting for him.

The next thing I woke up, it was 4am and he wasn't home. I felt my heart stop. In a panic, I woke Mathathle, who also didn't know where her brother could be. It was raining heavily as I ran barefoot downstairs to a friend in the complex, but there was no sign of my love. I kept calling his phone, but it was off. Then we phoned his friends, waking them up one by one; no one knew his whereabouts. I had this terrible feeling that something really bad had happened. I started calling the hospitals. Then my phone rang; it was my sister Momo. Calmly and quietly, she said, "Don't move. I'm coming over." As I ended the call, there was a knock on the door. Two policemen stood outside. They asked me if I was Lindiwe Hani. I nodded. Then they said the words that would play over in my head forever: "There's been an accident." My world stopped moving. "The driver has been killed. The passenger's in the hospital."

I remember everything in slow motion. Just like when I heard Daddy had been shot.

People started arriving. Mathathle broke down. It was all a blur. Fragments of the story emerged. Sikhulule had been just a few minutes from home. In the heavy rain he had hit a wall. And, just like that, it was all over. He was gone.

CHAPTER 13

Downslide

I was a wreck.

Over the following few days, sketchy details began to emerge around my boyfriend's death. Apparently, he had stopped at a friend's house and the two of them had gone off to a club. On the way home he had driven past his ex, the one who had scratched my car, to tell her she needed to leave me alone, that I was the girl for him. On the way back to the flat the car had hit a wall.

Khwezi immediately flew down to comfort me. I remember a blur of crying. And crying. And more crying. I listened to LeAnn Rimes's 'How do I live without you?' day in and out. I was in a terrible state. I tried to go to lectures but I was pretty useless on campus. I had been to an educational psychologist when I was at St Cyprian's so I went back to see him. He subsequently put me on sleeping pills and antidepressants. I used them like there was no tomorrow, in a weak attempt to try to ease the aching wound inside. I walked around in a shroud of death. I soon began swallowing pills throughout the day, especially sleeping pills, descending into a complete frenzy of using.

Between the pills, it was weed, more pills, all mixed with alcohol. From the moment I woke up I would start using and throughout the day I would get more and more off my head. The sleeping pills began to make me forget everything – who I was, what I was doing, why I was alive. My mom was very concerned, but didn't really know what to do with her 18-year-old daughter who was falling to pieces. So it was decided that Khwezi move to Cape Town to take care of me. She found work as a runner for eTV, so at least I had my sister close by, which was a great comfort for me.

But all that kept turning around in my mind, on and on, over and over, was that I was a jinx; I kill men and all the men I love end up dying.

I tortured myself, wondering why I had been given such burdens to carry at such a young age; first my dad, then my unborn child and the love of my life within months of each other. People say God only gives us what we can handle, but for a long time it felt like some awful trick had been played on me, that my life was over. I struggled to get through the days that simply tortured me as time licked away the hours.

The rest of 1999 was basically a total write off.

My using kept escalating. I was walking around like a zombie. Amazingly, I thought that if I took sleeping pills during the day they would help me stay awake! Both my sisters and Mathahle were at a loss as to how to deal with me. They finally took me to a GP, who told me in no uncertain terms to stop using the sleeping pills and alcohol together. So I stopped taking the pills during the day, but I couldn't stop the drinking and smoking. I loved my weed; I could smoke all day and all night, wrapped up in my bed in a cocoon of stoned delirium.

I tried to go to a lecture now and then and even tried to write an exam here and there, but it was all just a big mess really. Of course, I constantly lied to my mother about everything.

There was a tiny crack of light when Khwezi forced me to go on a road trip to Grahamstown. At this stage, people were making decisions for me because all I did was weep and sleep. So I was bundled into the back seat of the car, where I sat, quiet and depressed, listening to music all the way there. I often think my life has been like one long soundtrack. We played Tracy Chapman's 'The Promise' over and over again. It made me think of his touch, his kiss. I would never feel his warm embrace again.

The last time I had travelled to this Eastern Cape town was when Sikhulule took my hand in the moonlight, gave me his ring and told me I was his one and only, that we would be together forever. The trip brought back all those bittersweet memories, so all I did was cry. But I realised later that I really needed to go there, to release and connect with my feelings. The whole journey turned out to be a turning point.

Inch by inch, I slowly started dealing with my loss and the death of my love.

At the end of that year, 1999, we were invited to spend the millennium celebrations with my aunt, Sammy Ntsinyi, who was the South African ambassador in Italy. I flew to Rome ahead of my family. But of course, with hardly a foot off the plane, one of the first things I did was find hash and get high. It's amazing how an addict will always hunt down a fix, no matter where we find ourselves.

I was soon hitting my aunt's well-stocked liquor cabinet, polishing off all the Baileys with my cousins. On New Year's Eve, as 1999 ticked over into a new millennium, we hit the streets of Rome and celebrated. That night, surrounded by thousands of tourists and over 2000 years of ancient history, it felt like new beginnings were possible. The grief that had all but consumed me in 1999 seemed to be slowly ebbing away.

Back home in Cape Town, I decided to reregister at UCT and start my first year again. But soon the lethargy returned. All my resolutions and newfound enthusiasm, which had felt so tangible in Italy, began floating away. Khwezi, who had been my rock after Sikhulule passed, decided to return to Joburg to study Journalism at Bond University.

I was still staying with Mathahle, but after her brother's death, things changed in our flat. Again I found myself attending hardly any lectures, isolating myself and getting more and more stoned and drunk. I was lost. I lied to my mother about attending classes until I couldn't lie any longer. It was obvious that things were unravelling.

So it was decided that I should move in with my sister, Momo, who was working and living in Century City in Cape Town. But my drinking got so bad that not long after, having visited Mathahle at the flat, I crashed Momo's car. It had been a night fraught with tension, so many memories still alive and kicking in a space that was no longer mine. Naturally, I ended up getting trashed. I got into some stupid fight with friends, stormed off in a huff and next thing I found myself in the middle of an island on the N1. I had no idea how it happened.

I had all but given up on my studies before the year 2000 was even over. In December I decided to get a job as a waitress at Primi Piatti to make some cash. I'd promised myself to start the new year, 2001, at Varsity College and resume my studies at a new institution. I had high hopes. I was going to be strong and pour all my energy into my studying.

Perhaps a change of scenery was all I needed. It was clear that UCT had not worked for me. It hadn't occurred to me that the constant, self-imposed upheavals – changing flats, university, suburbs – were all just desperate attempts to avoid my challenges.

Not sticking to decisions would prove to be a pattern of self-sabotage that would haunt me for over a decade. Every time I hit a brick wall in my life, I would simply change places, locations, flats, houses, institutions. It would be a long time before I could see that the problems I was experiencing, coping with life on life's terms, were really all about me.

It was during that holiday season, as the year 2000 drew to a close, that I had my first real encounter with what would become the new Love of My Life, Cocaine.

CHAPTER 14

Sister, sister

Although Khwezi and I started our lives at each other's throats, by my late teens we were inseparable. Even though she had moved back to Joburg, we stayed connected by talking for hours on the phone every day, lighting joints together and getting stoned. I really loved weed. Eating while high, watching TV while high, driving while high, it felt like weed *was* me. Years later, weed would be by far the hardest drug to put down.

That December 2000, Khwezi's friend Sade came down to Cape Town. On my nineteenth birthday on 27 December, she and her sister picked me up after my shift at Primi to go out clubbing to celebrate. I had hardly closed the car door before I was offered a line of cocaine on a shiny silver CD. Although I had no idea what to do, I didn't hesitate. I took the rolled-up note and, in my enthusiasm, instead of inhaling it, I exhaled and blew coke all over the place. They were livid.

I felt like a real idiot when I confessed that it was my first time. Sade was genuinely shocked because she'd heard all sorts of rumours in Joburg that I was a coke head. They reluctantly chopped a new line and I took my first hit. This time I hoovered it all up. Almost immediately I felt a little more present and a whole lot more sassy, all grown up and sophisticated. It was by far the most glamorous drug I'd ever done. The rest of the night was spent snorting lines and clubbing it up until the following morning. I felt like a million bucks.

Over the next few days we carried on partying, drinking and snorting loads of coke, right through to New Year's. For the first time in what felt like forever, I was my joyous self again. This innocuous little pile of white powder had the power to lure out the extroverted, happy me, a part that I thought had been long dead after the grief and losses of 1993 and 1999.

And then, when January 2001 came along, I forgot all about cocaine and went back to my weed and drinking, without giving white powder another thought.

I started at Varsity College in February. Life seemed sweet; it finally felt like things were falling into place. I didn't realise it at the time, but back in Joburg Khwezi had become involved with a group of heavy cocaine users.

On 9 March, I was on the beach with friends in Camps Bay, smoking weed and drinking as the sun set, when Khwezi called. It was our usual, "Hey, how are you, what are you up to?" stoned-out chat.

The following morning, my mother's number lit up on my phone. Mama was hysterical. Did I know where Khwezi was? I hadn't spoken to my sister yet that day, so I told her I didn't know. Then she dropped the bombshell. A journalist had just contacted her to tell her that Khwezi was dead. I froze. My body and brain shut down. Then I frantically started calling people to try to find out what was going on. Immediately, I called one of Khwezi's friends in Cape Town who began calling friends in Joburg on another phone while I held on. Then all I heard was, "No-no-no!" And, of course, I knew it was true. My sister Khwezi was dead.

On autopilot, I called Mama back and confirmed the news. That was 10 March 2001, exactly a month before the seventh anniversary of my Dad's death. Less than two years after Sikhulule had passed.

It is hard to describe the internal devastation that ensued. That day I had to work the noon shift at Primi Piatti. I sobbed uncontrollably all the way to the restaurant. I know I could have called to say I couldn't come in to work but something inside me wanted to tell them myself. Maybe I just needed to be with people I really liked. So I wore my sunglasses and arrived there, sobbing. The manager, Eugene, comforted me as best he could, and told me to go home.

Back at Momo's place – she was working out of town – it wasn't long before friends arrived to help me pack to fly up north. I just sat on the bed, shocked and numb. Within hours I was on a plane to Joburg. I just remember being so cold. I was freezing. Like a mortuary.

By the time I landed I'd decided that I wasn't going to deal with my sister's death the way I'd done with all the other deaths in my life. I swore to myself that I wouldn't resort to drugs to try to drown my pain. That week the house was full of people, coming and going, just like it had been when Daddy died, but this time I had nowhere to run.

Soon a stream of conflicting details around Khwezi's passing emerged.

Within hours of her death, newspapers reported that Khwezi had died of a cocaine overdose. Then a few weeks later an autopsy report stated that she had died from an asthma attack, asphyxiating in her sleep. At that stage I didn't know what to think.

But from the outset I instinctively felt that there was something not right about my sister's death, that something sinister had happened to Khwezi – and that drugs were involved.

Before her burial, we all went to the morgue to see her. A few years before she died, Khwezi had had a beautiful blue dress designed by local couturiers Marc and Michael to wear to a wedding. She absolutely loved this dress, so we decided she should be buried in it. It was devastating seeing her in the coffin, so cold and lifeless. But I had decided that I wanted to do her make-up because she had taught me how to apply make-up, especially eye shadow, when I was just 14. It was then that I noticed a small cavity in her head, so deep that I could literally see her brain. No one could explain this hole.

According to our culture, the deceased needs to be brought

home before the burial so that the body can leave from the house. So Khwezi's body was put in a hearse and brought back home to Morningside. My sister was to be buried on a Saturday, so on Friday night the elders slept next to her coffin to make the transition to the afterlife easier for the deceased.

When I woke on Saturday morning I had already decided that I would not wear black. My sister had been so full of life, I didn't feel that dark colours would be appropriate. So I chose a tan dress. I was entirely numb and dead inside, perhaps in denial that Khwezi was no longer with us as I got ready in silence, moving quietly from room to room.

Many people came to the house that morning. After the viewing of the body, we left in a procession behind the hearse, the sadness hanging heavily in the air. Slowly we made our way to the hall we had hired in Boksburg. (Because Khwezi and I had not been baptised, there were issues about the service being held in a church.) Luckily, Father Stan, a priest in Boksburg who'd always supported our family, volunteered to conduct the service.

Although crowds of people came to my sister's funeral, I felt achingly separated throughout. Khwezi was to be laid to rest with my father in Thomas Titus Nkobi Memorial Park. At the graveside I read an essay she'd written in 1993 about Daddy and Daddy's death. It was only then that I began to cry. When all the male cousins, uncles and friends in Khwezi's life began to shovel sand onto the coffin, my heart simply broke.

For some reason, I remember noticing that a few women were wearing trousers, which upset me, almost irrationally so. Back at the hall, I kept to myself, smoking cigarettes as I watched groups of people laughing and chatting, networking at the funeral of my sister. That distressed me deeply, seeing people act as though nothing had happened, when I had lost my beloved sister, as well as my father and my Sikhulule.

In the weeks that followed the world heaved in silence. Any death is hard, I know, but it's not the days immediately after a death that are the most brutal – busyness and people can offer at least some distraction – it's the weeks that follow, when the empty, sad and lonely days sink in, when everyone else goes back to their lives.

I remember lying on Khwezi's bed, feeling like I would never be able to get up again. My cousin Alessandro played Bob Marley. I lay staring at the ceiling as he sang about how I wasn't to worry about a thing, how every little thing would be okay. I did not believe that it ever would.

After Khwezi's funeral, the rumours of foul play gained momentum. I became obsessed with the idea that someone had done something to her. There were whispers that she might have died hours before the incident was reported by the people, a group of local celebs, she was with. Others suggested she'd snorted bad coke – maybe she overdosed and people freaked out. Maybe someone killed my sister ... I was never clear about what happened to her.

The autopsy report remained cast in stone: the cause of death was an asthma attack. Officially, no traces of drugs were found in her system. I find that hard to believe. I know Khwezi was at the very least smoking dagga on a daily basis – we were both off our heads the evening of her death; I also know that the drug takes at least three weeks to leave the system. Ultimately, it felt like someone or some people were covering up the actual details surrounding how my sister died. Even today, I find it hard to understand why we have not been told the truth. Was it some misguided attempt to protect the 'Hani legacy'?

As time went by, I became more and more obsessed with the circumstances surrounding Khwezi's death; it was all I could talk and think about. Most of the time I just felt completely dead inside – except, of course, when I was drinking or using. Then I would just cry and cry. Despite the cloud that hung over the death of my beloved sister, after she died I threw myself into cocaine. You would think that the tragedy would have deterred me, but ironically it did just the opposite.

CHAPTER 15

After Khwezi

Instead of feeling glamorous and sassy like I had when I first used cocaine with Sade, I now found myself getting more and more emotional every time I shovelled a line up my nose. Irrational as it was, I told myself that snorting coke brought me closer to my departed sister.

By 2003, at the ripe old age of 21, white powder had taken over my life. I had left Cape Town by now and was back up in Joburg, studying English and Communications through UNISA, to which Varsity College was linked.

I moved in with my mom in Morningside. As always, Mama, the supreme coper, was just keeping on keeping on. We hardly spoke about Khwezi or the post-death depression that had once again descended on our family. Obviously, she was sad and angry, but just as she had always done, Mama was determined to forge ahead by putting one foot in front of the other and keeping a brave face, no matter what.

To make money, I got a part-time job at an ad agency. In between working and studying, I was hitting it hard, partying, drinking and coking it up. One evening, when my mom was away, we threw an impromptu coke-fuelled party at the house. One of the guests flipped out and had an epileptic fit. I panicked and immediately began calling an ambulance. My friends freaked out and dissuaded me: "You can't call an ambulance for a drug overdose at Chris Hani's house!" Fortunately, the girl recovered and there was no need for emergency services.

By now each day was like the next, mostly a blurry haze between the highs and the plummeting lows of coming down. I remember isolated incidents, small details, but I lost a grip on times and dates. Weeks passed, months slipped by and then it was another year of the same old same. Three years evaporated as though no one was watching.

My life was a mess. But, as with all 'good addicts', I was unable to see or confront any of the truth that was glaringly obvious to anyone who cared to look deeper, beyond the mask of partying and using. I simply surrounded myself with people who enabled my delusions.

In early 2004, I ended up having a very short-lived relationship with a guy – let's call him BBD. Within a few weeks I got the sickening feeling that I might be pregnant. I had read somewhere that your nipples get darker, so one morning I checked and, sure as fuck, my nipples were really dark. I immediately took a pregnancy test. Two lines appeared. Just to make certain, I took two more – with the same result. Positive.

Blind panic set in. I was no longer with BBD at this stage, so I knew I was totally on my own here.

As always when I was in trouble, I went to see my sister Momo. I thought she would freak out, but she remained really calm. She simply asked: "What do *you* want to do?" From her attitude, it was clear that she was all for me keeping the baby. "It's really not a big deal," she kept on saying. By the end of the conversation she had me starting to believe that I would be able to handle being a single mom and that she would be by my side.

Of course, initially I thought it was the end of the world, but within a few weeks I'd made my decision to see it through. I'd simply experienced too much loss in this short life of mine. I could not survive yet another death. This was a life. So, despite being petrified, I decided to keep my daughter.

But now the real challenge reared its head ... How was I going to tell my mom? I was terrified that Mama, who was so averse to anything that would sully the Hani name, would freak out. So we asked my aunt, Sammy, to tell my mother when she went up to Lesotho. I figured that hearing the news in another country would somehow soften the shock, plus it would give her roughly four hours' driving time to process it before confronting me.

Later I heard that, on being told the news, Mama had fainted, that her blood pressure had dipped and she had had to go to the doctor.

That evening, when I heard my mom's car pull up, I was shitting bricks. I have never been so scared in my life. She walked into the house, right past me and, without uttering a single word, headed straight for her room, closing the door behind her. Before I went to sleep I locked my bedroom door. I was irrational, terrified that she was going to perform an abortion on me in my sleep. Two days went by and not a single word from my mother.

Finally, I couldn't stand the tension any longer. I had to break the iceberg. Her fury was let loose. Of course, as I had expected, she berated me for being too young to have a baby. But I had my counter argument well planned: "But you were the same age when you had my sister." And when she brought up the trials of single parenting, I responded with, "Yes, I know it's hard; I've seen you struggling – you brought us up that way." But I think I really aced it when I said, "If I'm half the parent you are, then I'll be fine." She couldn't argue with that one, so that was it.

With newfound purpose, I was adamant that nothing or no one was going to stop me. Mama slowly started coming round and it was clear that she had finally came to terms with it when she bought me maternity clothing. Today my mother adores Khaya, who is the centre of her world.

For the first time in many years I experienced something really miraculous and beautiful as I went through all the stages of my pregnancy. Maybe it was my age, maybe it was because there'd been so much death and sadness in our family – but suddenly there was this new hope and new life, which I embraced with mind, body and soul.

Khaya's father, BBD, came to a few gynae appointments but my rocks during my pregnancy were Momo and my friend Lindi. I'd been working at a recruitment agency for just a month when I found out I was pregnant and for the rest of my pregnancy I happily went to work, while my tummy and boobs ballooned.

I stopped using completely. I couldn't even drink – the smell of alcohol made me sick. Cocaine was the last thing on my mind. Besides the odd cigarette here and there, the next nine months saw me the cleanest and healthiest I had been in over a decade.

Initially I was told my baby would be born around 25 December, but as she got fatter and taller in utero, the due date was moved to November. I was really excited because Khwezi had been born in November. I hoped she would be born by natural birth on the eleventh, on Khwezi's birthday, but from the outset the doctor made it clear that I might have to opt for a Caesarean as my daughter's head was super big, and I am rather small.

Finally, on 31 October I was booked into the Park Lane Clinic for induced labour. Although it was exhausting and insanely uncomfortable, I still believe my period pains were more intense than labour.

After 15 hours, however, I still wasn't fully dilated. Then, at the last minute, my beautiful, stubborn, unborn daughter decided to turn. I was now facing a breech birth. I remember thinking: "Look at this child, she's being a bitch already!" There was no arguing with my doctor now who immediately prepped for a Caesarean.

I never wanted my daughter to hear one day that I hadn't allowed her father to be at her birth, so I asked BBD to come into the theatre with me. He was there the entire night, finally witnessing the birth of his daughter at 08:45 am on 1 November 2004. October had passed, which made me very happy. All along I'd really wanted a November baby because I firmly believe – and still do more than ever today – that my daughter Khaya is a reincarnation of Khwezi.

We spent two nights in the maternity ward and I can honestly say I have never seen so many people visit someone in a hospital. People I hadn't seen for years, people I never expected to come, were in and out, queues and queues of people coming to celebrate the birth of a Hani granddaughter. It was the first time there had been happy news from the Hani quarter in over a decade.

I was in love with my daughter from the moment I set eyes on her. Not only did she remind me of Khwezi, but today she also reminds me a lot of my dad and when she was born she was the spitting image of her paternal grandmother, Gogo Tomato. My life after Khaya came into this world changed in every way, although of course in those first few weeks I was overcome with exhaustion. I also experienced challenges with breastfeeding from day one. I had inverted nipples, which caused problems with the milk flow, so I got a breast pump to express milk. I even joined a breastfeeding support group. I remember going there one day, having hardly slept the night before and feeling like some psychotic zombie, and someone in the group reminding me that sleep deprivation is one of the most effective methods of torture. I understood completely.

In those first few weeks I put myself under a lot of pressure, trying to prove to everyone – especially my mother – that I was coping. I had made this decision for myself and I needed to show the world that I was capable of doing everything, not just well, but like a superstar.

Although I embraced motherhood with everything I had, there were times during those first few weeks when all Khaya did was sleep, eat and cry, making me feel like a glorified nanny – bath, feed, change, feed. I was on the go all the time, a bottle in one hand, changing her with the other. Sometimes when she cried all night I saw myself looking at the wall above the bed and suddenly I understood how some mothers could lose it with their babies.

Then one day, she was just a few weeks old, she looked at me as I changed her nappy, and suddenly gurgled and smiled. I fell in love. Hard. I thought my baby, this special little soul, was the most perfect person in the world.

When it came to naming her, I didn't want her first name to be Nomakhwezi – meaning Morning Star – even though she reminded me so much of my sister. I wanted her to be her own person, with her own destiny. So I decided Nomakhwezi would be her second name – Khaya Nomakhwezi Hani. Khaya is traditionally a boy's name, so everyone kept telling me to name her Nokhaya but I hate the No attached to names. So she simply became Khaya, which means Home; it felt like she and I had come home to each other.

After I stopped breastfeeding, my iron resolve to stay clean and sober imperceptibly changed. I slowly began drinking again. At first, it was just a glass here and there, days would stretch between drinks. It felt like I had it all under control. Surely a glass once in a while was normal? Everyone did it. Why not me? Then a joint crept in, another drink here and there. And so I slowly started using again.

By the time Khaya was eight months we moved out of my mom's home in Morningside and found our own place. It had got to the stage where we really needed our own space. My mom had started telling me how to be a mother and I thought Khaya should only have one parent in the house and that was me. Additionally, I could see my mother's face every time she came back from work, the compulsive cleaner faced with Khaya's baby things and toys all over her spic-and-span home.

I thought she would be upset when I told her we were moving, but instead she said, without missing a beat, "How can I help you?"

So Khaya and I moved into a cute two-bedroom flat in a complex called Marble Arch opposite the Morningside centre, close to my mother but far enough away to feel independent. I had started working again, plus I had an amazing nanny to help.

So when I began drinking and smoking a little more regularly, it felt okay, like in some way I deserved it after so many months of being the perfect mother, tending to Khaya's every need. Why shouldn't I let myself have a little reward now and then? It felt different this time; I was happy, I was different. Gone was the girl who used to party until she blacked out, just so she could forget about death. Everything about my life had changed. I really believed the birth of my daughter had put the old using part of me to bed.

But I should have known that sleep can be deceptive. And addiction is like a snake waiting to strike at the first opportunity. By the time Khaya turned two, the other Love of My Life, the one I thought I had broken up with, came knocking once again.

One night I called in a babysitter and went to a friend's party. Within a few hours, I had a bank note up my nose and I was snorting that glamorous white devil again. I really thought I was in control before I did that first line; I hadn't even been craving it … Surely I was master in this house. But, as they say, when it comes to an addict, once the beast is awakened, there's no stopping it. One is too many, a thousand is never enough.

CHAPTER 16

Back with a bang

T he thing with drugs, and especially cocaine in my case, is that even if you've stopped using for the longest time, once you hit that first line, you simply go back to the place where you left off.

On the surface I had everything in place for Khaya. I was working, earning money, I had a sleep-in nanny – to the outside world it looked like I had really done a complete turnaround and my life was in order. It was easy to convince myself that I had earned it. If I wanted to party I'd leave Khaya with my mom for the weekend and see it as a well-deserved opportunity to break free of my responsible self and go wild.

The party animal in me was really awakened after I started working for a young, dynamic marketing and events company in 2006. It seemed like everyone there was drinking and drugging. Out of a staff of 15, 10 used cocaine, including the CEO. Friday drinks would become an all-night affair; the coke would be brought out and from there on it was balls to the wall. We'd have events during the week; late nights were made all the more bearable by copious lines of coke. It was everywhere.

When you drug at the office, and you're an addict and the majority of people are doing it, it becomes completely normalised. We wouldn't do it in the day, but come 5pm when the drinks were brought out, white lines would soon miraculously appear on the table.

The job entailed a lot of travel; there were events all over the country, which meant road trips, so coke was scored before we left and it would be just one long binge while 'working'. We did tonnes of events for alcohol companies so the booze flowed all the time. Things got really out of control. It got to the point where the CEO wouldn't pitch for work, so the staff felt justified going out for long boozy cocktail-fuelled lunches, during which time a dealer would be called to deliver the coke. And so it went on.

The company eventually went bust – no guesses why! Retrench-ments ensued, and it wasn't long before I was left without a job. What I did have, however, was a reawakened cocaine habit, very much alive and kicking.

And so I would just sit at home, in my townhouse in Riverclub, near Parkmore, doing nothing. Some afternoons friends would come around, the drinking would start and invariably someone would suggest a line, the dealer would be called and so it went down.

My pattern of using has always been to binge uncontrollably and then abstain, brought on by lows and soul-wrenching guilt. So at that stage I would take breaks, making deals with myself once I saw things were getting out of hand, promising myself that this was the last time. I would delude myself that I had the power to control and stop my using whenever I felt like it.

This is the anthem of an addict, the cycle of denial. The idea that we are in charge. That we 'don't really have a problem'. Back then I believed that my real issue was cocaine, so if I managed to stop using white powder, then everything would be fine. I conveniently ignored the fact that I was drinking and smoking it up daily.

Money-wise, of course, things had become unmanageable. Coke is a hellishly expensive habit so there were often times I would have to 'make it stretch', wangle IOUs from the dealer, who would either come to my home, or meet me at a prearranged spot.

I would wake up the morning after a binge wanting to kill myself. The downer after cocaine is deathly, the guilt and shame overwhelming. But denial is an iron-clad bitch and a few hours later I would reach for a drink or a joint and all my guilt would blur away. I would cocoon myself from reality, obsessing about ways to organise another line. The idea of just one line would make me feel better.

Cocaine made me euphoric. I was confident, funny, I could fit in and talk about anything. But of course that was just an illusion. In reality, I found I was getting more and more paranoid and violent as time went by. I would be aggressive, start fights – I seemed to be harbouring so much rage. Then, when I was high, I would often over share, dissolving into a mess of tears, weeping about my losses. In my warped existence, I told myself that coke made me get real.

The next morning the world would be a much darker place. With the downers came depression, sadness, lethargy. It could last for days – the regrets and self-recriminations, the promises to stop. "I'll never do this again" became my empty mantra. Before I knew it, my addict self was telling me that if I could just get one line, all those ugly, painful feelings would be forgotten.

While my unmanageability grew, Khaya was at nursery school, and when she came home, her nanny would be there to take care of things.

I landed another job, but the using continued. Lying came easy – phoning work to say I was sick when I was really just comatose from a binge and a hangover. I lied to my friends, my mother, my sister, the nanny, to my daughter, but of all those, the person I lied to most was me.

Of course, my mother was concerned. She must have known things were not okay, but in her usual 'sweep everything under the carpet' approach, we didn't talk about such things. She helped with Khaya, and she continued to be a wonderful grandmother. As my using escalated, she would tell me I was drinking too much. My response was to keep quiet, look the other way, change the subject. I don't think she knew about the coke, and if she did she was probably in denial about that too. I have learned that addiction is often a family disease and part of that disease is the secrets that we keep, brought on by shame and fear.

There were definitely times I knew in my heart I was an addict. I would often tell people, "I know I am an addict", usually when

I was high. But that momentary insight would get me nowhere, because soon I was lying to myself again: "Just one more time, and I'll stop tomorrow." Face to face with my addict self, I felt powerless over the urge to change my feelings by getting high.

Khwezi's death under those suspicious circumstances should have been a warning tale, but the loss of my sister only made me want to get high. I was careless, I had no regard for my own life. I didn't think beyond my immediate gratification, or even care whether I might die in the process.

But I couldn't escape the shame and guilt. I would often get the feeling that both my dad and Khwezi were watching me, bent over a table with a note up my nose. I knew how disappointed my dad must be, how worried and guilty Khwezi felt. Being high was the last place they wanted me to be. I knew that Daddy was not just disappointed; he was deeply concerned and scared for me.

During those years I avoided going to visit both my dad's and Khwezi's graves. I am not someone who enjoys visiting cemeteries anyway, but the drugs made me want to avoid the reminder of my heritage of sadness and death.

CHAPTER 17

Wasting time

I t's amazing what happens to time when you're using. It slips
away like oil. It disappears like dust after a storm. It was only
when I checked into rehab and got real about my life that I fully
realised how more than a decade had evaporated, with me in my
zombie-like state, a drug- and alcohol-induced haze.

A typical bender would start with me calling around to see what
was happening – a birthday celebration, a get-together. Before I'd
leave the house I'd call my dealer. In the early days it was much
more spontaneous; I'd be out somewhere and someone would say,
"Let's get a gram", and we'd all call the dealer together. In those
days it was for fun, to laugh and get high with a group of friends. It
was often just to even out the drunkenness. But now I was arriving
at every social event – a wedding, a funeral, a dinner party – armed
with my own drugs. I just couldn't live without cocaine. Now, if I
took one sip of alcohol, I craved a line.

I swapped a rolled up bank note for a straw to shovel the coke
up my nostrils. I mean notes were so unhygienic – who knew
where a dirty note had been! My own personalised straw seemed
so much more sophisticated.

I loved using alcohol and coke together. If I just used coke I
would get far too jittery and edgy, but the alcohol evened it out
and brought me down just enough to be able to cope with the

anxiety. By this stage my go-to drink had become whiskey.

The cycle of using had me imprisoned. As much as I tried to deny it and keep convincing myself that I was a good mother, there were more and more nights that I would black out somewhere and not come home to Khaya and her babysitter.

One night in 2012 I went to the house party of a friend of Khwezi in Parkmore. It was during the week, but of course I'd asked my live-in nanny to babysit. While most people bring a bottle of wine or a plate of snacks, I arrived with a gram. I proceeded to mix it all up with excessive drinking. I remember being really loud, dancing wildly and speaking a lot of rubbish, which made some people really uncomfortable. Later I was told how I'd lost control, slapped a friend and had to be physically restrained and forced to go to bed. I woke up the next morning in the same house with absolutely no recollection of what had happened. Panicking because my phone battery had died during the night, I raced to get home to take Khaya to school, terrified that something had happened to my daughter. Khaya, in turn, was in a terrible state, petrified that something had happened to me. I was overwhelmed by guilt at having put my little girl through such fear.

With me out the whole night, and unable to reach me, my nanny had panicked and phoned my mother and sister. Of course, there was hell to pay, followed by screaming matches between Mama and me.

Although Khaya was still besotted with me she could sense something was wrong. From then on she would get really scared and clingy whenever I left the house, anxious that her mommy wouldn't come home.

In waking moments, usually the following day, when the terrible cocaine blues descended, I was crippled by guilt for Khaya and self-hatred for myself. Then I would promise myself I would never do it again. I'd stay home for a few weeks, be the perfect mother, but then something would come up and the cycle would start all over again. Even when I wasn't using, cocaine was on my mind all the time. It really had me in the grip of its white powdery tentacles like a toxic lover.

People coming to see the aftermath of the bomb in Lithabaneng. This was before my time.

The damage to my parents' car.

Part of the roof fell down.

One of the few pictures of me as an infant. I was around six months old.

My cousin Thebe, my sisters Neo and Khwezi, my great aunt and myself.

During Christmas at Devcourt, with Khwezi and Momo.

In Botswana with Ntatemoholo and Malome Mophete. We stopped over to see Malome and his partner Jane as he wasn't allowed into Lesotho.

Khwezi and me with Aunty Jane. This was George's trip to meet Daddy.

Daddy and his girls at Victoria Falls.

In Russia with our translator.
The colour coordination was not planned.

Sight-seeing in Moscow.

Striking a tourist pose at the fountains in East Germany.

Sisterly pose in East Germany.

Daddy and me on a rock at the Black Sea.

I love this picture of me clutching Daddy's leg, Black Sea.

Momo, Ntate Makgatho and me, with Khwezi in the water. This holiday was filled with family activities such as boat paddling.

Momo, Daddy and Mama in Germany.

Daddy and me in Lusaka.

In between giants: Daddy, me and Uncle Steve Tshwete in Zambia.

The Hani girls on a cruise ship; nobody seems to remember where we were going.

Sammy, me and Khwezi at Ntatemoholo Sekamane's house.

Khwezi, me, Mama, Tsitso and Momo outside the SEDA residence. Mama worked for the Swedish agency for years.

The cutest nemesis ever, Tsitso and me in Maseru.

Khwezi and me; her hair was always on point while mine always looked like a mower had just been through it.

The girls in Mama's room at Devcourt.

My entrance picture for
Miss Ladybird (Devcourt).

Mama and me in our
lounge at Devcourt.

When Daddy came to visit in
Lesotho, family friends threw
him a party.

During our first few weeks
in SA, Khwezi and me in our
cousin's room.

Mama and Daddy in Umtata.

Playing dress up in Pali's
heels in Maseru East.

My cousin Selloane,
Gabi and me in
Dawn Park.

Celebrations at the Sexwale's in Dawn
Park.

Visiting
Nomathemba in
Maseru after we had
moved.

Our family portrait we used as a thank you card after Daddy died.

Khwezi and me in Bramley.

Visiting Makhulu in Cofimvaba.

Sammy and me in our home in Morningside Thembi Place.

St Cyprian's.

Saheti.

Cherie, me and Mathahle.

The Hani girls and Big Mummy Winnie at Mama's 50th.

At a party in Rondebosch.

Khwezi and me at our best, fighting in Disneyworld.

Khwezi and Momo dancing at Mama's 50th.

Judy and me at Mama's 50th.

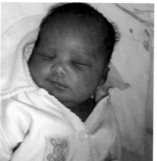

Trying to illicit a burp.

Minutes after Khaya is born.

My gorgeous girl at Mama's house.

Khaya's first trip overseas, Brazil

Ntatemoholo Sekamane in Botswana.

Tamkhulu Hani in Mafeteng.

Khaya and me in Hong Kong.

My rocks: Sbals, Zuko, Momo and Lukhanyo.

Tsitso, me, Selloane and Khaya.

Khaya and me.

The inscription at the back.

My handsome father in a picture he took just for my mom.

The way I love to remember him.

And yet, despite knowing I was traumatising my beloved child, something inside me just couldn't stop. By this stage I had lost many of my friends because I had become so aggressive and erratic; no one wanted to be around me, least of all myself. I have since learned that addicts use substances to change their feelings because they can't deal with who they are. At this point I was prepared to do anything to avoid having to be with Lindi.

There was a moment of real desperation in about 2012 when, after an all-nighter of extreme bingeing, I found myself driving to my mother's house and begging for help. This had been happening more and more regularly, the blackouts, not knowing where I'd been or how I'd got myself home.

As my mother looked at me, my hoarse voice like nails on a blackboard, pleading for help, I could feel her panic, her distaste and her shame. She said nothing, her icy eyes staring right through me, but "What about the Hani name, what will people say?" was written all over her face. She called my cousin, a doctor, and in cloak-and-dagger style, they bundled me off to a psychiatric hospital.

I was checked in under a different name. Of course. The people in white coats put me on pills, I slept a lot, I had a bit of therapy, but it really wasn't that effective. I stayed no longer than a week.

After leaving the hospital it was decided that I had to move back in with my mother in Morningside. By this stage, I could no longer be trusted to manage my own finances. Cocaine is a demanding lover; one who can render you homeless before you know it.

Staying with my perfectionist mom lasted no more than about four weeks before I found a new place. My mom has always been my trigger, so I knew I had to find my own space away from her constant judgement.

I managed to stay sober and clean for about six months. I got a job at an ad company, one where there was no crazy using in the boardroom. Things looked positive. I had all the resolve in the world to stop using, get my shit together and become a responsible parent to my daughter. I was determined to show my mother that I could do it. I tried to stay clean by controlling and disciplining myself, but all I was really doing was white knuckling, while my addict self did press-ups in the corner. I wasn't in recovery. There were no 'a-ha' moments, no self-discovery – I came no closer to understanding the beast of addiction in me.

And then one day, just as things were looking good, out of the blue an idea came into my head. "You've been so good, you haven't used for six months, don't you think you deserve to be happy? How about just one hit? Then you can stop and carry on being responsible."

It took one line and I fell straight back into the arms of the Love of My Life. In no time I was boozing and using harder than ever. And my shame and deep-seated sense of uselessness and failure now almost consumed me. The time off had meant nothing – in fact, it just made me hungrier, and the hole inside gnawed deeper.

Now the isolation set in. I stopped going out. I couldn't face parties or people. I managed to force myself to go to work, but a lot of the time I just holed myself up inside and used on my own. From bingeing only over weekends, I was now using in the week, two to three days in a row, sometimes more. The desperate calls to work to tell them I was sick were on the increase. Of course, inevitably, I lost my job at the ad agency. Somehow, I managed to keep it together and find a new job at a PR company, but soon my using put paid to all attempts at holding onto responsibility. My cocaine-induced anxiety had now become so intense that on many a day the idea of leaving the house was just too much to handle. I was experiencing true drug psychosis.

It was 2014, I was 33 years old, and my life was *completely* unmanageable.

PART 3

Recovery

CHAPTER 18

Rock bottom

I f you ask most addicts how they got clean, there's often a pivotal event, a single 'a-ha' moment when something happens to wake us out of our stupor and denial. Sometimes it's a spilt second when the light finally cracks in, where we clearly see how very fucked up we are, that our using has defeated us. In our broken, desperate state, we are ready to accept that we need help. I like to see it as grace, when we are given a miraculous chance to change.

My rock bottom came in the shape of a series of events. It began after taking my daughter to school one morning in late June 2014. It had all started the previous day, when I went grocery shopping and tossed a bottle of whiskey into the trolley to have with dinner. My friend Flower was visiting, which inspired me to 'celebrate'. I was a real pro at finding any excuse to knock back a glass, which often turned into a bottle of amber liquid to toast anything from a birthday to a new blade of grass.

After playing Good Mommy and helping Khaya with homework before dinner, I called the dealer. I made some feeble excuse that I needed to go out quickly and raced off to meet him at an arranged spot, five minutes from home. By this stage I had already consumed at least three whiskeys. My heart was beating, my eyes shining like I was off on a tryst with some secret lover. A night of coke and drinking followed, of which I have no memory. Sometime during the night I blacked out.

I woke up the following morning, one gram of coke and three quarters of a bottle of whiskey later, with what felt like a tonne of bricks on my head. The gas heater was still on, the house lights ablaze and all my car doors wide open. Spinning out because I was late to get Khaya ready for school and make her lunch, I hurriedly woke her up, which gave her a fright. I didn't have time to make her lunch and promised to bring it before first break. Before leaving the house, still drunk and high from the night before, I quickly snorted a line and downed a shot of whiskey to calm my nerves.

Just after Khaya climbed out, I had an accident reversing in the car park at school. That's when the next blackout hit. I don't remember what happened next, but when the ambulance arrived, I was apparently psychotic, reeking of whiskey, kicking and screaming, completely off my head. Against my will, I was taken to Linksfield Mediclinic in the back of the ambulance. Later I was told that I'd kicked one of the ambulance guys in the crotch while screaming obscenities.

The next thing I remember I was waking up in the emergency room at Linksfield with restraints around my wrists. When my mother arrived, I was apparently horribly abusive, screaming at her how much I hated her, that she was the devil incarnate. I insisted that I only wanted to see my sister Momo. I was transferred to a private ward and given medication to calm down. During the night I decided that I wanted to crush the pills and snort them so that's what I did. When I finally woke up the next morning, calm now from all the drugs I had ingested, I was wracked with remorse. I thought I would die from the overwhelming self-hatred and shame.

I remember the doctor coming into my ward, me on those crisp white sheets, and him saying: "So what are we going to do from here? Are you going to go to rehab?"

Despite the intense embarrassment and remorse, my immediate response was "No", that all I needed to do was to go home. I could handle it. Clearly, Denial was still in the driver's seat.

So I went home, tail between my legs and, of course, everyone was on my case. But instead of listening to their pleas of "Don't drink", "Get yourself together, Lindi. You have a daughter" and "What kind of mother are you?", within a week I'd gone back to my old ways. You would think that the accident would have woken me up, but no, my love for drugs was stronger; it knew no reason and had no boundaries. Soon I was in full using mode again, worse than ever. When an addict feels shame, instead of stopping and controlling our using, we usually just use more to make us feel better and forget, even temporarily.

Friday came and, of course, I'd been using. Half cut as usual, from bingeing the night before, I was late (again) to take Khaya to her singing lesson. Afterwards I dropped her at my mom, went straight to the bottle store and immediately called the dealer. I arrived at his house quite chirpy (read: already drunk). He invited me to have a drink, which I naturally accepted. I spent the entire Saturday and night at his place schnarfing and drinking whiskey. It was pathetic. The dealer was the only person I had left in my life; he was my best friend. I had caused so much trouble with everyone – family and friends – that I had completely isolated myself. It was sitting on his couch, straw up my nose, heart racing, that it finally dawned on me just how messed up I was.

In that crack of light, it suddenly became clear as hell that I needed to go to rehab.

Armed with my final stash, I got myself home and made a call to Momo. When I told her I needed help, I was still as high as a kite, but something had changed. I was sick and tired of being sick and tired. Then, coked off my head, I proceeded to call everyone in my entire contacts list, telling them I was checking myself into rehab. Of course, I'm sure no one believed me. I still had a farewell gram waiting for me on the table, which I naturally hoovered up, but inside something profound had changed.

Later that morning I woke up feeling like hell on earth, shaking and ill. That familiar dark post-coke depression assaulted me, but for some reason this time it was different. I was done. I knew my using was over. Of course I was terrified, but deep inside I was more scared of not doing something.

That was 5 October. I'd still been schnarfing in the early hours of that morning, so I consider my first official clean and sober day as 6 October 2014.

Now I decided I had to put my plan into action.

I went over to Momo, still high and drunk from the night before. I was in that feel-sorry-for-yourself-post-slit-your-wrists using mood, lying on the bed in the cottage, dehydrated and hurling up bitter yellow bile. But between the tears and the sickness, my new resolve to get help remained strong. My mom's baby brother, my uncle Mophete, was called and he arrived to lend support to my sister.

My plan was clear. I told them I wanted to go to Houghton House. I asked Momo if my daughter could stay with her family while I was in rehab. Khaya would have all her cousins with her so she wouldn't be lonely while her mama was away for four weeks. I wanted her to be able to laugh at least once a day with my sister's three kids, within the safety of a normal, loving family.

The one thing I knew for sure was that I didn't want Khaya staying with my mom. In Morningside she would be all on her own, where she would more than likely be exposed to my mother's deep rage, further confusing and traumatising her.

Ironically, I thought Houghton House was in the upmarket suburb of Houghton, which meant I would be close to my sister and Khaya. It turned out that HH had actually moved to Randburg! But now was not the time for me to be elitist. Momo had already called to arrange that I be admitted the next morning, Monday, 6 October.

My greatest obstacle was to get Khaya back from my mother. I told my uncle he needed to go and talk to his sister to tell her that Khaya was to stay with Momo while I was away.

As I feared, my mother did not want to give me my daughter. She simply refused. She clearly got to my uncle, too, who returned from seeing her and tried to convince me that maybe Khaya should just stay with my mom, that it would be in her best interests. I said, "Over my dead body."

Of course, as expected, Mama was horrified that I was intending to book into rehab as Lindiwe Hani. She kept telling me I needed to check in under an assumed name. But I was insistent that I wanted to stop all the lies and pretending because for too long I'd been deceiving myself and everyone in my life. I knew this time that if I was to get better the lies needed to stop.

As the day unwound, I began to feel stronger. By late afternoon I had had enough of my mother trying to call the shots. I decided I was going to go over to Morningside and fetch my daughter myself. That was my deal breaker: unless I could get Khaya, I was not going to go to rehab. At this fragile stage, Momo was so desperate for me to stick with the plan that she drove me over to my mom's place herself. She had to stay in the car, outside the complex, because my mother hadn't spoken to her in 10 years. That was my mother. She was hardcore.

I soon discovered that the security guard at the entrance boom had been instructed not to let me in. So I waited for a car to come through and, as the gates opened, I ran in, with the poor guard chasing me. Talk about Jerry Springer. You cannot make this shit up!

I got to my mom's gate screaming my head off, calling, "Khaya! Khaya!"

My daughter came to the door, all sad-faced, saying: "Yaya won't let me open, Mommy."

It wasn't long before my mother appeared, but while she ranted at me from the front door Khaya darted into the garage and pressed the garage door remote. I ducked in before my mother could close it, and grabbed my daughter and her stuff. All this while my enraged mother spewed her usual angry accusations. "You're nothing but a drug addict!" I screamed back: "Well, what's new? Open the newspapers – everyone's a fucking drug addict! At least I'm willing to do something about it."

My love-hate relationship with my mother, which had been simmering dangerously for so long, had finally come to the boil. As I left with my daughter, my mother raged after us: "You're going to ruin your child!"

My parting shot was: "Well, you'd know all about ruining children."

I was shaking as I led Khaya back to Momo's car. I could tell that my little girl was upset, confused by all the drama that had just erupted. Gently I tried to explain to her. "Baby, everything you heard Yaya screaming, about me being a drug addict, it's true – but Mommy is going to get some help. Soon I will explain everything to you properly."

When we got back to my sister's house, I sat Khaya and her cousins down and told them I had a bad drinking problem. I didn't tell them about the drugs because I thought it would be too much for these young kids to process. Khaya was nine at the time, my nephews Khanyo, 8 and Zuko, 6. My niece Nani, who was just nine months old, was clearly too young to understand. I explained to them how I needed to go away so that I could get better. Khaya had already told her cousins about the drama in Morningside with my mother. I had to laugh when one of my nephews said: "Maybe Yaya should go away. There's nothing wrong with you, Aunty."

I even asked Khaya if she would prefer to stay at my mother's, but she was clear. Always the sweet child, concerned about everyone's happiness, she said would like to visit her Yaya but she would rather stay with her cousins.

Thank God my nine-year-old understood that her mommy needed help. And I'm grateful that I didn't leave it until she was 18 because by that stage my using would have irreversibly destroyed far too much.

The SMSes from my mother to Momo and me came in like machine-gun fire, berating my sister, insulting me as a mother, threatening that she was going to come and fetch my daughter. I really didn't want to walk into rehab worrying about whether my mother would make good on her threats; if my daughter wasn't safe there was no way in hell I was going to go to HH. Messages and calls from other relatives my mother was clearly talking to poured in, most of them trying to convince me that my mother should keep Khaya.

I realised I needed to put some precautions in place before I could go with a peaceful heart. On Monday, after dropping Khaya off at school, I had a meeting with the headmistress and my daughter's class teacher to tell them the truth. "I have a drug problem," I told them. "I am off to rehab and my sister Momo will be in charge of Khaya while I'm away." It felt so good to be honest and real. I explained that Khaya was only to be handed over to my sister, that under no circumstances was my mother allowed to fetch her.

My next stop was to tell my boss, Alan, about my plans. I was on a mission. Before Monday was over, I had also spoken to Khaya's dad, BBD, and his mom, Khaya's grandmother, to inform them of my plans, and both were in full support of my decision. We signed an affidavit explaining I was giving temporary custody to my sister and that Khaya's father was aware and unopposed to it.

Then it was off to the police to get it stamped and official.

On Tuesday I went back to my place to pack clothes for rehab and all the things Khaya would need for the next month. All this time I was still receiving a flood of calls from relatives attempting to convince me that my mother should keep Khaya, trying to trip me up with, "Your mother's been through so much." My angry response was: "Well, who fucking hasn't?" By this stage I'd had enough of her manipulations. I told them, one after the other, that I was done with letting my mother get her own way.

"Over my dead body," I said. "My daughter's happiness will not be the bargaining chip to keep your cousin or sibling happy." It was the first time in many years – perhaps my entire life – that I had managed to firmly say no to Mama.

There was a moment, however, when my mother's tirade even got to Momo, my strongest ally. When my sister suddenly suggested that maybe, for the sake of peace, Khaya should go back to my mom, I really dug my heels in. I was not prepared to go to rehab unless I was guaranteed that my daughter would stay with my sister. I knew I could only get well in rehab if I had just myself to think about, nothing else. Momo then made a promise to fight for Khaya with every fibre of her being and not give up.

That Wednesday, I went into Houghton House to ask advice about my daughter and the legalities around temporary guardianship. They suggested I go to Family Court as they'd seen many addicts with similar situations to mine. Family Court, in turn, suggested I take out a restraining order against my mom. But by this point she had become very quiet. I think family members must have spoken to her and she seemed – finally – to have accepted my decision. It also felt a little extreme taking this type of drastic action against her, so I decided not to pursue the idea.

So it was that I spent the rest of that week getting things in order. Having those few days gave me time to settle Khaya in. The thought of using never crossed my mind – I was on a mission and nothing could stop me. In moments of self-doubt, I did think that maybe I could stop using on my own, as I had managed many times before. But I also knew that I would stop for days, even weeks, but that I could never *stay* that way. Something always happened: something sad, something happy, a wedding, a funeral, something that would inspire the thought, let me just have one hit. I knew inside that I couldn't guarantee that this wouldn't happen again.

But as much as I knew I had to go to rehab, I was terrified of actually checking in. My intense missioning that week, the drive to get my business in order, was clearly a delaying tactic. But the clock was ticking. There was no turning back. I had told the entire world that I was 'off to rehab', and Khaya was used to the idea, excited to stay with her cousins.

However, by Saturday morning, almost a whole week since my announcement, my sister was growing concerned that I was getting cold feet. She suddenly looked at me and said: "Girl, you've got to go."

I was all packed and ready to leave, but being the queen of procrastination, I decided to cook the family a final meal. Lasagne. We had a wonderful lunch and then I spent ages washing the dishes. It was almost 4pm now. I had run out of things to do.

I don't think I've ever felt more terrified in my life. But there were no more excuses, no more delays. It was time to go.

CHAPTER 19

Checking in

I walked into Houghton House at 5pm on Saturday, 11 October 2014, six days clean and sober. My little entourage included my daughter, my nephews, my sister and Malome Mophete who drove us there.

It was a warm summery evening; family visiting time had just come to an end. The smell of meat braaiing wafted across a beautifully manicured garden; the pool in the centre, surrounded by exotic palm trees, sparkled. People were playing cricket. It really looked festive and serene.

My nephew stared in wide-eyed amazement: "This is a *hospital*? I want to come here!" It looked more like a happy holiday camp from some high-end brochure promoting some exotic destination than a medical facility.

In the admissions' office, the nurse on duty explained the procedures and rules before I signed myself in.

The first thing that was taken from me was my phone. Panic. How was I meant to speak to Khaya? On seeing my anxious face, the nurse explained that this was done to remove distractions and to isolate the inmates from the outside world, in order for us to begin concentrating on ourselves. I was told that during the first week, no calls were allowed. Thereafter I would be able to use the public phone.

The nurse then read out a list of items that were not allowed: razors, books, medication, drugs. Of course, my ever-vigilant daughter piped up with, "She's got books!" So all my books and mags went back with the family. I felt completely vulnerable; stripped of my distractions. But there was no turning back …

And yet, despite feeling nervous, relief was by far the greatest emotion. I could sense, too, that my daughter felt a burden lift at the idea that her mommy was going to get better in this happy-camper environment. So I kissed my daughter and family goodbye, and told them I'd see them in a week, the following Saturday, at Family Time. Khaya seemed happy; there were no tears, just smiles.

Once my family had gone, the nurse searched my bags – you'd be amazed how many people check into rehab with drugs stashed in a compartment of their suitcases or in or on their persons.

Now it was time for the forms:

List all the drugs you have ever used.

I remember ticking marijuana, LSD, ecstasy, alcohol, cat and cocaine. I suddenly felt quite limited and inexperienced. The list went on forever; there were so many drugs I'd never used: tik, heroin, crack, GHB, ketamine, nyaope. I was like, "What's this? What's that?" I felt like a drug virgin.

Alcohol was on the list and although I ticked it, along with dagga, I really didn't think I had an issue with either of these. As far as I was concerned, cocaine was my only problem. If I could get a handle on that then I'd be able to happily drink and smoke – life would be perfect. Little did I know that over the following four weeks I would be rudely awakened to the idea that I was an addict, that *addiction* was my problem, not the drugs I used.

When I got to *When last did you use?* the nurse was clearly shocked that I was already six days clean. Most addicts check in trashed and in withdrawal.

After all the bureaucracy was completed, as a new patient, I was sent to detox as part of the standard procedure, but I was obviously given no medication to facilitate withdrawal. I was grateful that I had come in clean and of sober mind. It helped me get used to things almost immediately. Other people I met who came in high, like the Benzo Bitches, or the smack heads, took at least three or four days to detox and acclimatise.

I think the most significant change in me since all the previous times I had tried to clean up was that this time I knew, without a sliver of doubt, that if I carried on using, I was going to die. There was no other way this story was going to end. I saw with absolute clarity how the nightmare would unfold: I would die and my mother would land up getting Khaya. I imagined my daughter growing up, becoming a teenager, knowing her mother had died because she was a drug addict. I could see Khaya inheriting this terrible burden of believing my love for her and hers for me wasn't enough for me to stop.

I already knew that my drug addiction, the terrible hole inside me that craved for more, was fuelled by loss. I didn't want her to experience this same feeling – the untimely loss of me and, as a result of her own loss, her feeling like shit about herself, which would more than likely send her into a spiral of using. I could see this destructive cycle as clear as day, this terrible image of my daughter as a drug addict.

I knew it had to stop now.

And there was also a little part of me, as sad and depressed as I was at that moment, that really wanted to know what it would feel like to experience some happiness in my life. I think deep down, some-where inside, I felt I deserved it. This life I had lived up until now – there had to be more to it. A tiny part of me was ready to find some joy.

⟲

Amy Winehouse sang about people telling her to go to rehab, to which she went, "No, no, no." And look what happened to poor Amy. For me it was exactly the opposite. I wanted to go and, once I was in there, everything inside me just went: "Yes, yes, yes."

After signing all the forms I was assigned a detox bed, along with two other new girls: Lupita, an alcoholic from Zambia, and Lerato, a pill addict from South Africa. Detox was right next to the nurse's office. In case you spazzed out in the middle of the night, the nurse would be on call.

Now it was time to meet all the other inmates gathered around the pool. The smell of meat sizzling on the braai filled the early evening air. Jan, a tall, sturdy Afrikaner, introduced himself as Head of Res; he was clearly running the show and enjoying his power trip. With an air of self-importance that only someone who had almost completed his time in rehab can assume, he welcomed us newbies and I was assigned Lupita as my recovery buddy.

As we sat down to eat, I was suddenly surrounded by a swarm of addicts: "So, what are you in for?" I would soon discover that that's the first question everyone's asked in rehab. My response of, "Cocaine" elicited a few "Ooh, larney!" responses.

After dinner it was time for my first AA meeting. That night had such a profound effect on me. It was a 'speaker meeting' during which Dave, a pharmacist, who had been clean for about 16 years, shared his story. I related so much to what he had to say. Throughout his share, I kept thinking, "I've done this", "I've done that". Strange as it may have seemed to an outsider, it made perfect sense to be sitting in a circle, listening to people who were just like me. For the very first time in a very long while, maybe in my entire life, I felt I belonged in this group of strangers. At the end of Dave's talk everyone had to say how they felt about his share. That was my worst, being put on the spot. As it came closer to my turn, my heart thumped against my chest. I felt super exposed with all these eyes on me. I think I said something lame, like: "Thanks for sharing, I was really inspired," hoping the next person would say something as quickly as possible.

After the meeting it was time for the Welcoming Ceremony where us newbies – Lupita, Lerato and I – sat in front, while the rest of the group welcomed us with, "Good luck – you're in the right place," and "If you work hard you'll make it." Then it was our turn to tell the group what we hoped to get out of rehab, after which we had to do something like dance or sing. I sang a silly nursery rhyme and said, "I'm here 'cos I'm a coke addict and I want to get to understand the demons that made me use."

Although I'd only been in this place for no more than three hours, miraculously I felt pretty much at home. By the time we got back to our detox room, Lerato had started withdrawing. I, however, was feeling pretty upbeat. Finally I'd done something positive, finally it felt like I might just have a chance at getting something right in my life.

I slept well that night without any medication.

I woke up early on Sunday, another 'free day', to discover that chores played a huge role at HH. I guess addicts become so lazy, so unfazed by the basics of everyday life, that this was a way to kick-start us getting our shit together.

I was horrified to discover that straight up it was time to clean our rooms as well as the communal bathroom. Had we come to a joint that costs R50k for four weeks to be the cleaners? And we couldn't do some half-arsed job because after breakfast the Head of Res, Sergeant Jan von Rehab, and the nurse did inspection. For a moment it felt like I was in that army movie *Private Benjamin*, with Jan marching around and inspecting. The cleaning worked on a point system – if you got under 1.5 you had to do extra duties. We managed to scrape in with a pathetic 2.

Then it was time for the whole house to go for a walk in the surrounding suburb, and from 10am it was open day for visitors. Because I was allowed no visitors at this early stage, I spent the blue-skied summer's day around the pool, bonding with Lerato, the Benzo Bitch who was still deep in withdrawals.

For the first time in years, as Lerato and I shared the intimate details of our lives, war stories about our using, I felt a little safer. We both agreed that we were sick and tired of being sick and tired and desperate to kick our habits.

My good mood was dampened, however, when Sergeant Jan approached me and, in his thick Afrikaans accent, interrogated me as to why I hadn't done one of my assigned tasks: washing the dishes after making the sandwiches. His berating me in front of all these people humiliated me. I looked at him and thought, I actually hate this motherfucker. From then on, whenever he came near I got a slight panic attack. Thankfully, Jan's stay at HH was almost over.

My bruised ego was, however, forgotten when we began to play 30 Seconds, which made me laugh harder than I had in a long, long time – like I had as a child before the darkness set in. And then suddenly, in the middle of our game, we heard this crazed screaming from inside the house, as though all hell had broken loose. "Well, fuck you! Fuck yooooouuuuu!"

All the families, kids and inmates, who'd been serenely bonding in the sunshine, stopped what they were doing, aghast. Two roommates had gotten into an almighty argument. Apparently one of them, Claire, had locked the cupboard door in the room she shared with Candice, a blonde botoxed northern-suburbs number. It transpired that Claire was not permitted to lock doors because her big problem was that she was abnormally secretive. She was actually something of a weirdo, very skittish, and always clutched tightly onto her handbag, no matter where she was. We, of course, were highly suspicious that she was still using.

Candice – who had probably been very beautiful, but now had a face that had been worked on within an inch of its life – was screaming in a high-pitched kugel accent, "Who the fuck do you think you are? How dare you fucking lock the room? I'll fuck you up!"

Lerato and I looked at each other: What the fuck was this? Then Botox Candice came out to apologise. Slowly everyone, slightly shell-shocked, went back to what they were doing. Soon after the explosive drama, the families began to pack up and leave. It was time for the weekly NA meeting, attended in conjunction with the people from The Gap, the secondary-care house next door, affiliated to Houghton House,.

As I drifted off to sleep that night I thought about my day. Besides the drama with Captain Jan von Recovery and the catfight over locks and cupboards, my first full day in rehab had been life-affirming, beautiful even, filled with silly games, bonding and laughter.

If this was rehab, then I was definitely in the right place.

CHAPTER 20

Rehab gets real

C ome Monday morning, I was quickly jolted out of my little rose-tinted cloud of ignorant bliss. The counsellors were all back and I soon discovered that the real work was about to begin.

The first thing on the agenda after breakfast and chores was something called Clearing. All the inmates had to sit in a circle to 'clear' any issues that had come up in the house. Of course, the incident between Botox Candice and lock-obsessed Claire was raised, and Candice apologised to the group for the previous day's explosion.

Once we had 'cleared' the air, everyone was put into the week's groups, in which we had to attend sessions together. All the new inmates were assigned a file and a diary in which we were expected to write every day and hand in every night to our respective counsellors. For some reason, though, I did not receive my recovery tools, and this put my newly clean nose completely out of joint. My paranoia and urge for instant gratification kicked into overdrive – why was I being left out? I made a huge fuss about it until I finally received my stuff a few days later. Maybe they were pushing my buttons to gauge how I would respond, I don't know.

Once a week we were also divided into gender-specific groups so that we could discuss issues such as abuse, being molested, how we used sex as a weapon or how many partners we'd had –

issues we might not feel comfortable talking about in front of the opposite sex.

Finally it was time for my first meeting with my personal counsellor, the tall, young, bespectacled Etienne. I was very glad I'd been assigned a male counsellor – I have always felt more comfortable opening up to males – and took to him immediately.

Within minutes of us meeting, Etienne told me straight out: "I'm going to put in 100 per cent if you put in 100 per cent. If you put in 60 per cent, that's what I'll put in from my side."

During that first session, he asked me a series of questions about myself: my background, my family and what had brought me here. I was in pieces throughout that initial encounter, sobbing like a child. If only I had known how many more tears would follow. At the end of the session he asked me who in my family was supporting me. I told him it was my sister and he responded that she would then be the person he speaks to throughout this journey. He quickly picked up that my mother and I were clearly not on speaking terms.

I had gone into Houghton House knowing that there would be a moment where I would have to own up to who I really was: Lindiwe Hani. In that first encounter Etienne told me that one way or another people were going to find out, that if I was going to get honest and work through my stuff, I needed to own my identity from the outset. That's why I had chosen to book myself in as Lindiwe Hani and not under some pseudonym, he reminded me.

On the second day, we were expected to tell the group our personal stories. I mentioned that my dad had been killed and I used the word 'assassinated' deliberately. I knew immediately that when Candice, who was in her forties, asked me, "What year was this?" and I responded with "1993", she knew who I was referring to. My words had hardly left my mouth when I saw her dashing off to spread the village gossip.

Within minutes, I had people coming up to me with: "We hear you are Chris Hani's daughter."

I could do nothing but say, "Yes, I am."

It was actually a huge relief to get that out of the way right at the outset.

Of course, the usual Chris Hani Admiration Society predictably followed. Immediately, it felt like I, Lindiwe, began fading into the background. I knew I needed to bring the focus back to me, Lindiwe the Addict, so I said, "Before I am Chris Hani's daughter, I am first and foremost an addict. And that's the reason I'm here."

There was a long moment of silence. Then Sergeant Jan, rather unexpectedly, said: "Well put, Lindiwe." From that day on, he and I got closer. For the first time ever I felt like I had earned respect on my own merit.

ᘒ

The concept of Just For Today soon became a pivotal part of my daily recovery. In our groups at the beginning of each day, we were given topics such as, "Just For Today group will not start until I have spoken" or "Just For Today I will tell you about all the masks I wear and why". After being given our Just For Today slips of paper, we would stand in a circle and read the Just For Today from the NA book.

Just For Today:
JUST FOR TODAY my thoughts will be on my recovery, living and enjoying life without the use of drugs.
JUST FOR TODAY I will have faith in someone in NA who believes in me and wants to help me in my recovery.
JUST FOR TODAY I will have a program. I will try to follow it to the best of my ability.
JUST FOR TODAY, through NA, I will try to get a better perspective on my life.
JUST FOR TODAY I will be unafraid. My thoughts will be on my new associations, people who are not using and who have found a new way of life. So long as I follow that way, I have nothing to fear.

Although initially I had no clue why all the fuss was being made about Just For Today, I began to love this reading. Over the following four weeks I would begin to understand how those three simple words would become the cornerstone of my recovery. It soon became a mantra, honouring the idea of the present. Addicts tend to dwell on the past and fear the future – as do most people, actually – but this time warp affects us intensely as addicts. It's often what drives us to use, because very often we've lost the ability to stay in the now. At an Alcoholics Anonymous meeting I met a guy called Frank who described it brilliantly: "If you have one leg in the past and one leg in the future, you're pissing on the present."

Before I came across the JFT philosophy, the idea of never using again seemed impossible to commit to. But with JFT all I had to think about was not using today, for just 24 hours. That idea slowly began to make sense to me. And as one day became the next, so could the time between my present and my last drink and drug. Baby steps rather than trying to run a marathon before you are ready.

After the reading, we'd go around in the circle and tell the group what our particular JFT was. These would be our mission for the day. The one that everybody dreaded was "Just For Today group will not begin until I share my consequences" – that was a real horror! As addicts, we dreaded 'fessing up to the shit we'd done.

In the evenings during the week, we went to a few outside Narcotics Anonymous and Alcoholics Anonymous meetings, where we met other addicts who had a lot of clean time, who were living the Just For Today way of life. Listening to people who had been clean for a few years was really inspiring; hearing how they were now productive people, responsible parents, how living a clean and sober life was possible. It was a real revelation one night at an AA meeting when I came face to face with people I'd partied with in my old life who were now sober. They were so happy to see me, as though the prodigal daughter had returned, but it annoyed me deeply when they said, "We've been waiting for you." At this stage, I was still in denial about how addicted I'd been and that people out there had even noticed!

The next tumble from the land of the rose-tinted clouds came in the form of Chores. In that first week I was assigned CUPS. All the new inmates were given this humbling task because it was the worst. There's rigid hierarchy in rehab; like school, the newbies get all the shitty duties. But before long, new newbies arrive and soon you're moving up the ladder and the new intakes are having to do the chores you hated. You can spot the seniors, the ones with just a week left, a mile away. The know-it-alls invariably dish out words of wisdom to whoever will listen.

Doing CUPS meant that all day and every day, between counselling and group, you were washing cups. Addicts drink copious amounts of coffee and tea, so the cups just pile up wherever you look. And Heaven help you if there were no clean cups, because those fucking inmates could really bitch. I have *never* washed so many damned cups and mugs in my life – before breakfast, after breakfast, before tea, after tea, before lunch, after lunch. It just never seemed to end, right up to the end of the night, which meant there could be cups first thing in the morning too.

But what I did – even more than wash cups – was cry.

For those four weeks I wept buckets; tears that had been frozen and stored up for years just seeped out. You'd go back to the other inmates, red-eyed and clearly an emotional wreck, and everyone would ask sympathetically, "Counsellor?" We were adult crybabies bonded by our tears. For years we'd all been using substances to block out our emotions and now those long-forgotten, locked-away feelings were all coming out by way of what seemed like a never-ending river of tears.

Every night we would sit in a circle and listen to each other's life stories. But in those first few days, although it often felt like I'd found a new little family among all these weird and unusual characters, there were times when I wondered whether I really was an addict. When I listened to some of the stories of people who were really down and out, those who'd sold everything for their next hit, who were now undeniably on skid row, having lost their careers, their families – everything – a part of me thought: "Well, I'm not as bad as that one. I still have a home, I still have my child. I have never stolen or sold my body for drugs. I didn't do crack."

A part of me wondered: "Do I really belong here? I'm not that bad – maybe I'm not really an addict!"

But I soon learned that the details don't matter – what we'd done and how much we'd used and lost was immaterial. Instead of trying to look for the differences, we needed to rather look to our similarities. And there were many that knitted us together.

Doing the work required by the 12-Step programme also levelled us all out; there was no denying that we were on the same playing field. Every afternoon, time was set aside for us to answer worksheet after worksheet pertaining to the 12 Steps of Narcotics Anonymous. But it was the first step, Step One of NA – "We admitted that we were powerless over our addiction, that our lives had become unmanageable" – that had us writing for what seemed like forever. We had to write 60 stories on Step One alone. Before I even started mine, I heard from almost every other inmate how absolutely hellish the first step was. For starters, we had to write five examples on our unmanageability, five on our financial problems, five on dangerous situations, and so it went on. And you couldn't just do it half-heartedly – you had to read the step work aloud to your counsellor so there was no escaping. As much as I resisted doing it, once half my notebook had been filled, I really got to see the consequences of my using, carved out in black and white.

Once out of the three-day detox room, I discovered that the rooms at rehab were pretty cool. Okay, they weren't five star and we did have to share – which, of course, being such a queen of isolation, was my worst – but they were tastefully decorated and the beds were comfortable. Naturally, there were no TVs, radios or music systems because rehab is all about removing distractions from our inner journeys. All that was left to do was to create our own music, which meant we did a lot of singing. Belting out 'Amazing Grace' carried me through many piles of unwashed cups.

But don't be fooled. Rehab wasn't all love, roses and bonding. I experienced my first bad vibe on the day we moved out of detox into the room upstairs assigned to me and the other two newbies, Lerato and Lupita. Although I was still very much a pushover at this stage, a real people-pleaser, I managed to assert myself when it came to choosing my space. As soon as we got to the room I dibsed the bed at the far end and Lupita took the one opposite. Lerato then began bitching because she was stuck in the middle. When I put my foot down, she was furious, which made me extremely anxious. Our relationship kind of went downhill from then on.

When another Benzo addict, Ethel, needed a room, in a flash I offered to move downstairs with 17-year-old Liz. Lerato and Ethel would hunch up in the smoking area like two old women, commiserating with each other on how hard everything was, how hectic the side effects of their meds were, how bad their withdrawals were. They drove me crazy with all their moaning. One day I complained about them to another inmate, referring to my ex-roomies as the 'Benzo Bitches'. The idiot went and told them, and from then on things deteriorated even further.

When it came to some of the other inmates in the house, I was taken aback to discover how many black larnies were in rehab. There were five of us with political connections, including the son of a premier, the child of the CEO of a top black corporation and the granddaughter of Zulu royalty.

One of the few people who I initially clashed with, but who I eventually grew to love, was the Nigerian nurse, Franca. We'd often joke about how they could have hired a Nigerian to dish out medication, because when she would call in her thick, staccato Nigerian accent, "Come take your medication", we'd be like, "So where are the drugs?" We couldn't help but be reminded of our dealers, many of whom came from West Africa.

In those first few days, vulnerable and wounded, I was freaked out by Franca's take-no-prisoners attitude, which I saw as punitive, but soon discovered that it was just her manner and that her heart was that of a lion.

In the first week, filled with counselling, groups, AA\NA meetings, self-discovery and washing cups, I was so exhausted and exhilarated that I hardly had a moment to think about my loved ones. But suddenly Saturday arrived, which meant it was time for my first visitors' session.

My sister and brother-in-law had already attended a family session earlier in the week. Along with other 'addict' families, they were advised on 'how to live with an addict' and 'what kind of people addicts are'. I think it was really important for my family to feel that they weren't alone in the whole drama that was my addiction. I will forever appreciate how supportive they both were during this time, especially my brother-in-law, who is one of a kind, a truly outstanding human being – my 'Sbals', as I like to call him – and the brother I never had.

If Momo had been married to any other type of man, who refused to accept me with all my faults and dramas, I don't know what I would have done. He was like a real hands-on dad to Khaya, taking her to school some mornings, fetching her from music, stepping in as a father in so many ways.

On the day of our first family visit, before our beloveds arrived, a few of us sat at this big window in the front of the house to wait for the cars to pull up. We looked like a proper bunch of caged-up inmates in our loony asylum, waiting for the outside world to visit us.

My heart almost burst when I saw my sister's car arrive, and Khaya and her three cousins tumble out. My daughter was overjoyed to see me, but I could sense too that she had settled well and was thrilled to be among her cousins. By the end of the day, it was with great relief in my heart when I kissed her goodbye. Despite her age, not yet 10 years old, she instinctively understood that her mom was in a safe space and was getting better.

For the rest of my time in rehab, my sister and the kids would visit every Saturday and Sunday without fail. They would bring a picnic lunch, and the kids would be in their swimming costumes, in and out of the pool, having fun in what seemed to them to be a happy holiday camp. Throughout my four-week stay, my mother, however, refrained from visiting.

CHAPTER 21

Owning up, showing up

Letters were a big deal in rehab. I discovered that they are powerful self-development tools, creating self-awareness on issues and insights that often remain hidden until written down.

One of the most memorable letters I wrote in treatment was to my addict self, a letter that required brutal honesty, owning up to all the pain I'd caused people in my using life, and all I'd caused for myself. Then there was the letter that I had to write to my drug of choice, cocaine:

My dear Cocaine

I originally didn't think that this would be a difficult letter to write due to our acrimonious break-up, but as I put pen to paper I find it difficult to say goodbye to you forever. There has been this part of me that has held onto the thought that we might reunite even for a spell, but now I realise that will trigger the same destructive pattern we have had throughout our entire relationship. Our relationship is toxic but due to me holding on to you for dear life, and you being the last standing thing in my life, I can't imagine life without you.

When I think about it even our initial connection was because I was broken, lost and in pain and I believed that you would distract me from dealing with that. That was unbelievably stupid on my part. What followed were years of destruction in my life. The good times we had don't outweigh the bad. I fondly recall the times I felt incredibly low and was unable to share my feelings with the people around me and I could get lost in your always embracing oblivion.

Throughout my life I always regarded myself as strong. I thought I dealt with all the pain of loss that came my way. "I am Lindi," I constantly told myself, that there was nothing God wouldn't give me that I couldn't handle. Boy oh boy, I have never been more wrong. The minute you walked into my life there was Euphoria but, as the years went by, that dissipated. Instead through my obsessive nature to keep you close I acted inappropriately, embarrassed my family and couldn't even be a present mom. It would be so much easier to lay all the blame at your feet but that would not be accurate. I allowed the destruction into my life. Not only did I welcome it, I embraced you with open nostrils. That was the only time I had a sense of being myself, the illusion of having everything together. But all I was, was a muddled-up, insecure little girl screaming for help!

The downward spiral that became my life was so chaotic but as much as I really wanted, even prayed to get you out of my life, I still kept coming back. I can't even look at myself in the mirror from all the shame I feel. My behaviour was so uncharacteristic but I felt as though I was hanging in the air watching myself become more lost each day. There came a point where it couldn't happen anymore.

I am trying to get my life where I believe it deserves to be not just for Khaya but also for myself. It's so difficult because even now as I am getting better I still feel your cold crushing hand squeezing my heart. All I know is that I don't want anything to do with you anymore. You have left me crashing down and debilitated. I am slowly and painfully picking

myself up. You have no role in my life anymore.
    Lindiwe Hani

Putting it all down on paper allowed me to exert some power over that which had almost destroyed me.

Our families were also asked to write letters to us. Everyone dreaded being asked to read them aloud. It was very painful and exposing. In group, the counsellor would walk in holding something and we'd all watch, terrified, while whispers hissed around the room: *He's got a letter ...* It soon became clear that not everyone got to read their letters out loud, that if you were chosen to read your letter, you were probably in some kind of denial, clearly someone like me, who went in and out of thinking: "I'm not that bad" and "Maybe I'm not really an addict".

My turn came about two and a half weeks into my stay, when the counsellor walked into group one day, looked straight at me and said, "Lindi here's your letter from your sister."

Momo started off her letter by saying what an awesome sister I was.

Dear Lindi

I really don't know where to start this letter, but it certainly is not because I am at a loss for words (never!), but because there is truly so much to say and so little time. I could have started with how blessed I am to have a sister like you who is my rock (yes, even with this addiction) and true north, east and south west star. And this comes from someone who considers herself strong and a survivor. I don't think you realise what an impact you have had and continue to have on my life. I know you think I take you for granted and maybe I do sometimes. But you have spoilt me, nurtured me and stood with me when our dearest Mother was acting up as usual. You love my children like your own, everyone always tells me they wish you were their sister. But, guess what, you are MY kick-ass sister. And that is why you need

*to get well, girlfriend, coz if both Love [her husband] and
I die today – all my kids are yours. It's official – the will is
there in black and white.*

But the tone soon changed. Momo didn't play around when
confronting me on my relationship with our mother and how
much I allowed Mama to bring me down.

*Lindi, you need to set serious boundaries with Me [Mama].
I cannot dictate how and what. She made it much easier for
me by simply cutting me out of her life so I don't have to deal
with her shit (scuse my French). You cannot allow another
person, whether she gave birth to you or not, to abuse you
emotionally at will, insult you, call you useless, debase you
and tell you that you will never amount to anything. Anyone
will tell you that if you continue to hear something often
enough – you run the risk of starting to believe it.*

Soon the mood of the letter got even more serious, with some hard
truths about my using. She reminded me of the night she and Sbals
took me out to dinner after hearing gossip about me.

*I was very cautious and told you what I had heard and told
you to "tone down this alcohol use". You were upset and
cried, threatening to leave the restaurant. I actually was
unmoved at the time as I felt I couldn't let you misbehave
and not confront you. I just didn't know about the drugs as
I am naive like that and keep to myself, so I generally don't
hear the latest Joburg gossip – and anyway who would tell
me in my face about your drug use ...
The first time I knew you were definitely on drugs was the
day you had a "car accident" in the school parking lot. I was
at one of my usual meetings when Malome called to tell me ...
I decided I would see you later as I was avoiding the drama
with Me [Mama] there too. Then I got a call around lunchtime
to say that you were screaming my name and that you wanted*

*no one but me, despite Me telling the nurses I wasn't allowed
to come. I sat on the stairs at work in the basement listening
to this drama unfold and went weak at the knees. I honestly
couldn't imagine what was going on. I tried speaking to you
and you cried and cried. I prayed (not literally, I struggle to
pray on a normal day) to get to hospital in one piece without
having an epileptic seizure, which can happen if I am highly
stressed. When I got there you were a "hot mess", woman ...
clothes from the previous (or whichever day), looked clearly
like you hadn't washed, you were shaking and cold in spite
of heaters, blankets, fans you name it! Yho, what a sight, but
you maintained a sense of humour and everyone asked why
I didn't come earlier as they didn't know you were such a
nice and funny person. Supposedly that day you kicked the
paramedics, wouldn't get into the ambulance, kicked one of
them straight in the crotch and was described as 'aggressive'.
That was a shock to me. I don't know that Lindiwe they were
talking about. When you got to hospital the poor nurses got
shouted at (or is it screamed at), you wouldn't co-operate
pulling drips out and generally misbehaving, including telling
your mother off when she tried to be nice to you. There was
definitely an alien that had invaded my sister's body. Even
Matumelo mentioned that you get so angry (bohale) when
you are high or is it when you are craving "the things you are
on" were her words. Geez, that's not my sister. I told her you
were kind, sweet, helpful, loving and damn beautiful inside
and out. I was showing them your old photographs and they
were asking if that is you?*

Momo also pointed out my inability to handle my own finances,
how she and Sbals were always offering to help by going through
my bank statements to see what I was doing with my salary.

*Promises to open your financial affairs to Love (even when
I promised to butt out) went unmet; instead occasionally
when you had a glass or three too many, you would complain*

143

that I didn't understand you were struggling financially and didn't offer to help ...

It only dawned on me that the situation was dire when you tried to buy a car and it wasn't working and eventually you wanted us to buy it for you. I was clear that was not going to happen, certainly not with the number of 'unexplained' car accidents you were having. Malome also mentioned that cocaine is expensive ...

She hit hard when she went on to ask whether, even though I was always talking about wanting to get married, in reality who would marry me when I was so messed up. That really cut to the bone. But perhaps what impacted me most was when she brought up our beloved sister Khwezi.

You need to get yourself healthy and off those drugs and alcohol forever, my love. They are destructive and will waste your life. I tell you my greatest fear is that you will end up dead like Khwezi. I don't mean to have Neo's pity party but two sisters dying from drugs would just about burst my tumour!

I wept when I read those words out loud. It was powerful stuff. Nothing quite like a hardcore letter to burst my well-constructed rose-tinted bubble to wake me up to the fact that through my using I had deeply hurt the people I loved most.

Then I had to tell the group how reading the letter made me feel. I took a deep breath to control the tears and told them how consumed by guilt I felt reading her words in her handwriting. Basically, I saw what a harbinger of pain and suffering I was, what a burden I'd been to my sister. Momo's letter had launched a crazy roller coaster of emotions, of guilt, pain and shame.

It was during that session that my denial about my addiction began to dissipate. Up until that point I'd still been bargaining with my disease, sitting on my throne of denial. That letter brought me right down to earth. I had finally landed up in a place where I could really start the hard work on myself. But this realisation also sent me into a serious spin of craving. For the first time in weeks I ached for a drink, a line, a deep pull of a joint – any escape into oblivion. If I thought for a second that I had slain my addict, I was finding out just how sly and present the beast could be – literally, just one line or one drink away.

After the session I went straight to the nurse for some headache tablets. I was refused and told to "stay in my feelings". That day my deep craving, especially for weed, grew more intense; all I wanted was to get totally stoned, to run away from my sore and open self and fly off somewhere into the big blue sky. But of course I couldn't. I had to sit with my pain. I had to put into practice my Just For Today and watch myself hurting and experiencing for real that "this too shall pass" without the aid of a drink, a puff or a line. Slowly I was learning to sit with me. Just for today.

Something remarkable happened to me in the days that followed the reading of Momo's letter. A veil of lies was lifted. Finally, I got to see myself clearly, my dark truths and stark defects. And the world didn't come crashing down. I was okay.

I can only describe it as a feeling often explained in church as "a peace descends that transcends all understanding". And in this newfound space of acceptance I sat with myself and began to process all that had happened over the previous weeks: the hard, sometimes aching days where there was nowhere to run or escape to, my sometimes overwhelming impulse to sleep rather than face the reality of the hurt I'd been carrying inside me for so long, the endless tears, my trivial altercations with others, the relentless exposing of self – all part of a journey that was set to save my life.

Finally, I could see that my problem was much bigger than just cocaine, that I was an *addict* – and that I could not use any substances, be it alcohol, weed or coke, without slipping back into the downward spiral. Alcohol was a biggie for me. I think that all this time I'd been keeping a backdoor open, reassuring myself that when I got out of rehab I would at least be able to continue drinking without any serious repercussions. So it was a huge victory for me when I finally surrendered to the idea that I could not drink in moderation. But perhaps as important, I had learned to reach out to and be vulnerable with a group of people, say no to those who disrupted my peaceful space, ask for help and, in turn, be kind and caring to others who needed mine. It was incredible to feel like I belonged and that I had something to offer.

I had grown up as the daughter of Chris Hani and yet, for as long as I could remember, I couldn't shake the sense that I was useless. Up until I went to rehab I had felt like a failure and there was nothing I could do to redeem myself. My father was such a huge figure, such an icon to so many people, that it felt like I could never be anything close to what he achieved, so why even try? Of course my addiction made me feel my worthlessness even more.

Now, clean and sober for the first time in so many years, I felt the possibility that maybe, just maybe I could play a meaningful role in this world. But that didn't mean I had miraculously recovered and was instantly ready to face life. There were still days when I was absolutely drained from unruly emotion and self-punishment.

I was thrilled when, after 21 days, I was made Head of Res. Now it was my turn to welcome the newcomer, allocate tasks to newbies and oversee the house as Captain Jan von Rehab had done when I walked through those doors.

Just after Momo's letter, about a week before primary treatment ended, I was asked about my plans after I completed my 28 days. At every opportunity, Etienne and my other counsellors urged me to sign up for secondary care at The Gap: "You of all people will really benefit from this, Lindiwe." Although they thought I'd done well, they clearly didn't think I was ready to go back into the Real World. I knew they were right. I had but touched the core of my disease. There was still so much work to be done.

Before making any decisions on whether I wanted to enrol, we were taken on a tour of The Gap, right next door to Houghton House. It was an upmarket joint, lots of open spaces, tastefully designed with an industrial look. The residents appeared to be living a less constrained existence than us inmates in primary. They seemed so confident and worldly wise, which intimidated the shit out of me. At Houghton House we were like a bunch of wayward kids, all immature and gung-ho. I immediately noticed a huge flat-screen TV and books everywhere, unlike in Houghton where what we read and watched was monitored 24/7.

I discussed the prospect of The Gap with Momo because, clearly, if I were to make plans to be away for another four weeks, she would need to be on board to carry on looking after Khaya. In her usual supportive way, she said, "Whatever it takes to get you healthy, I will back you."

I decided not to even broach the subject with Khaya. I knew she was missing me and that she would probably resist my plan. She had been sending me little letters throughout my time away; now I tortured myself by reading them over and over.

Saturday, 18 October
Mom, I love you so much when you are not with me my heart is in pain. Everyday you are so special, anytime you feel sad just take a memory scan and look at all the good memories
LOVE Khaya

Sunday, 19 October
Mom, I just saw you and I just realised I miss you very much. I feel so mad even when I cant tell my friends, it makes my heart burn in flames.
Love Khaya

fRIDAY 30 hALLOWEEN
I am feeling sick because Khanyo is wiggling his thing. Zuko is also doing it like twins. Its my birthday tomorrow and I am happy because I might have friends but I am sad also because I am not spending time with you and I wish you could have my party. I love you to the heavens and hells to the end of the earth to the moon and back.
Love

147

On weekend visits she kept telling me she didn't want me to go to "that Gap", because of what her friends would say. "They keep asking questions, Mama," she said, all big-eyed and worried. She had told her mates I was away in Cape Town on business. "Now what must I say when they ask me, Mama?"

It almost broke my heart when I read her letter a week before I went into secondary care.

Sunday, 2 November
I am feeling sick I am dying thinking about another 30 days,
I will want to die. I know I will see you more often I just
dont want you there.
  Feeling sad
  From Me

I was wracked with the guilt for all the nonsense I had put my child through, but I managed to stand firm. I explained that there was nothing I could do about it because I needed to focus on our future together, that I needed to follow through with these plans because my getting healthy would ultimately benefit her, and she would just have to tough it out. That was really hard for me, asserting myself in the face of my daughter who was clearly struggling with my decision. Once I showed her around The Gap and she fell in love with the tree house, her resistance seemed to dissipate. After all the irresponsible decisions I had made in active addiction, leaving her with the nanny, coming back home blotto at all hours of the night, sometimes not coming home at all, at last it felt like I was doing something right. "This is an investment for our future," I promised her.

To appease my nagging guilt, I first tried to barter a week back at home before starting at The Gap, but my counsellors were adamant that I start straight away. Although that initially pissed me off, I was at the point where I was ready to do anything. The last night at HH was an emotional one, especially when Shamiel, one of the guys I had really connected with, said that I was one of the "great ones to have passed through the gates" and, like my dad, I was "leaving behind big shoes to fill". It really felt as though he had seen my true worth even though I was still battling to see it. For the first time in many, many years, as I moved from HH next door to The Gap, I felt that Daddy would have been proud of me.

CHAPTER 22

The Gap

O n 8 November 2014, a week after Khaya turned 10, I moved into The Gap. I was all too aware of how, after checking out of HH as a senior, I was starting again, a little fish in a big pond, among a group of strangers, leaving all my connections behind. At the braai on the first night, I felt completely out of my depth, surrounded mainly by big white guys. After helping to wash dishes, I immediately escaped to my room.

But soon, just as I had in primary care, I slotted in. Life's like that; one day you're the new kid on the block, the next you're part of the scenery. I discovered, too, that I really liked the people in the house and embraced my new freedom. After completing certain tasks, we were given permission to go out for eight hours on weekends, we had our own kitchen, there wasn't a set bedtime and we were generally allowed to manage our own time more freely.

But if I thought that I was on some cushy holiday, I was soon in for a rude awakening. Once the week began it felt like there was nowhere to run to at The Gap. At any given time someone was either looking at you or for you.

The work we did on ourselves, in group and mini-group, was super intense. It was all aimed at becoming aware of our addictive behaviour, our flaws, and making major changes so that we would go back into the world better equipped to deal with life's challenges, which were for certain going to put our sobriety to the test. With all the intro- and extra-spection, it felt at times like I was a squirming insect under an unforgiving, all-exposing magnifying glass.

I basically came into The Gap with a hit list. I wanted to deal with my dad, my sister Khwezi, my mom and my boyfriend, Sikhulule.

In my first group session I spoke about Khwezi and almost immediately the tears started flowing. That set the tone of honesty and willingness for the rest of my stay, for me to really tackle my stuff. I made a pact with myself that nothing was off-limits, that I had to face it all.

Dealing with Daddy brought up unimaginable emotional pain in me. Talking in group about the love and loss of my father made me weep so much that it felt like the end of the world. But not just normal tears; I was overcome with that ugly crying, when you can barely breathe, never mind talk, between the gulps and gasps and sobs. As I struggled to gain control over my emotions, I was sure people were getting irritated, but they were amazing. They simply sat there, listening, holding me in their silence, allowing me to simply let go of the pain and emotion that had been buried deep inside for what felt like forever. After I calmed down, Alex – the head counsellor who I was really intimidated by – gave me the ultimate stamp of approval when he said, "That was a good share."

He had a reputation for brutal honesty; if he didn't feel someone was really disclosing, he had no problem responding with, "That's bullshit." His relentless honesty permeated the way we dealt with each other in 'clearing sessions', in which you tell people something 'nice' and something 'not so nice'. I was told that I seemed 'really nice' but that I tended to isolate. In truth, the accusation was nothing new. In HH, every time I experienced too much emotion I would take myself off for a nap. It got so bad that napping was eventually banned. It was imperative that I got to grips with my tendency to run away and escape because that had been at the core of my using.

One of the most precious lessons I learned at HH and The

Gap was to connect with people again, to forge real and deep friendships. The community aspect really worked for me, allowing me to open up and rely on people, people to whom I might never have given the time of day in the Real World. I learned to see my own shit, talk about it and deal with people's differences.

I experienced one of the most emotionally life-shifting sessions at The Gap when we were tasked to create a Family Sculpture. Basically, you use your fellow inmates to represent members of your family. In my case, someone was Daddy, another was Khwezi and someone else my mom. I got to address each one of them and say what I really felt and how they'd affected my life. Once again, I nearly drowned in my sea of tears.

When I addressed Daddy I told him how angry I was with him for dying, for leaving us with Mama. Just as we had become a little family after we all moved back to South Africa to be together in late 1990, he had to leave us, unprotected from our mother. With him dying, I had no one to love me unconditionally as he loved me. I sobbed as I told him that I no longer knew what love was, that all I had left was this burdensome legacy, one that I had failed to live up to. I was in pieces when I told him how sad and sorry I was that I had disappointed him. But I also thanked him for watching over Khaya, who reminds me so much of him – she really looks like Daddy and has his strong, survival-oriented character. I told him how sorry I was that he would never get to meet his granddaughter.

When I confronted Mama, although I expressed anger, I thanked her for doing the best that she could. But I also told her that she had been harsh and, even though she said she loved us, there were many times that we didn't feel loved. I vented my anger for forcing us to portray this persona of the perfect family – the Chris Hani legacy – that put so much pressure on us. I told her how her fierce protection of that legacy had in so many ways constricted and suffocated me, propelling me deeper and deeper into the black hole of using.

When it came to Khwezi, I had to dig really deep. I told her what a mess I was after she died, that I felt like she'd abandoned me. I told her how much I missed her, how alone I felt after she had left, because I had lost someone who I could really talk to. I finally reached a bittersweet peace, understanding that by dying she had escaped her suffering in this harsh world. After Daddy died, having seen his bloody, bullet-ridden body, she had been carrying so much pain. In dying she had been freed. In the session, I got a sense that Khwezi regretted leaving me behind, that if she could have taken me with her she would have.

After these family sculpture sessions it was the group's turn to give feedback. Sometimes you'd have people saying, "I didn't feel it", or "You were holding back", but after I finished the entire group was like, "Girl, you did it!" I felt both euphoric and drained at the same time. I had held nothing back. I knew my life depended on my honesty and willingness to get real. If I didn't deal with my stuff here, how was I ever going to be able to go back and live any kind of authentic and decent life? But, most of all, how would I be a proper parent to my beloved Khaya?

I was so desperate to change and get better that a voice inside me just kept saying: "This is it, Lindi, you have one chance to get this right." So I simply surrendered to everything. I didn't question their motives or their methods. If the folk at The Gap said, "Jump," I simply said: "How high?"

Before you could leave The Gap you had to have completed Step 4 in the 12-Step Programme: "We made a searching and fearless moral inventory of ourselves." This entailed a huge amount of written work that required you to explore in great depth and detail all the damage you had caused, to pinpoint where you went wrong and be absolutely fearless in taking responsibility for all actions rather than blaming everyone else.

Although I found it incredibly hard to motivate myself to start, I eventually managed to get it done. Once this mammoth task was complete, Step 5 – considered almost a confessional step in which you have to, without reservation, share your wrongs with another person – loomed ahead. I decided to put this off until I had left The Gap.

As time ticked nearer for me to leave my place of safety, I

153

became horribly conflicted about how I was going to make it out there in the Real World. It was already nerve-wracking just going out for a few hours a week. Even the joy of spending time with my beloved Khaya saw me counting down the minutes before I was safely behind the walls of security and routine at The Gap.

In one of the final groups before I left, it was time to deal with my mom. I ranted on, moaning about things she had said and done to me since childhood. Then Alex suddenly stopped me. "Lindi," he said, "you're not that powerless 12-year-old girl any more – you're now an adult with choices. Do you really think your mother is going to change? The only thing you can change is the way you react to her."

Of course, in my mind all I wanted to say was, "Fuck you! You don't know my mom; you don't know how hard it is," but I listened and I actually heard it; I completely got it.

It was another of those empowering, life-shifting moments, realising that my mom would never change – the only thing that could change was the way I reacted to her. I'd always felt so powerless around her. And, come to think of it, how I dealt with her was how I dealt with many people in my life: keeping quiet, not saying anything, people-pleasing, building up debilitating resentments that simply sent me off on a spiral of using, where I could heap blame on everyone else for all that had gone wrong in my life, all to justify my drinking and drugging.

I dreaded leaving the safety of The Gap, leaving my beloved Daryl and Robert, who had been so instrumental in my healing. How would I deal with all the people in my life, but especially how would I deal with my mother? That all-important word, 'boundaries', suddenly appeared in my 'recovery vocabulary'. It was truly a pivotal moment for me.

CHAPTER 23

Life in the real world

My mom hadn't called or visited at all while I was in primary or secondary care. She appeared to be in complete denial that I'd gone to rehab.

I had my first encounter with her one morning a few weeks after I'd checked out of The Gap. I was in my bedroom, making the bed, when a face appeared at the window. I got such a fright that I screamed, and when I realised it was her, I screamed even louder.

When I let her in she told me she'd heard rumours that I was on drugs. I looked her straight in the eye. "Where do you think I've been for the last two months?"

"I have no idea," she said, unfazed.

"You know exactly where I've been – in rehab," I fired back. "You know that I have a drug problem and now I'm dealing with it." I continued to stare her down. "I need to not see you for a while. I know that you're an amazing grandmother to my daughter, so that's a non-negotiable relationship, and whenever you want to see Khaya, you can pick her up or I will drop her off. But, as for you and me, we don't have a relationship until further notice."

My heart was beating triple time, but I knew it was either her or my sobriety.

She was clearly shocked; she tried to remind me of my using and how much money I'd wasted.

I told her I knew all these things; I knew what I'd done wrong, I knew how much pain I'd caused her. "But I also know you are not good for me right now, so until I am stronger we can't resume our relationship."

Then I asked her to leave. She said nothing as I opened the gate and she drove away.

Once she was gone, I burst into tears. Wow, how I cried! Saying 'no' to my mother was one of the hardest things I'd ever done. I'd been afraid of this woman for most of my life, never able to live up to her high standards. When we were kids we would hear the garage door open and we'd all run around tidying up. Feet off the couch, almost standing to attention – filled with such fear.

From that day, that first encounter after leaving The Gap, my mom began to respect the boundaries I had set – for the most part, anyway. She continued to see Khaya, and of course we greeted each other and exchanged polite pleasantries, but something profound had shifted between the two of us.

It's been a slow process, and she still sometimes tries to push her own agenda, but now it's much easier for me to simply say, "No" or "Please do not speak to me in that manner. This is what I want to do."

The balance of power in our relationship has changed dramatically. She was clearly not gung-ho about me sharing my story in this book but she has backed off. She may even like it.

☾

I left The Gap at lunchtime on a Monday. Part of me was half expecting a parade to ululate at the gate, "Whoo-hoo! She did it." Instead the streets of Johannesburg remained disappointingly the same as I made my way across town to my sister's home, with two months of sobriety under my belt and expectations galore. In theory, I had it all worked out: armed with my AA Big Book, a sponsor and a carefully written-up plan on how I was going to cope, I felt prepared. But instead of heading straight home, I decided to spend the night with Khaya at Momo's. In truth, I was petrified to walk back through the doors of the place where I'd spent so much time getting high. What if it acted as a trigger, hurtling me back into using? Although I had flushed away all the weed and drug paraphernalia before going into treatment, I was obsessed that there might be the lure of ghosts around every corner.

The following morning I summoned up courage to go back home. As I pulled up in the driveway and turned off the ignition, for Khaya's sake I put on my coping mask, feigning excitement and enthusiasm to be back but, lawd, my heart was beating a rap attack. While I told her to go ahead and see if everything was as she remembered, I sat in the car, frozen for at least 15 minutes, desperately trying to pull myself together. But as per usual I had 'awfulised' the event out of all proportion. On entering my home for the first time in two months, instead of wanting to call the dealer for a gram, I took in the familiar rooms and just breathed.

Thankfully, two months in treatment had humbled me. I knew that the only chance I had of staying clean and sober was to follow all suggestions, so I continued therapy with Etienne, attended NA meetings and signed up for three months of 'aftercare' three days a week, which would commence in January 2015.

One of the most pressing issues I needed to deal with after getting out of The Gap was the issue of work. I knew I wasn't ready to head straight back into the nine-to-five, and was hoping to get a reprieve until the new year. In the week before I went into treatment I had nervously approached my boss, Dave, telling him that I was an addict and that I was admitting myself to Houghton House for four weeks of rehab. After blurting it all out, he'd looked at me rather coldly and said, "Well, I'm glad you've told me, but did you lie to me while you were working here?" He was clearly upset when I responded with, "Yes."

Now, two months later, as I waited for my meeting with Dave in the HR office, the head of HR informed me that while the boss was very unhappy with the situation and didn't want me to return to my job, I shouldn't worry – the job was still mine and that I should just listen to what he had to say to me.

The first thing Dave said when he joined us in the office was how great I looked. I knew he was right – eight weeks of treatment and a strict regime of kettlebell workouts had inspired the loss of a whole lot of alcohol-induced fat.

Almost immediately, however, Dave proceeded with a lengthy lecture on how, because of the lies I'd told him, he no longer trusted me. I listened in silence. What really irked me was when he said, "Well, either way you're a winner – you got sober so even if you don't have a job you will have your sobriety." What a snivelling, patronising asshole. Without a word, I stood up and walked out. The only thing to do was to let it go and keep moving.

Without a job and faced with the realities of the Real World, those first few weeks adapting to life and learning to be comfortable around the new me were incredibly challenging. I couldn't watch a movie because I was so used to doing it high. I even found cleaning the house and reading a book really hard because everything I had done before rehab had been centred around using. Cooking was weird, too, as I'd always had a drink or a joint when I was in the kitchen. I was a child again, not knowing what I liked, or how I fitted into this new and intimidating world.

When it came time to do the 'confessional' Step 5, I was wracked with anxiety at the idea of having to confess 'my sins'. Finally, I summoned up the courage to meet my sponsor at a quiet little coffee shop in Parkview. Once again I'd 'awfulised' the idea long before it came to be. Just as with a heartfelt confession in church, unburdening the weight of the darkness and shame, accumulated from all my using, brought unexpected serenity and peace to my soul, a feeling that no money could ever buy.

But, like all feelings, serenity is not a permanent state of mind. I had checked out of rehab slap bang in the middle of the clang and clutter of the festive season, a time when most South Africans are in blotto mode. The idea of my first Christmas clean and sober in almost two decades terrified me. To add to the pressure, my beloved Danish cousin Tlalane, her husband Carsten and my gorgeous nieces Chilli and Jamilla were about to arrive. As much as a part of me was truly looking forward to spending time with them, the last time I'd seen them was in Denmark in 1999, when I'd been permanently stoned on prime Danish weed and hitting the sauce daily. What if we had nothing to talk about? What if they picked up on my social anxiety? What had they told my nieces? My brain went round and round, 'awfulising' the entire idea of the visit.

The plan was to go to Durban with my sister and the kids, meet the Danes there and then all travel together to Lesotho to spend Christmas with the rest of the family.

A few days later we received news that my beloved brother-in-law, Sbals, had unexpectedly lost his father in Port Elizabeth. We now all had to make our way to the Eastern Cape, but I had the bright idea to first take the kids – my two nephews, Lukhanyo, Zuko and Khaya – to Durban for a week. You have to love my gumption. Talk about hitting the ground running!

Clearly my new resolve, fresh out of treatment, to be a responsible and committed parent made me underestimate how challenging it would be to look after three boisterous children on a countrywide road trip with no other adults in sight.

I've never been more grateful for the Serenity Prayer. We drove down to Zimbali just outside Durban, and as far as holidays go, it wasn't too shabby. But the ghosts of addiction were alive and kicking – the last time I'd been to Zimbali was when I was still drinking catatonically. Although I was as well prepared as possible, with my counsellor and sponsor on speed dial, I felt the intense ache of loneliness and pressure as I tried to relax around the pool and go on long walks. Plus, having to address the constant needs of the three kids was a real wake-up after having spent eight weeks in treatment where I'd been surrounded by support with only me as my sole focus.

Before driving to PE, Khaya needed to fly back to Joburg to attend her father's wedding and as I waved her goodbye at the airport I fought back tears as I marvelled at how much she'd grown. En route to the funeral, I decided to break the journey to spend the night in Mthatha with my St Cyps friend, Sherry, who had no idea that I'd just got out of rehab.

At some point on that long, scenic south coast drive, Sherry sent me a message to ask whether I was in a whiskey or wine mood. Immediately my mind started doing flick-flacks, suddenly obsessed about drinking. Surely I could have a whiskey? I'd been so good; maybe my problem wasn't alcohol. I was bombarded by the internal dialogue of an addict in bargaining mode; it's incredible how easily it can happen if you take your eye off the ball.

But when we arrived in Mthatha, instead of ordering Jack on the rocks, I asked for water and told Sherry the whole sordid tale of my using and how I'd just got out of rehab. Almost immediately I wished I hadn't, and promptly followed up with, "Maybe a whiskey won't kill me." Thankfully, she immediately responded with, "Nah, let's rather have a smoothie – I actually think I'll join you." I mean friends, hey. Pure love.

And so that fleeting moment of temptation passed. I think most addicts face that crossroads after treatment, that instant when you're given the choice to either stick with sobriety or slide backwards again into the dark hole of using. That was my moment.

Back home after the festivities with the family in Lesotho, I realised that although I had phoned my sponsor while I was away, being without the stability of my NA meetings had put my recovery at risk. It was clear to me that my approach to my entire social life had to change.

From then on, during that first year after rehab, for the most part I stayed far away from parties, events and socialising. I was very honest with family and friends about the challenges I was facing. I realised that if I lied about anything, I would regress and more than likely relapse. And instead of resenting the fact that I was an addict, I found myself looking forward to attending NA and AA meetings. I even began chairing one.

☾

The day I celebrated my one year clean and sober on 6 October 2015 honestly felt like one of the greatest achievement I had ever managed to chalk up in 35 years. Three-hundred-and-sixty-five whole clean-and-sober Just For Today days of staying vigilant and honest.

Two days later while driving, I heard Melinda Ferguson talking on Radio 702 about her book *Crashed*. The last time we'd seen each other was back in early 2014, at a *True Love* cover shoot for a story titled 'Children of the Struggle', when I'd been in the depths of my using.

As I drove, listening to her voice on the radio, Mel's words to me then, "You should write a book", rebounded. I reached for the phone and sent her a message. She responded almost immediately: "I often think about the idea we discussed about the book." My entire being went *Yes!* Although I was proud of my one year in sobriety, I had hit a wall around what I was to do with the rest of this life.

I've been feeling so despondent about the future, I responded.

Despondency is often a sign that there's something beautiful on the horizon, she typed. *I feel we can do this book, and your dad is going to guide us.*

We met face to face on 4 December 2015 for our first meeting. We jotted down ideas, set up dates, scheduled a string of meetings, and discussed the idea of applying for a writers' grant. As at the inception of most projects, details were murky, but the will to proceed was there. Little did I know how challenging the following year would be. Confronting my hurt, my darkness, but by far the toughest of all would be coming face to face with the Bogeymen, my real demons.

PART 4

Facing my demons

CHAPTER 24

Making the call

'm one year and four months clean and sober when I meet up with Mel in late February 2016. The notion that once you get clean life gets easier has been systematically dispelled over the year since leaving The Gap. Living life on life's terms back in the Real World, that's when one is faced with all one's defects and bad habits. Sobriety simply means that a life-long journey of real work on the self begins.

Since committing to writing the book, I often walk into meetings with Mel slightly apprehensive, mainly because I know I haven't delivered on my writing. I'm not sure what makes it so hard for me to meet a deadline. Since I've got into recovery, I've become achingly aware of it.

I've recently joined Bootcamp. Waking at 04:30am, forcing myself from the womb of my bed, before the birds have tweeted, to meet my trainer at 05:15am. I'm desperate to force myself out of my inertia. I long for things to change. It feels like I've been reclining on the couch in my head for far too long. The thing is I don't understand this fear that cripples me, which leaves me like a patient knocked out on an operating table every time I'm supposed to come up with material to meet a deadline. Much the same happened in rehab when I was told to work on my life story. It took forever for my words to meet the page.

Mel thinks it has something to do with childhood trauma, that once-safe world that was violated. "When we lose our trust in the outside world, when something happens to us beyond our control, we often internalise that break of faith and stop honouring our own commitments," she says. I think it may also have to do with the self-doubt I was riddled with during active addiction, probably even earlier, which meant that I never stretched myself, in case I failed. Whatever its root cause, I have no idea how to fix it.

We agree to meet at a Middle-Eastern restaurant on Grant Avenue in Norwood and, as usual, I arrive empty-handed. I have run out of excuses – weddings, birthdays – none of them seem valid any longer. But this time round my non-delivery has taken on a far more serious tone. I can see the frustration on Mel's face. Over the last couple of months, she's been hard at work pitching our story to various funders to get financial support to help us write the book. Up until five days ago we've been pretty much working in a financial vacuum.

But things have changed. The Taco Kuiper Fund, a grant agency funding investigative projects, has approved our application and seeded us some money to develop the book. Almost overnight, the main thrust of the work has changed from being a simple biography to one that needs to have an investigative angle, looking for answers and details around my father's death. The pressure is on for us to come up with material that has 'investigative integrity' in which we intend to embark on a journey where I will come face to face with my father's killers, Clive Derby-Lewis and Janusz Waluś. The Bogeymen. Reading our proposal document feels like a story about someone else, not me.

I try to hide my anxiety as we sit down to order coffee. As usual when I feel pressure, my head starts searching for an exit, whirling around in loops of panic, barely able to stay in the moment and process the new gravity of our situation. It wants to leave, run, check out the building.

What started off as my secret project, one that's been safely hidden away in my head for almost two decades, has not only suddenly grown legs, but has careered off into what feels like a Usain Bolt sprint. But instead of embracing the moment like Mel seems to be clearly doing, I feel crippling fear at having to expose myself.

Before our coffees have even arrived, however, Mel's contagious enthusiasm has us launching into a plan of action. It seems logical that the first killer we hit on is Clive Derby-Lewis. He's been out of prison for almost a year, after receiving medical parole at the end of May 2015, released into the care of his wife, Gaye. According to his lawyer at the hearing, he's supposedly close to death from stage-4 lung cancer, said to have just two months to live at the time of the hearing.

But it's been nearly 10 months since he was freed and there have been no death announcements in the press. "We need to try to get hold of him as soon as possible. We don't want him dying on us," says Mel, somewhat insensitively.

My co-writer is curious as to whether he's ever made attempts to contact me personally, to show remorse for the role he played in my father's death. She alerts me to a news report in June 2015, in which his wife Gaye stated that her husband wouldn't try to contact the Hanis "again" as they had tried too many times, and it was clearly "a futile exercise". This is news to me. I have never been told about any of these attempts.

"I have no idea how to get hold of him," I say. "Probably the best way is to try go through his lawyer."

In a flash, Mel, the Google queen, grabs her iPad and comes up with a name. "Advocate Roelof du Plessis." Another round of Googling has her finding a PDF list of Brooklyn Pretoria-based lawyers; there's a cell number next to Du Plessis's name.

Next thing I'm grabbing my phone and punching in his number. I often confuse myself – I'm either frozen with fear, caught in inertia, or ridiculously impulsive. This has been a moment long in the making – if I don't act now, my ever-present companion, fear, will get the better of me. I'm suddenly grateful to be hanging out with Mel. Action can be a catchy thing.

The phone rings. It feels as if I've exited my body, watching myself from the ceiling, a tiny girl from Mini Town in a white dress waiting for a prince. Suddenly it feels more macabre, like I'm on *The*

Game Show of Death about to meet my fate. As much as I'd like to hang up the phone and run, right now there's no turning back.

The ringing is incessant. I'm praying it will go to voicemail. I've already decided not to leave a message. Then a voice cracks through the fear.

"Hello, is this Advocate Du Plessis?" I almost choke the words out.

"Yes. Who is this?" An Afrikaans-speaking man on the other end responds.

"My name is Lindiwe Hani and I was wondering if you are the lawyer representing Clive Derby-Lewis?"

"Yes, I am he." The advocate sounds guarded.

My heart is beating through my bones.

"As I stated, my name is Lindiwe Hani. I am Chris Hani's daughter. I was wondering if you could help me get in touch with Mr Derby-Lewis as I would like to meet him."

Why the fuck am I being so polite when all I want to do is rip the phone apart?

The conversation unfolds as though I'm on autopilot, two strangers talking about numbers and names. Organised Lindi, polite and restrained, is in control. I am barely breathing. The advocate himself sounds thrown – this is not a call he's prepared for. He tells me he will convey the message to Mr Derby-Lewis.

Then more words tumble out. I need to make things clear. I tell him I want to meet Derby-Lewis in my own personal capacity, that I have not been sent by anyone, and that there is no political objective or agenda. Just me and Derby-Lewis. No press, please. That's very important. Definitely no media.

"I recently read that he's been trying to get in touch with my family but I've never received any such information …" Now my words rush out, tangled in nerves; it's almost a plea. "I know he doesn't owe me anything but this would mean a lot to me."

I'm watching from the ceiling, a manic woman in her new white dress, almost begging her father's killer's lawyer to plead her case for a face to face. It's absurd – a bit like I'm asking a boy out on a date, filled with dread that I'll be rejected. I suddenly feel the urge to burst out in crazy laughter. This can't be normal.

He promises to relay my message. He wishes me a good day. The call ends.

Mel and I stare at each other shell-shocked. Our eyes are huge. I relay word for word what just went down. Before I've managed to finish, my phone rings again. It's the advocate. Oh my fuck! I thought we'd have to wait for days, maybe weeks to hear back from him. But in this new terrain of warped speed and time, things are happening fast. What happens if Derby-Lewis doesn't want to see me? Again that feeling of asking a boy out and dreading rejection.

Du Plessis has spoken to Mrs Derby-Lewis and, yes, they would like to meet. He informs me that I will have to go to them to their home in Pretoria, because Mr Derby-Lewis is under parole restrictions. He gives me a number. I grab a pen. "Phone Gaye after 5pm today to set up a meeting."

The game show bells clatter victory. Glitter rains from the heavens. I have a date. Oh my fuck, this is happening – this is crazy. Within 10 minutes, my double-decade-long desire to meet the man who masterminded Daddy's death has been set in motion. I am just one call away.

Now the guilt descends. The shame. How can I be so fucking excited to meet the man who's been so instrumental in the destruction of my family, my life? This can't be normal. What will I say to him? What words will be appropriate? Oh my fuck, what will my mother say! Terror grips me. What have I done?

Then fear turns to rage; snakes of decade-long anger swallow me.

It's all supposed to be much harder. How can it be so easy for him to agree to meet me – the daughter of the man he killed – in just a few minutes? How can he not hesitate? Is he not scared, ashamed, put out? Fuck him, fuck him, fuck him! I'm a blur of emotions; everything around me has slowed down, except my mind and heart.

And then the anger turns inwards again. Fuck you, Lindiwe. What's *wrong* with you? How can you be so excited to be so close to making a date with your father's killer?

◯

It's 4:55pm. Tick tock, tick tock.

I've been trying to stay busy in the kitchen for the last hour, blasting Yolanda Adams 'I'm Gonna Be Ready' at full volume, trying to capture the Holy Spirit while Rocky Balboa-ing the air in front of me, Bootcamp style. At last, the hour hand on the kitchen clock shudders 5. I dial, the phone rings twice, then immediately the call is dropped. Engaged. I realise I've been holding my breath. I exhale. Push redial. This time it's picked up by a man.

"Hi, may I speak to Gaye Derby-Lewis?" My heart's thundering Morse code.

"She's not here at the moment ... May I give her a message?" A posh, slightly British accent.

"May I ask who's speaking?" I'm channelling business-like Lindi.

"This is Clive."

Hey, Clive! Simple, run-of-the-mill Clive, the guy at the *Cheers* bar where-everyone-knows-your-name Clive. Good, old, jolly-hockey-sticks Clive. Him.

Surely not Clive, the bogeyman puppet master from my terror-filled dreams?

"Hi, Clive, this is Lindiwe Hani, Chris Hani's daughter," I respond, without missing a beat.

"Oh, hi, Lindiwe." All familiar. Like he might be greeting a long-lost friend. "Should I ask Gaye to call you back?"

He did hear me say 'Hani', *right?*

I take my second breath in five minutes.

"Well, actually, it's you I'm looking for. My name is Lindiwe Hani." Just in case he didn't get it the first time round.

Long silence.

Then Clive: "I've been waiting for this call for a very long time."

I exhale slowly. Well, that makes two of us.

His voice suddenly changes, strained.

"My lawyer mentioned your call today," he continues. "I would love to meet you." The pace quickens. "Earlier on I pressed the wrong button trying to answer your call." He stumbles a bit, over-explains. Okay, so maybe I'm not the only one who's nervous.

"Well, let me look at my diary ... What day suits you?" *Stop sounding so desperate.* I clutch my phone, white knuckles. "I'm tied up until 8 March, seeing my doctors."

Ah, yes, the stage-four-two-months-to-live cancer. Lest I forget the reason for his parole.

"Shall we make it the ninth then? I'll send you an SMS to confirm," I respond.

"I look forward to meeting you. Take care of yourself," the architect of my father's murder says before hanging up.

Now I'm left alone in my kitchen. This is unfuckingbelievable. I'm shaking all over. I need to sit down. I want to scream, laugh, cry. It can't be real. What is this, who am I, who is this somebody speaking through me? And then the self-recrimination from that deep, dark hole within. What kind of a moron has a normal conversation with her father's killer? Yep. That's right. This idiot.

Yolanda is still belting it out, urging me to prepare my mind, my heart for whatever comes, telling me I'm going to be ready.

The next day I break out in eczema.

○

The night after I speak to Clive, I dream. Like I used to dream when I was 11 years old, when my sleep descended into nightmares of someone breaking into Dawn Park to murder Daddy.

Now in my dream I walk through a tiny house, a combination of our home in Dawn Park and my grandfather's house in Maseru. There's an open patio with grapevines growing overhead. The dusky light makes it hard to see the figures that loom in the shadows of the fruit trees. The trees we were once forbidden to touch. Although I can't see his face, I know that the man in a military uniform who lurks in the shadows, watching from a rocking chair, is Clive Derby-Lewis. Gaye appears beside him, like a portrait shot of husband and wife in an old, faded photograph. As she opens her mouth to speak, I lunge at her, my hands around her throat. In the darkness I hear voices shouting, telling me to stop.

I wake. Alone in the blackness of my room, my heart thunders, shocked by a surge of adrenaline, the pure and clear urge to kill.

The next morning my mother sends me an SMS telling me that Janusz Waluś is to appear in court today to reapply for parole. Oh my God. Does my mother know what I'm planning? She always knows when I'm up to something. Guilt is a bitch.

As I drive Khaya to school, the early-morning radio breaking news blares reports of Waluś's parole application. I have not been aware of this. I almost slam into the car in front of me when I hear that Roelof du Plessis is his lawyer. Hands gripping the wheel, I wait for my name to come up: "And in breaking news, according to Roelof du Plessis, the lawyer for both Waluś and Clive Derby-Lewis, who was released on medical parole in May last year, Lindiwe Hani, the daughter of the late Chris Hani, has approached Derby-Lewis for a meeting."

What a cock-up. What have I done?

There's an ad break. Nothing about my meeting. "And now it's time for Eye Witness Traffic."

I'm safe. For now.

The following day I visit Momo. I need to talk to someone who's got my back. I've told no one besides Mel of my plans to meet Derby-Lewis. Secrets keep you sick. That's what I learned in rehab. But if this one comes out, if the scavenger media get hold of this, I'm done for.

Almost immediately I break down and confess how wracked with guilt I am, how much terror I feel. She always gets me, dear faithful Momo, my rock, who's been there for me through all my craziness over the years, no matter what. She has a copy of *The Citizen* newspaper showing a front-page photo of our mother's sad and angry face taken the day before outside the court, haggard and bereft. I'm even more distressed when she suggests that with Waluś applying for parole, with the media on high alert, perhaps this is not exactly the right time to have approached Derby-Lewis. A million fingers of self-recrimination point back at me. How could

I have been so stupid? If only I'd known about this crazy timing. But even before her words are out, we both know without having to say it: There never will be a right time. Now is as good as any.

○

A few days later I'm in full mommy mode, organising the tuning of the piano, trying to keep busy with the everydayness of things, to deafen the raging committee of doubt that's taken full ownership of my head, when my phone rings. Without looking at the call screen, I pick it up.

"Hi, Lindeeweh?"

"Hi," I enthuse. I'm unguarded, friendly, expecting the piano tuner to be on the other side of the line.

"I wanted to say we saw your mother—"

"Wait, who is this?" I interject.

"This is Gaye."

"Gaye who?" I'm genuinely confused.

"Derby-Lewis. How many Gayes do you know?" replies the cheeky fucker.

Oh my god. Why is she calling me?

"Gaye by name and not by nature," she merrily cackles.

My eczema itches.

"Hi, Gaye. What can I do for you?" I take a thousand steps back. My voice has changed; it is guarded and restrained. I'm still kicking myself for sounding so stupidly friendly when I picked up the call.

"We saw your mother on TV yesterday. She does still appear to be so very angry. She says we show no remorse. So we were both wondering what actually is the point of you meeting with us?"

I'm thrown. Long pause. I gather myself.

"The request to meet Mr Derby-Lewis has nothing to do with my mother. I want to do this in my personal capacity." My heart plummets. Is this devious cow trying to pull out of the arrangement?

"Oh, okay," she drawls. "It's just that she is still extremely angry so we were just wondering ..."

My mother's "still extremely angry"? I am taken aback by her callousness, her blind inability to see why my mother may possibly still "be angry".

"So I will see you on the ninth?" I am cold, matter of fact, practical.

"Yes, I will send you the directions for our get-together."

"Our get-together." My fingers tighten around the phone. Her throat. I've just given new meaning to white knuckling.

"Good. See you at the meeting." I emphasise the last word.

Over the next few days the eczema keeps spreading, twisting through my skin in angry red welts. I feel like scratching my insides out. I'm holding it together on a wisp of faith and a prayer. I have to keep repeating to myself: "This is about you, this is about you." I know I have to go through with it. It's a gift that's been handed to me. No matter how diabolical the meal served at my father's killer's table will be, I have to do this. For me.

CHAPTER 25

Meeting
Mr Mastermind

M y alarm clock rips me out of sleep. It's 9 March 2016. For
a moment I lie in the pitch dark before my brain thuds
me into the knowing that this is the day I'm going to meet Clive
Derby-Lewis. Outside it's dull grey and dreary – perfect weather.
I wouldn't be able to reconcile myself with a bright, sunny day.
My stomach feels like a cancerous mess as I pack Khaya's lunch
and hurry her up for school. I act overly bright and normal as I
deliver her in one piece, praying that my usually highly intuitive
(and nosey) daughter won't sniff out the fact that I'm about to
embark on meeting her grandfather's killer.

I've been trying to deflect the gravity of meeting the mastermind
of my father's murder by stressing for days about what to wear.
On the drive home from school it feels as though my mind has
been invaded by a reality fashion show. I mean, what does one
wear to meet the orchestrator of your father's death? Sunday best?
Casual I-don't-care torn jeans and a nondescript shirt? A don't-
mess-with-me business suit?

My first choice, my Fidel Castro T-shirt, was loudly thumbs-
downed last night by my relapse prevention counsellor, Elli.
She's told me in no uncertain terms that making a Fidel fashion

statement is "beneath me", that I should just dress like "the lady I am". She's suggested jeans, a white shirt and heels; "simple and elegant channel Jackie O," she said. She got me with that. I love me some Mrs O.

Now, as I stand in front of my wardrobe, I know I don't just need to channel Jackie's style but, more than anything, it's her composure I'm after. I end up choosing the jeans option, opting for a black flowy top instead of a white shirt, which uncannily I don't own, and my black I-feel-sexy-and-strong heels. To top it off, just to add a Communist twist, a red blazer. That should add a bit of bloody drama.

The idea of a 'lunch' with the Derby-Lewises has made me nauseous from the outset so, as Mel – GPS activated – tries to navigate herself around the estate I live in, I prep my 'survival pack'. My lunchbox cooler bag is packed to the brim with health bars, fruit and water. I try to quieten the voice of Polite Lindi who's obsessing how to decline the meal that is sure to be offered today. How do I decline without seeming rude? Damn your manners, Lindi!

The heavens open as Mel and I set off from the East Rand to make the journey to the Derby-Lewises' home in Pretoria. Gaye has already checked in a couple of times this morning, warning me of street closures due to student protests. And just for good measure, a couple more times to see whether I'm still coming. I get the distinct feeling that both she and her husband are highly suspicious that I'm not intending to honour the arrangement. She has begun signing her messages off with *G* instead of Gaye – it feels far too cosy, too familiar. I mean, who *is* this woman?

I have absolutely no intention of cancelling the meeting I've been planning for most of my adult life, but the weather has played havoc with the roads. According to Google Maps, what should be a 45-minute journey is being flagged as one closer to 2.5 hours. As we snail behind trucks and cars along the busiest highway in Africa, Miss Manners rears into a near panic attack. The mist is thick, the downpour so intense we can hardly make out the vehicle in front. The windscreen wipers of Mel's teeny rental creak at a pathetic pace, defenceless against the river that pours from the sky. There is absolutely no way that we are not going to be horribly late.

Thankfully, Google soon diverts us onto a short cut.

"My father is sending us a message to say: you are two crazy bitches—" I announce.

"—or he's blessing us," interjects Mel, trying to stay upbeat.

I am not convinced.

My eyes become increasingly heavy as we drive. I keep having to jolt myself from dropping off, vaguely listening to Mel as she chatters through the storm. She notices me zoning out.

I tell her that whenever I'm anxious, I feel like sleeping. In fact, I remind her, it got so bad in rehab that I was banned by my counsellor from taking naps because he had realised it was my way of avoiding emotionally draining situations. As far as stressful scenarios go, having a lunch date with the man who was instrumental in my father's death is enough to induce permanent narcolepsy.

As Google finally alerts us that we've reached drizzly Pretoria, I realise just how much I hate this place. Growing up, it had the reputation for being the place people went to and never returned.

We pass through Waterkloof, a suburb that appears to be the neighbourhood for notorious criminals: Oscar Pistorius, the Waterkloof Four ... When the GPS alerts us that we are 200 metres away from our destination, we stop the car, grab hands and half whisper half plead the Serenity Prayer.

God grant me the serenity to accept the things I cannot change, the courage to change the things I can and the wisdom to know the difference.

My heart's all but leaping out of my rib cage as Mel buzzes the entrance button to the facebrick, gated complex. It resembles one of those retirement villages where every unit looks the same. I'm relieved it's not some sprawling mansion; I don't know how I would stomach that.

Almost immediately we hear a woman's voice, which we assume to be Gaye's, informing us that she's coming to the gate to open for us.

As we snail along the bricked communal driveway, a figure in a large printed kaftan emerges. Gaye. When we draw closer, she peers into the car and stares at me. Not a polite once-over, but a proper eye-piercing look. She's clearly as curious about me as I am of her.

Thankfully, Mel breaks the contact to ask her where to park. My anxiety is off the radar. I've given up my power way too soon to this middle-aged, bespectacled matron.

Gaye talks non-stop as we enter the townhouse. I'm immediately struck by how dark and oppressive it feels. The horror scenario is complete as I spot the cat – evil clearly lives here. There are two people sitting in the lounge, a man and a woman who is introduced to us as 'a friend'.

An old, thin, bespectacled man rises from a chair on the opposite side of the room to greet us. Surely this isn't Clive? Where's the firebrand moustachioed man with a full head of foxy brown hair? The Bogeyman from my dreams since 1993?

As he extends his hand to greet me, I notice a big white plaster on his arm. My first thought is how well placed it is, lest we forget that he is a long-term cancer sufferer. But other than looking much older, he looks fit, not like a man who is dying, with 'just two months to live'. Two months that ran out a year ago.

Miss Manners steps up to the plate as my hand, on autopilot, reaches out to meet his. There's no blackout or bolt of lightning as our skins touch. For a second, I breathe. Maybe, just maybe, I can do this.

I steal surreptitious glances when I think he's not looking. The man before me is time-worn, his pants perched high in the middle of his gut, T-shirt loose-fitting, his arms riddled with age spots. But I can't escape his eyes, which pin me to my chair. Perhaps for him it too feels like a ghost has come to visit.

So far I haven't said a single word. It's as though I've left my body in the chair while my mind drums panic. The conversation quickly turns to the weather. In the car I had told Mel that this was likely to happen. It's clear that the heavy rain is diverting much of what would otherwise be uncomfortable silence. I'm always fascinated by how people love to latch onto the state of the skies whenever there's an elephant in the room, one that is too big to deal with.

After a few minutes of asinine discussion I break in with, "As much as I appreciate you agreeing to see me, this is not really a social visit. I have questions that I would like some answers to." Before he has a chance to respond, Gaye interrupts, which she seems to have a habit of doing, and brightly suggests lunch. She proudly tells us that she's made a pile of sandwiches and a quiche. She breaks the news like she's Nigella Fucking Lawson. Playing the ever-gracious hostess, she offers drinks all round.

This is the moment I've been dreading, the one I've played over and over in my head ever since the word 'lunch' was mentioned in our communication. I decline the offer. I do not wish to drink tea or coffee, let alone break bread with my father's killer, nor his wife.

My, "No thank you, I don't have an appetite," clearly affronts Gaye.

"You won't eat anything, Lindeeweh?" It's more of an accusation than a question.

"I would rather eat my leg than imbibe your food" remains on the tip of my tongue.

"When you see the food, I'm sure you will change your mind, Lindiwe," says Clive, trying to placate his wife. "I can tell you it's delicious."

But I'm adamant. The air is now fraught with discomfort as Nigella huffs off into the kitchen to play the hostess with the mostest. Mel leaps up to charge her phone and I'm left alone with Clive, the air hanging thick in silence. I try to breathe into my space; I've made a deal with myself: no small talk, no Miss People-Pleasing Lindi. So I sit in silence.

Clive clearly can't stand it.

"So how old are you, Lindiwe?"

I summon my tongue to form two short words.

"I'm 35."

"35! You don't look a day older than 25." He is trying to compliment me. I nod.

"And what do you do, Lindiwe?"

"I'm in communications. PR and Marketing."

"That's a good thing to be in," he says. He's trying hard. "They always need people in that area."

More silence.

I have not come to sit at my father's killer's table to chitchat about the weather or PR, to eat with him or forgive him. It is neither in the realms of my ability, nor my will. I do not want to sip coffee or toast reconciliation.

There is nothing that will ever bring my father back, back into the world of his fatherless children, back into the arms of his widowed wife, back to the helm of our nation to steer our floundering, leaderless ship.

So why have I come here?

I want to stare down The Bogeyman. Look Fear in the eye. Make eye contact with The Monster. I want to feel how The Lion Heart of my father beats in me.

And right now sitting tight with my quiet is the bravest thing I can do.

Finally after what feels like days, Mel and Gaye return to the lounge.

Mel decides to cut to the chase.

"Okay, so we are all here today and this is clearly not an easy situation for anybody."

"Well, we do our best," Gaye cuts in.

"It's especially hard for Lindiwe," Mel cuts back. "She has some questions—"

Before Mel can finish I feel a surge of courage and find my voice.

"I appreciate everything you are doing to make me comfortable, but this is obviously an uncomfortable situation. I am here today because there are some questions I need to ask you."

Without waiting to hear any of my questions, Clive goes into lengthy detail to dispel the idea that there was any conspiracy theory behind my father's death. I'm immediately curious why this is the very first thing he would choose to tell me, to assume this is the main reason for my visit. I'm also offended by the smugness in his tone as he takes control of the floor. "Over the years, as you know, there was a lot of opposition to me receiving amnesty, in the second parole and in the third medical parole hearing.

Somewhere along the line someone came up with the story that there was a big conspiracy behind your father's murder. In prison I was visited by Penuell Maduna, Steve Tshwete, and even at a later stage Jacob Zuma. And the reason behind the visits was that they believed that Thabo Mbeki had had something to do with your father's murder. I had – and have – never met Mr Mbeki, never mind planned a murder with him. Mandela introduced the whole conspiracy theory after your dad died, saying it was part of a National Party conspiracy, then Winnie Mandela accused members within the ANC of conspiracy. This idea grew in people's imaginations. Surely if I could have gotten myself out of prison by telling 'the truth' I would have."

Clive is on a roll now.

"As I said at the amnesty hearing, what benefit would I have had, from withholding information? That would have been totally stupid of me and I don't think I'm a stupid person. Surely, if I had been part of a bigger conspiracy, it would have been in my interests to lay the blame at another party's door, in order to secure my release."

Although he has not been an active politician for decades, he evidently hasn't lost his take-command-of-the-podium touch. He now moves on to blaming the SACP who, according to him, has for many years been fanning the conspiracy theories. "The SACP has continually accused me of not making full disclosure, while using your father's death to justify their existence."

I feel that if I don't interject at this point, I will explode.

"I am not that interested in the whole conspiracy theory idea right now, Clive. What I need you to do is to please walk me through the planning around my father's death. From conception of the plan to the actual execution. I am curious as to your thinking at the time."

But Clive has other plans. Ever thorough and logical, he now tells me that he would like to begin by telling me the history of the Conservative Party. He explains that it's imperative to understand this in order to see how he arrived at his decisions. He meticulously proceeds to paint a picture of the political landscape leading up to 1993, the year Daddy was shot.

Initially I choke back irritation; I don't feel like another diversion. But Clive's a natural historian and before long I'm drawn into the history of his party, which up until today has been foreign territory to me.

"I was a senior member of the Conservative Party at the time," he explains methodically. "We were winning against the National Party. Every year we got closer and closer. We had a policy that as far as possible we would use the democratic process to gain power. However, when the NP started doing really badly in the elections in 1987, we started winning more by-elections, and soon we secured control over what was then known as the Transvaal province. In the 1989 elections we won 40 seats, so we were clearly heading for power."

Despite being 80 years old, his passion for politics is palpable as he continues to sing the praises of the CP. It feels, absurdly, like he's almost trying to recruit me. I try to gently but firmly steer him back to my original question, but he's clearly on a roll.

"In 1992 along came Mr De Klerk and the NP did really badly," continues Clive. "We could see we were on our way to victory. De Klerk even admitted this, that he no longer had the support of the electorate. So what did he do? Instead of holding an election, as he was morally bound to do, he held a referendum."

During Clive's speech, Kaftan Nigella moves in noisily, sets her 'meal' out on the coffee table, and proceeds to ceremoniously dish out the quiche and triangular little sandwiches. I've been off quiche since soggy boarding school fare so I naturally judge her on that. She could have at least served something to make me regret my decision to abstain.

Gaye dishes up for her hubby and, like a parent, tells him, "Eat your food, Dad." Clive takes his plate. He's clearly noticed my face, perturbed by his wife interrupting an important moment between us. He responds by telling her, "Lindiwe would like some answers, which is fair enough." I find myself instinctively appreciating that gesture. The fact that he's read the room.

He proceeds to explain how a referendum was much easier to manipulate than an election, and how the NP basically cooked the results. "Despite all the crooking, the NP still only received 51 per cent of the vote, which was hardly a convincing result. The question posed to the electorate was also very ambiguous. 'Do you agree we must proceed with negotiations?'"

De Klerk broke all sorts of promises, explains Clive and when it was revealed that the NP had only in fact secured 48 per cent of the vote, the CP realised that they had the balance of power. According to Clive, the CP believed the democratic process in South Africa had been compromised and that violence now was the only option.

"I, as a senior member of the CP, was obliged to make sure that we didn't lose power. My decision was that we had to stop this process with as little bloodshed as possible. A month before he was shot, your dad announced in the newspaper that the MK weaponry that was still in Angola must be brought back to South Africa. It was quite clear to us that this was an act of war."

I ask him if he'd only planned to kill Daddy within that month. This was clearly not the case; the plan to assassinate my father had sprung to life the previous year.

"From September 1992, it was decided at a CP congress that the time for violence had come," explains Clive.

I'm confused. "Why after all this dissatisfaction with De Klerk? Why mark someone in the ANC rather than the leader of the National Party?"

"Because it wouldn't have had the desired results," says Clive. "Our strategy was that, as a result of our actions, there would be huge chaos in the country. The security forces would then be obliged to step in to restore law and order. To do that they would first have to declare martial law, because the government had lost control. After that a fresh election would be called and we believed at that stage that we would have won."

Clive defends his ideology, saying the CP's confederal approach was not racist because it would give everyone a vote, black and white people. But in their *own areas*. "We strongly believed separate development would work."

"You mean separate but equal?" My sarcasm is lost on Clive.

183

"Exactly. When it came to voting, if you lived in a certain state you would vote there," Clive continues to explain.

"So basically," Mel interjects, "people would be forced to vote on racial lines?"

"Oh no," says Clive, "it would be ethnic. Zulus would vote for their government, Tswanas would vote for their own government." It's clear, sitting in his lounge, that 23 years in prison have done nothing to change his political thinking. He still believes that this flawed approach was the near-perfect solution.

"So," says Mel, "what would happen in a place like Soweto?"

"We had a plan that Soweto would become a—"

"Bantustan," I offer. Dryly.

"It would be a city state," explains Clive. "We were trying to give everybody equal representation; we believed that after everything the Afrikaner had done for the country, they were entitled to their share of it."

His thinking boggles my mind. He now begins to talk about the Freedom Charter. My frustration is mounting. I have had just about enough of all these long explanations. We've clearly veered far from my initial questions.

"Can you please get back to what I asked you?" It's my turn to interrupt. "When did you earmark my father and how did you go about my dad's assassination?"

Clive begins by introducing a certain Polish man to the tale, by way of Janusz Waluś. He now explains how, in 1986, he started an organisation to bring English and Afrikaans conservatives together.

"Waluś heard about a meeting we had planned for in Johannesburg, which he then attended. Afterwards he approached me and said he would like to support me, that we had a good thing going, and it was necessary that we all stick together. So that's how the two of us met."

Waluś and Clive soon became buddies, with his new Polish friend regularly visiting the Derby-Lewis household. "Janusz, who worked for his dad, lived in QwaQwa at this stage, but whenever he came to town he would visit and we would discuss the situation in South Africa. As you know Waluś came from communist Poland; he and his family had experienced such great suffering under the communist state that they emigrated to South Africa. As things deteriorated with the unbanning of the ANC and SACP in 1990, it became clear that we were moving towards communism. Now Waluś decided to really commit and become involved."

I assume it must have been at this point that my commie father became a red-hot topic in their conversations.

Clive explains how hard it was to trust people during this time. "If you had three Afrikaners in a room, one would invariably be a traitor, so one had to restrict the numbers."

Waluś and Clive began meeting to discuss a strategy to get "rid of the communist threat".

"I believed that a small spark could get the whole country together; chaos would unite the Afrikaner. Then we would strike a big blow against communism, which has never been successful anywhere in the world."

By now I'm hanging onto every word, waiting for Daddy's name to crop up at any moment.

"When I told Waluś that something dramatic would have to happen, that we would have to take out a senior member of the Communist Party, Waluś said if there was any shooting to be done, he would do it."

Just like that. Like a plumber volunteering to unblock a drain, Clive Derby-Lewis had his Polish hitman.

Mel now asks, "Had you ever done anything like that before?"

"No," says Clive emphatically. Well, I guess he was obviously not going to suddenly 'fess up to a whole lot of other killings.

"And you never thought of taking out Nelson Mandela?" continues Mel.

"No, that was another falsity that the media contrived at the time, to make out that the address list we had was actually a hit list. There were other names on the list besides your dad's name, Lindiwe. At the top of the list was Mandela; Joe Slovo was also there, as well as a number of journos, like Tim du Plessis."

'The list' sounds rather dodgy, a list of 'enemies of the CP' that just happened to have the name and address of my father who was assassinated, but that wasn't actually a 'hit list'? I ask him to explain this 'list'.

"Gaye drew up the list because she was working as a journalist for *Die Patriot* newspaper at the time and she was investigating the affluence around certain people, with a view to exposing them for having received money from overseas," says Clive.

Gaye has been bursting to butt into the monologue that's been unfolding for the last 30 minutes; now it's her turn.

"We called them the 'Gucci Socialists'," she smiles smugly at her clever title. "They were all talking about everyone being 'equal' and 'we're all so poor' – in the meantime, they were all running around in BMWs, with overseas bank accounts. So I was doing a series of articles on these people. Some of these Gucci Socialists and other people on the list were journalists, like Tim du Plessis, who was promoting these people who were going to destroy our way of life. So the 19 on the list were people who were not who they pretended to be."

"So you were saying that Chris Hani was a Gucci Socialist?" asks Mel incredulously.

I can't help but smile at the idea of my dad as a Gucci Socialist, my dad who freaked out every time my mom bought us new clothes, who gave away most of his clothes to the comrades, who drove around in an embarrassingly old Corolla, who couldn't bare wasting anything on any level.

Gaye is clearly having to defend this ludicrous idea.

"Yes, well there were some articles that said he was sending his kids to private schools while he was purporting to have no money. It was the hypocrisy of all these people, pretending to be poor and all for the people, while living the high life. Chris Hani was one of them."

She talks about Daddy like I'm not in the room. Clive seems embarrassed by his wife's outburst and steers the conversation back to my question on how he and Waluś went about targeting Daddy.

"So, Lindiwe, in September 1992 we discussed the idea and

Waluś said he would do the shooting. I made it clear that no one else should be harmed, no passerby; there was only one target," says Clive.

"How did you get the address?" asks Mel.

"From the phone book," Gaye almost laughs at how easy it was. She again takes the floor.

She explains how a journalist friend, a man by the name of Arthur Kemp who worked at *The Citizen*, and who was also a stringer at *Die Patriot*, simply looked in the phone book and found our home address in Dawn Park. "He also got Mandela's address for us and Joe Slovo's. I told him I needed them for articles."

Then Mel asks the million-dollar question: "So, Gaye, did you know what your husband was planning?"

"Oh no, no, no," Clive is quick to interject. Mel and I glance at each other.

It's extremely unlikely they would both suddenly admit that Gaye had anything to do with it when the story that's been out there for over 20 years was that she had absolutely no knowledge of her husband's plans.

Clive attempts to steer the conversation back to answering my question on the planning of Daddy's murder, but once again Gaye silences him. "Let me finish my story, Dad." There's clearly an awkward atmosphere in the room. Nonplussed, she carries on.

"I showed my list to Ferdi Hartzenberg, the editor of *Die Patriot*, and told him about my idea of writing a number of articles about the Gucci Socialists and he said go ahead."

Gaye's on a roll as she explains how one Saturday, in February 1993, she had to rush out to go and canvas for the CP in Krugersdorp and so left all her papers, including the list with all the names and addresses on a table in the house. "Waluś came by, saw the list and that's how he got the address for your father."

Her explanation sounds suspicious, way too convenient. Of course, this would suggest that Gaye had nothing to do with giving either Clive or Waluś info that would incriminate her in Daddy's murder.

"I have to say I find this all a little hard to believe," says Mel. "I mean, you two are clearly close and politically like-minded. When you were together in bed at night, you mean to say you never once mentioned that you thought Chris Hani needed to be taken out?"

The couple insists that Gaye knew nothing of the assassination plot.

Clive steers the conversation back to the plan to kill Daddy, saying that although my father had been chosen as the target, "I still had serious misgivings about the whole story."

According to Clive, he got Waluś the gun (a Z88), but he didn't give him ammunition or the part of the gun to enable the silencer. This was omitted, according to Clive, in order to maintain control over the shooting, as he was still unsure whether this was really in fact a workable plan. He also told Waluś not to execute the plan on a long weekend, clearly meaning the Easter weekend, which started on Friday, 9 April, as there might be too many people at home.

As I listen to the details of my father's assassination unfold, I'm surprised how calm I am. I always thought that it would be much harder to hear than it's proving to be. It's Gaye who seems anxious, fidgety and agitated as Clive carefully goes through the details like a soldier marking time.

According to Clive, Waluś then took matters into his own hands and shot Daddy unbeknownst to him. "I was having tea with friends in Krugersdorp on Saturday, the tenth, and got a helluva shock when I heard that your dad had been shot. I thought someone else must have done it; I didn't think it was Waluś because I hadn't given him the go-ahead. I never heard a word from him that day. The last time I'd seen him was the beginning of April. I tried to call him but I couldn't get hold of him."

I hang onto each word spoken by Clive. Finally, I am hearing what I've come for, the small details that have haunted me since I was 12. Clive suddenly looks a lot frailer. The room has gone dead silent. I am in control.

"Then what happened?" I ask.

For a long while he seems locked in thought, unable to talk. Finally: "It was a nightmare."

"Tell me about it," I say, sarcastically.

"It's difficult to explain—" he breaks off.

The room shudders in silence.

"I'll tell you my nightmare if you tell me yours," I say, gently coaxing him.

"My nightmare was being responsible for somebody's death," he says shakily.

"So what happened in your mind when you realised it was Waluś who had done it?"

"I didn't know how it had happened because the last time I saw him he didn't have ammunition. I couldn't work it out. He was arrested shortly after leaving your house. Only once it was on the news did I realise that Waluś had in fact done it."

For almost a week Clive heard nothing and tried to go about his daily business, hoping his Polish friend would refrain from dragging him into it.

"What was going through your mind that whole week before you got arrested?" I ask.

Clive is clearly struggling to go there, his voice betraying the strain. "The agreement between us was that if he was caught, he was on his own. I was really hoping he would stay quiet, that the whole thing would go away. There was nothing really to connect us except that we were both members of the same club, but so were many other people."

But Clive's hopes were soon dashed.

"The following weekend the security branch got Waluś full of liquor; they made him think they were on his side. They made him feel safe, to get him to open up, and said he should tell them who helped him so they could protect this person."

Clive was subsequently arrested on 17 April 1993 for the murder of Daddy, exactly a week after Waluś shot him.

"We were out canvassing for the CP in Krugersdorp on that Saturday afternoon. We came home and were drinking a cup of tea," says Gaye. "The next thing there was a flurry of noise and heaven knows how many policemen stormed into our home."

"Twenty-two," says Clive.

"They arrested Clive," continues Gaye.

"And did they tell you what they were arresting you for?" I ask. There's a long pause.

"They actually didn't." It's as though Clive's realised this for the first time. "They just said they had a warrant for my arrest."

"They did tell you," Gaye contradicts her man. "Remember, it was on the television at the same time. While they were arresting him, before they got out of the door, it was all over the TV."

Was Gaye arrested at the same time, I ask.

"No, the reason they arrested her later was to force me to tell them the full story because I was refusing to talk," says Clive. "As far as I was concerned, it was an act of war and I had no reason to explain anything to them."

According to Clive, he was ill advised by his advocate, Hennie de Vos, appointed by the CP. He was told that because the state had no case against him, he didn't need to testify in court. "What De Vos didn't tell me was that if I didn't testify and the state produced circumstantial evidence and I didn't refute it, it becomes prima facie. So that's what happened."

Gaye was arrested in the early hours of the morning of Wednesday, 21 April. "I wasn't charged. I was arrested under section 29 – detention without trial – where they can do whatever they want to you and you just simply disappear from life."

Officially, section 29 was defined as 'Detention for interrogation'. It basically gave the state power to hold a detainee in solitary confinement without access to lawyers, family, friends or anyone else other than state officials or people such as interrogators, magistrates and district surgeons, for "the purpose of interrogation". The period of detention was effectively unlimited until "all questions are satisfactorily answered".

"At Benoni police holding cells I was given a statement that said I was part of the planning of the murder," continues Gaye, "saying all sorts of things that I was supposed to have done and I was told to sign it. I absolutely refused to. After each sentence I wrote, *No Comment*. I had no legal counsel. They woke me up at all hours of the night to ask me questions about the murder. After ten days inside, they told me I had to write a statement, so I wrote about the articles that I wrote for *Die Patriot* and how I was a member of the CP. I was told I would have to be a witness in the case against my husband, but the next thing I was taken to Pretoria court and charged with attempted murder and conspiracy. Finally, I was allowed out on bail under very severe conditions. Then I started consulting with an attorney as I was the only one not in prison."

Gaye has the floor now; this is her tragedy, her nightmare. At times it sounds like the Gaye Derby-Lewis pity party. I wonder whether she realises how many people over the dark years of apartheid were arrested under section 29. I doubt she senses the irony.

"I told the lawyers, 'I'm going to testify'," says Gaye. "I didn't have anything to hide; I was getting suspicious that Clive wasn't going to be able to defend himself. I argued a lot with the attorney, De Vos. He was a terrible man, a chain smoker, and now he's a judge. He threatened me, saying, 'If you testify, the blood of your husband will be on your shoulders [sic].' But as little as I knew about the law, I knew I had to testify and, in the end, because I did testify, I was acquitted. If I hadn't I probably would have gone to prison for murder too."

I now bring the conversation back to Daddy's death and remind Clive that my sister Khwezi was there on the day that Daddy was shot, that it was Khwezi who ran out, dodged a bullet, saw Daddy's lifeless, bloody body and ran down the road screaming for help.

This clearly makes Clive extremely uncomfortable. "It must have been very traumatic for her," he stumbles.

I'd say.

The room has grown quiet.

"One regrets these things," Clive finally manages to say. "As you know, I told the TRC amnesty hearing, and every time that I applied for parole, that I've been trying to meet with your mother for years to personally express my regrets. But that never happened. Lindiwe, I am glad I can do it with you today. I don't feel proud of what happened. I don't feel any degree of satisfaction around what happened. But the circumstances in the country were such that things developed. But I can tell you, it's not gratifying to know that you are responsible for somebody's death under any circumstances. I don't know if it's any consolation, but your father must have been quite a man because of the support he had from the people. And the fact that he was the target is some kind of indication of the esteem he was held by his people. Lindi, I am really sorry we have had to meet under these circumstances."

I listen. I am utterly confused regarding my emotions. On one hand I know that I should be angry, furious, but it's difficult to muster that emotion. It feels as though Clive is telling me his truth as he sees it – strangely, I find myself respecting that.

"There was no personal motivation in this," says Clive. "I know that might be difficult to understand, but I had nothing personal against your father."

I receive his words. I almost feel empathy for the position Clive once found himself in in the political climate of the time.

More silence widens between us. It feels appropriate.

Finally, Clive breaks it. "Are you sure I can't persuade you to have a cup of tea?"

It's either the weather or tea.

I don't take up his offer.

"Do you have grandchildren?" I ask him.

"Yes, I do. I don't see them very often except for on Skype. As you probably know, I'm confined to this complex, under house arrest. I can't even go to church on a Sunday."

His voice is filled with regret. My father will never see Khaya. I still don't think he sees the irony.

"So when you look at it all," says Mel, "your whole plan to cause chaos in the country after Chris was shot, for a kind of military coup to take place – none of the things you hoped for and planned for ever happened. You united black South Africans even more. A father and hero of the people was killed, you and Waluś went to prison and the ANC became the ruling party."

"And you also elevated the next president, because Mandela had to go on TV and calm everybody down," I add.

"So, did you ever feel that the plan had backfired, that what you hoped for became in fact the opposite, that you got what you dreaded and feared?" asks Mel.

"Up until the AWB debacle, it was working," says Clive, "but when they went into Bophuthatswana, they messed it up. Terre'Blanche was a bit of a nutcase; he saw himself as some kind of a leader, which he wasn't, so when he went in, he wasn't supposed to be there. The agreement was between Constand Viljoen, the CP and the Bop government, which was supposed to give our forces weapons on arrival but with Terre'Blanche and his maniacs shooting innocent people, the Bop government simply refused to keep to the plan."

Gaye goes off on a rant about Zuma and the present government. I look straight at Clive and say, "You know by killing my father you indirectly gave us Zuma?" The irony of fate is clear. "In retrospect, have you ever had any regrets killing my dad, who would have in all likelihood become president after Mandela?"

"I didn't know your dad as a leader – I saw him as a communist," says Clive. "I didn't know if he would have been a competent leader. But when you look at what we are sitting with now, anyone could have been better than Jacob Zuma."

"Did it feel disorientating when you got out last year?" Mel changes the subject. "Twenty-three years had passed."

"One thing I learned in the army was to adjust," says Clive stoically. "Within 24 hours I had adjusted. One of the problems with my parole conditions is that I can't attend church. That's a contravention of the Constitution. I have to deal with a parole officer who is an SACP member and who will victimise me at any opportunity."

"But," interjects Mel, "you must understand how someone who belongs to the SACP, whose leader, whose hero was brutally murdered, must feel towards you —"

"But it's 23 years ago—" says Clive.

"He's a state employee," Gaye butts in. "His personal political persuasion should have nothing to do with his duties."

"I think now, more so than ever, instead of fading away into some memory, Chris Hani has become more and more of an important symbol in the nation's psyche," says Mel. "Many people think, if only we had had Chris Hani leading our country, things wouldn't be like they are today under Zuma. So Chris Hani is still very present. And you of course," she says to Clive, "are directly associated and responsible for the death of that dream."

"Plus, after the death of my dad, there was such a scramble to soothe people that nothing was dealt with," I say. "No anger, no disappointment, no pain. So, as a result, the generation that was born afterwards is feeling that anger and taking up that fight now. This is as a result of Mandela's leadership and the TRC, the rainbow nation farce. There's no way we can move forward without an acknowledgment of the past. Going through the painful process of acknowledging and then forgiving was never done. A plaster [like the one on Clive's arm] was put over the gaping wound and now it's seeping."

Clive is quiet, almost mesmerised. He simply stares at me. "Why don't you get involved in politics, Lindiwe? You are such an impressive young woman."

"Because I don't want to die. I have a daughter who is the age I was when my dad died." I say this half-jokingly, and I am not sure if the irony is lost on the Derby-Lewises.

It's time for Gaye to paint a picture of how hard things have been for them. "We struggled so much and we worked so hard—"

"We're still struggling," says Clive.

"We used to have money," adds Gaye. "I travelled the world. We had furniture, a house, a car. We weren't rich, but we were comfortable. We lost 23 years of our life."

I can only but stare at this woman. Some of us lost much more.

"So what are your plans now, Clive?" I turn away from Gaye.

"I carry on. I'm an old man now. I'm 80. I try to move around as much as I can, to keep going."

And then, from out of nowhere, Gaye says: "So, what are we going to do about Jacob Zuma?"

I almost burst out laughing.

"I'm sure this is how a certain discussion happened 23 years ago," I say. "Fade back to Waluś and Clive: 'So, what are we going to do about Chris Hani?' ... Let's not go there!"

Before leaving, I ask Clive what his biggest regret has been.

194

Gaye offers, "The whole Hani thing." But either Clive doesn't hear, or he chooses to ignore her. He is lost in time, a high-waisted old man creased in resentments for the old National Party. "That we couldn't stop the treachery of FW de Klerk. He didn't have the permission from the South African people to unban the ANC and SACP, but he did it anyway. Things could have been very different in South Africa. Our policies in the Conservative Party, a confederal system like Europe, would have given prosperity to all. Everything that went wrong and haywire in South Africa originated with De Klerk."

As we get up to leave, I shake Clive's hand. Gaye goes in for a hug. I would have preferred to embrace Clive.

As we drive home, the rain has stopped. I am filled with many conflicting emotions, still in utter disbelief at how weird the whole meeting has been. Parts of me feel guilty that, somewhere inside, I liked him and believed him. I feel even more guilty that I might even like to see him again.

However, in the days that follow I can't help but feel an anticlimax, uncertain as to whether he has been entirely genuine with me or not, which leaves me with a hollow emptiness.

But at the same time, I am strangely at peace, as though a weight has been lifted off my heart, removing the poison of animosity. It feels like, in the bigger scheme of things, I made a difference. I confronted the unimaginable. Not only did I survive, but I managed to sit through my fear and confront the man who I for so long saw as a monster. I saw that he was just a man. I have a sense that I have left him with much more. When, in November 2016, eight months after our visit, I hear that Clive Derby-Lewis has succumbed to cancer, I feel sad for his children, who have lost a father.

CHAPTER 26

After the visit

The day after meeting with Clive and Gaye Derby-Lewis, Janusz Waluś – the man who pulled the trigger of the gun that killed my father – is granted parole. It's 10 March 2016, the anniversary of my sister Khwezi's death. Exactly a month to the day of the twenty-third anniversary of the day my father was murdered. I hear the news on Radio 702 as I'm driving back from dropping Khaya at school – in 15 days, it appears, my father's killer will be released from prison. I am still sleep hazed, exhausted by the previous day's momentous events, when my mother's voice on the radio jerks me alert.

She is furious at Judge Nicolene Janse van Nieuwenhuizen, who has ruled on granting Waluś parole.

She is nothing but a racist. To her, black lives don't matter. She hardly made mention of my husband's murder in her judgment.

Listening to my mom voice her anger, I am shocked and saddened that she hasn't called or mentioned this breaking news to me before speaking to the media. This is typical of my mother. Sometimes it feels like her identity as Chris Hani's widow precedes the needs of her children. For as long as I can remember it feels as though her life's purpose has been to preserve my father's legacy. For 23 years, I've been watching her live in the shroud of her loss; Limpho, the grieving wife of

Chris Hani, has been her world, her mission, her identity.

I remember as a child, in the years that followed my father's death, wanting to scream, "Hey you, look at me! It's not only you who's hurting, it's not only your loss – we have also lost our beloved father." Growing up, my mother's stance gave us no space to stand up, to be seen and counted.

That's how it was until I got clean. These days I've been understanding more and more how hard it must have been for her to keep our broken family together. I have been accepting that she is but human and, despite her sometimes abrupt manner, she has always had her children's best interests at heart.

In the backed-up traffic, my mother's anger continues to staccato through the radio static.

Janusz murdered my husband in cold blood ... All I want is for Janusz and whoever is supporting him to tell me what happened and tell me the truth.

It's there and then that I make the decision to find a way to set up a meeting with the man who pulled the trigger. Before he is released from prison. Whether my mother likes it or not.

The following day I decide to make the call. It's Friday. Ever since I made the first call to Derby-Lewis's lawyer a few weeks ago, I've been experiencing the fruits of taking action. This time Mel is not with me to support or egg me on. Today I am the mistress of my own destiny. I have the courage of a lion.

I punch in the number of Advocate Roelof du Plessis who helped me connect with the Derby-Lewises. He tells me to jot down a number and advises me to speak to Waluś's lawyer, Julian Knight. Without hesitating, I make the next call.

Julian Knight answers almost immediately; he doesn't think there'll be any problem with Waluś agreeing to meet with me. He thinks, however, that the prison will require a social worker present. I immediately go on the defence. "I'm 35 years old, a grown-up; I don't need anyone monitoring or babysitting me. I need to do this alone. I don't want any third party facilitating this."

Knight sounds doubtful that the authorities will agree; they are strict and the procedures will in all likelihood need to be followed if I'm to be granted access.

He promises to get back to me.

As the call ends, another comes through. My mother. My personal bloodhound. I feel the panic rising. I scratch the crease of my inner arm where my eczema resides.

Oh my fuck, what does she want? Does she know about my meeting with Derby-Lewis? Has she sensed by some weird telepathy that I am up to something? She's always had this uncanny sixth sense when I'm doing something she disapproves of. It's been like this for years.

The phone rings mercilessly. Accusingly. If I don't answer now, she'll keep on calling. Heart pounding, I pick up.

Almost immediately, like a confessor in Guantanamo, I blurt it out as soon as she greets me.

"Mama, I've decided I need to speak to Waluś. I've already spoken to his lawyer. He is busy helping me to set up the meeting." There. It's out. I wait for the bomb to explode.

First there is silence, that long icy silence that Mama is so good at, then all hell breaks loose. Her words are her weapons. They once had the power to machine gun me down. Not so much any more.

The tirade ends with her slamming the phone down on me.

I am breathless. Shaking. Scratch, scratch, scratch. My arm bursts into a frenzy of itches.

The SMS alert clangs in. I can barely force myself to look at my phone's inbox full of my mother's vitriol and self-pity.

I feel small. Afraid. I am that numb child again.

"Put those bloody boundaries up," I hiss to myself. I try to call Mel. Her phone goes to voicemail. It's only the Serenity Prayer that's going to get me through this.

ↄ

I wake up on Saturday morning feeling like I have a hangover. I have the dull thud of a headache, a scratch at the back of my throat. I'm too exhausted to do Bootcamp.

For a moment there's a flash of perspective. Despite feeling like crap, I realise how grateful I am for being clean and sober through all this. Imagine how unmanageable it would be if I was boozing or using. But, I soberly remind myself, none of this would actually be happening if I were still in active addiction. These are the fruits of my recovery: action and purpose. I reach out to Mel when her phone's back on; she suggests I take the day off, re-energise, take time out to recover from the past few days of madness.

By the afternoon I'm feeling a whole lot better – until a call from an unknown number catches me off guard. It's a journo from South Africa's biggest Sunday newspaper, the *Sunday Times*. It's clear the story of me wanting to meet with Waluś has been leaked. The journalist informs me that an "impeccable source" has alerted the newspaper that I have contacted Knight to set up a meeting with my father's killer.

I dissolve into a ball of familiar terror; my mother's threats and manipulations pound back at me – oh my God, what have I done? All I manage to say is "No comment" as I drop the call.

I call Mel. I can hear she's trying to stay calm but is as thrown as I am. We're confounded as to who has alerted the media: the lawyer? The prison officials? Someone on our side? It's weird how this whole thing has suddenly taken on a sinister feeling of 'sides'.

Mel reassures me I have done nothing wrong, that it's my right to seek answers, to find the truth, to get some closure. I try to take her words to heart but the terror has gripped me. I am 35 years old, a grown woman. I have a right to make my own choices, but once again I feel like I'm drowning in my mother's fury. All I want to do is sleep. My escape tactic. Oh God, I feel so tired.

○

I wake up on Sunday around 04:30am. The world is still inky black as I mission out of my little cocoon to find the Sunday papers at a nearby service station. I have hardly slept.

In the car, heart pounding, I confront my terror. There's nothing on the front page, thank God. I turn to page two. The story screams at me with a huge headline: *Hani's daughter's request to Waluś.*

They have managed to come up with an entire half-page article based on the news of Waluś's parole – there are only two paragraphs around me wanting to meet with him, which they have verified from "an impeccable source". My response of "No comment" is all they have from me.

I call Mel as soon as the light breaks. She dashes out to get the offending article. Later, to cheer me up, Mel comments that at least they have sourced a good pic of me. It's a much-needed light moment. The photo is from the *True Love* magazine shoot where Mel and I first met two years ago, where she'd first suggested I write a book about being Chris Hani's daughter.

Writing a book had been something I'd dreamed of doing for many years, but back then – unbeknownst to Mel – I was still in the grips of addiction. And although I felt a surge of excitement and smiled and nodded in agreement as we concluded the interview, I knew at that stage that I would never be able to be honest about my life and my using. There were just too many skeletons in the closet. The shame and darkness of my battle with drugs and alcohol back then obliterated any desire I might have had to come clean or to have the courage to put pen to paper. For God's sake, back in 2014, the night before the cover shoot, I had been on a huge coke bender. At that stage in my life I was nowhere near facing my demons.

But now, staring at the sensational page-two headlines, where the media bottom feeders were trying to get in on a story that was really mine to tell, I knew that there were no more excuses left for me to hide behind. It really was time to own my story.

CHAPTER 27

Janusz Waluś – A killer at my table

I decide to wear black to meet the man who murdered my father. Black feels right. Black skirt, black shirt, black stockings, black jacket, black boots. Black is my armour. Only my lips are red.

This time, unlike the rain-drenched, traffic-impeded journey to meet with Clive Derby-Lewis, both the weather and the busiest highway in Africa have come to the party. The sky is a big, blue, cloudless dome umbrella. The traffic is clear. We make the journey from the south of Joburg to Kgosi Mampuru II prison, formerly known as Pretoria Central, in under an hour.

I have been obsessed with Janusz Waluś for what feels like all my life, plagued by questions that have invaded my brain since I was 12. But today my mind is silent, my nerves dead. The last few days I've been working hard to keep expectations low. It's as though I've been neutral-bombed.

At the entrance to the prison, the smiling, pretty high-cheekboned prison official has details of Mel's rental car written on her hand. I called them in to Reverend Kekane, the prison's chaplain, on our way in. As per procedure, our car is searched.

Mel makes small talk about the prison with the two officials who sit in the back of her tiny Ford Figo rental as they direct us towards the area commander's office. I stay silent all the way.

A smiling Reverend Kekane is there to meet us. I've been communicating with him for the last few weeks around the permissions and protocol of the meeting. He's an upbeat Presbyterian, open faced and nattily dressed in black with a red tie. With Mel similarly attired, black and red seem to be the going colour combo for the day. I have told the Rev on numerous occasions that I need to see Janusz Waluś alone. I've insisted that this is a personal journey, to sit in a room alone with my father's killer, look him in the eye and ask the questions that have been holding me hostage since 10 April 1993. I am insistent that this is the only way I'm prepared to meet him.

Perhaps the Rev has merely agreed to this request to placate me, to get me here, for I am soon to discover that this is not the plan.

From the Reverend's office, we're led back down along the red polished stone passage to the area commander's office. It's a very unprison-like room. Painted in warm ochre tones, colourful landscapes adorn the walls, the curtains an organza green sheen. The talking point soon becomes the gleaming wooden cabinet behind his large oak desk – an array of silver trophies, medals and statues – accolades to prisoners' sport and musical achievements.

The area commander is a small, stocky fellow. "I loved your father very much," says the Reverend. "I was in the middle of conducting an Easter service when the congregation was informed of your father's death." After 23 years, I've grown used to people needing to tell me what they were doing the day my father died.

Out of the corner of my eye I see Mel take out her phone, push the record button and place it nonchalantly on the table, as it reverts back to home screen. I am not sure whether I am furious with her or relieved that she intends to record this piece of history. It appears that neither the Reverend nor the area commander have noticed.

They begin to explain the planned procedure for the meeting. They are clearly proud of their Victim Dialogue programme and I now discover I am a prime candidate for this initiative.

My throat starts closing. My eyes darken. I have already made it clear that this is not what I have come for. I do not wish to be part of any agenda of the prison system or government initiative, to be a pawn in a bigger play.

"I want to see him alone," I announce emphatically, forcing myself to keep my anger in check. Who are these people who think they can dictate the terms of this meeting?

The two men glance at each other. The Reverend cuts in.

"Lindiwe, our Victim Dialogue programme has been very successful in bringing perpetrator and victim to sit at a table, for the victim to ask questions and get the answers that they deserve."

The area commander adds his weight. "You see, Lindiwe, we don't allow the victim to be alone with the perpetrator in a room. This is because of past experiences; it's completely against prison procedure. We cannot leave you locked up alone with the man who killed your father. People would think we were mad."

"So I am not meeting Waluś alone?" I can't help but reveal how upset I feel. I wanted the visit to be small and intimate, not with a room full of people.

"You will be alone with him. You can ask him any questions, you will not be restricted in any way, but we will be here in the room with you."

Clearly, he does not see his own absurd contradiction.

But this is non-negotiable. If I can't do this meeting my way, then it's off.

I can see that Mel is clearly caught in the middle. On one hand, I know she is here to support me, but she knows we have a book to write. She touches my arm and cautiously suggests that I conduct the first meeting according to the procedure that's been laid out.

I irrationally want to scream: "Don't touch me, bitch!" I'm highly irritated – with her, with everyone in the room. This is *my* meeting. It's *my* father we are talking about here. Who are these people who think they can dictate terms to me?

"What if I come in as a normal person?" I say. "Apply to see him as any of his visitors would? Would you then give me permission?"

This has clearly thrown the two officials. They scramble for an answer, "Yes, that could be possible ... but, but, but ... this is not an ordinary visit."

From their perspective, it's clear: I am the victim and Waluś is the perpetrator.

"The thing is, I know what I'm doing," I respond, stubborn in my decision. "I have been waiting for this meeting for 23 years; there is nothing that Waluś can say that will hurt me. I have said from the start I don't want to be a part of this victim/offender dialogue – I want to meet him alone. Please respect my request."

But the two officials are insistent. After much to-ing and fro-ing, it's clear that it's non-negotiable: the only way to meet Janusz Waluś is to do it the prison way. This is an official process and there is no way of getting around the red tape. I swallow and try to keep my powerlessness, my raging anger, from getting the better of me. *God grant me the serenity to accept the things I cannot change* silently whirs in my head.

Finally, I nod. "Okay, I'll do it. But this is only an introductory meeting. Then we can take it from there. Next time I want to see him alone."

Once again, I feel like I'm being told how to meet my father's killer just like I was told how to mourn him when he died. I am swamped in the lava of my resentment.

Visible relief washes over the room; it's only me who's fuming.

The Reverend thanks me for accepting the prison's conditions and begins to explain how the process is going to unfold.

"We are going to invite the offender into the room. We will be here and your friend will be here to support you. You are free to ask him whatever you like and you are free to interact with him in whatever way you choose. Just one thing before we bring the prisoner in, we know you have been searched but do you have any objects in your possession that could be seen to be unlawful, a sharp object maybe?"

Mel brings out her red lipstick, brandishing it like a sword. There's laughter all round.

We take a five-minute smoke break before returning.

☽

It's clear that Waluś has been held in a room nearby. Within minutes of our return, the door opens and he's led in, accompanied by two prison guards. Dressed in orange prison-issue overalls, he walks in head bowed and takes his place at the far end of the table.

This is the moment that's been playing over in my head for what feels like centuries. Inside I feel completely dead. I'm in my movie mode again, where I watch events unfolding like some detached spectator.

The Reverend takes over and does the introductions. He suggests we pray. Waluś bows his head, gratefully. He looks highly apprehensive. He clearly doesn't know what to expect. That makes two of us.

Perhaps he's expecting an onslaught of anger. Besides firing bullets into my father, the only experience he's had of the Hani family over the last 23 years is my mother's unrelenting anger every time he's appeared in court.

For years I've obsessed over the questions I will ask my father's killer and now I am here before him. It feels like the most momentous thing I've ever experienced. Where do I begin? I summon courage from deep within.

"Hello, Waluś. How are you today?" I'm business-like. Cool, calm, Jackie O.

"Hello, Lindiwe. I am well, thank you."

I take a deep breath.

"I would like to ask you some things about yourself. Like where do you come from? Where were you born?"

"Okay, Lindiwe," his voice, still heavy with a Polish accent, is barely audible. "I was born on 14 January 1953 in Poland, in a town called Zakopane, which is in the south of Poland. I come from a family where there were three children, myself, my older brother and a sister."

"Thank you. What was it like growing up in Poland?"

"It was very hard growing up in communist Poland. My father, who was a businessman, lost everything because the government kept taking over businesses. Whenever his business was doing well the government would introduce some tax, even backdate tax and so whenever he could show some success in the business, the government would make sure to take as much as they could and then the business would have to close down. The communists destroyed Poland and many people suffered because of their policies."

He relays this information, hardly taking a breath.

As he's talking, I'm amazed at how my recovery brain's kicked in: "Find the similarities rather than the differences."

"Is that why you decided to come to South Africa?" I'm surprisingly composed, like some interviewer doing a Q&A on *Oprah*.

"Yes, Lindiwe. There was no future for me in Poland. My brother and father left for South Africa in the seventies and I joined them in 1981."

"What kind of business was your father involved in?" Next question. So far, so good.

"He was involved in different businesses but there was a time when I was very young that he was involved in the chocolate business. So I remember I could get a lot of chocolates and sweet things. That is perhaps why today I do not like to eat the sweets."

He gives a little smile; almost immediately his face straightens, back into seriousness.

The chocolate detail intrigues me. It's the first time I have seen a glimpse of human emotion. I want to know more about the young boy Waluś. I ask him if he had a happy childhood.

"I must say I had a very happy childhood, Lindiwe. Even when my parents fought and after they separated when I was 13, they did not make their problems our problems."

"So, tell me about yourself when you were a child. What kind of a boy were you? Were you shy, were you a nerd, were you a naughty child?"

The tension in the room eases. For the first time Waluś smiles openly.

"Yes, Lindiwe, I was what you say – not a very good child sometimes. I didn't have much achievement at school. I liked sports, I liked being outdoors and I was what you say mischievous sometimes. I was not the model child."

"Tell me some of the things you did." I am hoping to hear that this is where he pulled the legs off beetles, tortured cats, where the seeds of his monster were sown.

"Sometimes I would not go home after school. I would stay out and play with my friends. My mother was the one who was at home so she would take care of punishment, but for more serious things it was my father who disciplined us. But it was never serious lashings or such things."

Mel decides she's had enough of my questions about little Waluś and his shenanigans at school. Out of nowhere, she leads the elephant into the room.

"Not everyone has it in them to kill another person. The majority of people don't ever think of killing a fellow human being. What was your state of mind during the time, 1993, when you found it so easy to shoot Lindiwe's father?"

I am immediately flooded with anger and resentment. This is exactly the reason why I wanted to do this interview alone. I didn't want to head straight into questions about my dad's murder. This is the man who has always held a morbid fascination for me. I want to get to know him.

"It wasn't that easy ..." Waluś is thrown and struggles to respond.

"Okay, maybe not easy," says Mel, "but what I want to know is what was going on in your mind before you shot Chris Hani? It sounds like you came to this country with so much anger – someone who can kill like you did must be a very angry person. I mean, you volunteered to be that guy, the killer. You must have felt a confidence inside yourself ... to kill ... so maybe not 'easy', but what made it possible for you to do such a thing?"

"I am not sure if you can understand this but maybe it had to do with our national political history in Poland. We have been between Germany and Russia for a 1000 years," Waluś chooses his words slowly and carefully. "We were often attacked from both sides ... Maybe this makes us Polish people more susceptible to be performing some violent act."

Mel won't let it go. She doesn't notice the look on my face. "I can't imagine that most Polish people are sitting in prison on murder convictions?"

"I am just trying to find an answer to your question," says the man in orange with the silver hair and startling blue eyes.

"So, when you sit in your cell, alone with just you and your past and the memories of what you have done, when you think of your deed, 'I have killed a man,' what do you think of, of the you inside yourself?"

"I am trying to understand … I try to answer this question." Waluś is clearly finding it hard to answer Mel's barrage of questions. "In a war situation, you find yourself capable to do such a thing."

Now it's the area commander's turn to intercede. He explains to Waluś what Mel is trying to get at – when he, Waluś, self-reflects, how does he feel when he looks back on his deed?

Waluś seems frozen. There is something inside him that is struggling to answer this question.

Mel tries again. "After you carried out your task to kill Chris, did you feel a sense of accomplishment? Clive obviously saw something in you that was capable of being the killer, so I am still trying to find out what was it in you that made you that person that Clive chose to be the assassin … Was it hatred?"

"I would say it was more hatred for the system than hatred for the person I killed," Waluś finally finds words. "It felt like our way of life was threatened … where the country was going down the same way as it had gone down in Poland with the communists."

I've had enough of the rest of the room running the show. I interject with a question that's been on my mind for years. "Were you brought up knowing how to shoot?"

"Yes." He looks straight at me, almost grateful that I'm asking the questions again. I don't blame him. He is under no obligation to be here and now he's at the mercy of these three, who all clearly seem to have their own agendas. "As I was growing up, I was taught to shoot when I was 11 or 12 by my father's brother, my uncle; he stayed in our house for many years. He was a hunter. I had an air gun and this gun it had small power. I learned to shoot target, but always in a very safe environment."

"Are you a racist? Were you a racist? Did the fact that your target was a black person make it easier?" I ask Waluś quietly.

He takes a moment to find his words. "The thing is, when we were talking about a political solution in the CP no one wanted to listen to us, we believed in a system where you [he clearly means black people] had your homeland. We wanted to have our homeland because we believed in separate development."

"That sounds just like apartheid," I say.

"Well," says Waluś, "you can call it apartheid, but I don't see anything derogatory about people having to live separately and not interacting." He corrects himself quickly. "I am not saying not interacting, but definitely not living under one-and-the-same government."

"But," says Mel, "why would it be so offensive having an integrated government?"

"You could see the way the other countries like Zimbabwe were going ..."

I am very clear on what I'm about to say next. "The problem I have with this is – you come from Poland, a country where there are not many black people, and then you come to a country like South Africa, where the majority of people here are black, and you think in your mind that black people can be subjugated by separate development. And then you say you didn't have ill feelings towards black people? Did you see black people as equals?"

"We are all created equal," says Waluś.

His words sound like a cliché. I don't believe him.

"That's the Bible," I say.

"I am trying to ... see all people as equal."

"But that's now; I am talking about how you felt about black people then?"

He almost stumbles. "I wouldn't say then ... that I didn't see them as equal." I still don't believe him.

Mel interjects. Slap bang to the chase. "I am sorry, but anyone who belonged to the Conservative Party was racist, was anti-integration, was anti-democracy, was anti a black government. It would really help if you could admit your feelings around this, your mentality at the time when you shot and killed Chris Hani. We are talking about Janusz Waluś in 1993 and for you to avoid that … and say, 'No, I didn't have those racist feelings' – it feels like you are lying."

"I have never treated black people badly; I have never had fights and arguments."

"But you killed a black man."

The obvious swallows the room.

"But I did not kill him because he was a black man," says Waluś. "It did not have to do with his race, it had to do with his politics. Please try to understand this, race did not play a part in this …"

The prisoner at the far end of the table is clearly feeling cornered. But it suddenly occurs to me that in his world, in the Polish head of Janusz Waluś, perhaps the fact that my dad was a commie was far more dangerous than the fact that he was black.

Before I can voice my realisation, the area commander intervenes. "Your answers to these questions are problematic. There's a conflict in your answers. On one level, you say you believed black people should live in separate homelands, yet you say you were not thinking along racist lines?"

There is a part of me that almost pities this man, grey and gaunt in his lurid orange overalls. Sitting in front of three black people and Mel, being interrogated about his racism.

"I think the problem is that you are answering from your viewpoint today," I say. Am I trying to rescue him? "And it can't be easy talking about racism in a room full of black people. You see, Waluś, I don't feel there is anything wrong in admitting who you once were. So, if you happened to be a racist right-wing person in 1993, who believed that black people were monkeys, it's actually fine to admit that now. A lot of people felt that way."

And then from almost out of nowhere, he says, "We all know that we as white people developed first as a race, that we were responsible for civilisation."

The room breaks out in a belt of surprised laughter – huge relief as the truth finally resounds.

"There's the Waluś I've been waiting for," I almost shout from the rooftops. "Welcome, Waluś!"

He grins. It's a bashful look. He is shocked, a little confused maybe, and a whole lot relieved by how happy I look.

"Now tell me," I continue, "how difficult is it for you these days, surrounded by so many of us? They are all over the place now …"

"The thing is, Lindiwe, I have met a lot of black people here in prison who are so decent. It is not very often pleasant to be in jail, but it is pleasant to be with some of the people I have met." He looks at me straight in the eye.

"So, do you feel you have changed since 1993?" Mel asks.

"For sure," he says, "but I don't want you to think I suddenly am claiming this has been my road to Damascus or something. It's been a process."

"Did you make good friends in prison?" I ask.

"Look, in prison you must be very careful in making friends. You must be very selective with whom you can get close and who you can rely on."

"I read somewhere you were attacked in prison." I want to hear more about this incident, which took place back in early 2014.

"Let me tell you what happened … I was in the section one floor down – it was a man who was working as a cleaner, he was connected to the gangs. He was a 26 or whatever. I don't know because I never got involved in such things. But he was always very polite; he was also reading books, like me. I always say reading books can be better than studying – it gives you wider perspective. In prison I have read many, many books. Now this man, he always helped me, when we put our names down for the—" He pauses for a second, looks at the AC and says, "Can I disclose about the phones here?"

The Area Commander laughs and tells him to go ahead.

"So here in prison we have one phone, for let's say three sections of about 300 people. You have to put your name on a list to keep some order. This man was always helping to put my name on list. So, on this day of the attack, we pass the gates – he said,

211

'Go forward,' because they wanted to close the gates and the next thing he came at me from behind. Then all I see is this red curtain of blood. Blood on the floor made me slip and I couldn't catch him. At that moment Clive was walking past so, as this man ran out, he hit Clive on the head. I don't think he even knew why he did this, he was so full of drugs."

As he speaks, I feel weirdly protective of him, imagining the unsuspecting Waluś incapacitated as he slipped on his own blood.

Now that he's brought up his buddy Clive, I decide to ask him about his relationship with his co-conspirator. "Do you miss him since he's been released?"

"We were good friends, we always helped each other, but he is gone now. There are so many people in jail who you can miss. But someone is always leaving, getting transferred, so you can't afford to get too close to people."

My plan for today has been to get to know "Waluś the man" a little better. To make him feel a little less afraid and unthreatened so when I get to ask him about Daddy's murder, he will be able to be as honest as possible with me. I have already decided to only approach that on our next visit. Clearly, Mel and the other two have not been on the same page.

When the session comes to an end, the Reverend asks Waluś if he would like to say anything to me.

This time the grey-haired Polish man looks me long and straight in the eye.

"First of all, I want to thank you, Lindiwe. I cannot tell you how much I have appreciated meeting you; you are a very brave, very courageous woman. If it means anything to you, Lindiwe, I am very, very sorry for what I did to you and your family ... I am very, very sorry." He seems overcome with emotion. I feel the lump in my throat too.

Then it's my turn.

"Waluś, you were under no obligation to meet me. I appreciate you coming today and I value your honesty. I know this must be difficult for you, as it is for both of us; I thank you for your time."

The area commander announces that lunch is about to be

served. It's after 2pm. Waluś, the prisoner in his orange overalls, gets up to leave.

"You are invited to eat with us," says the AC, unexpectedly.

Waluś is clearly thrown. He hesitates, asks if he is really invited, then awkwardly sits down again. He has not expected this. Somehow, unlike with the Derby-Lewises and the forced quiche lunch, where I could not eat a morsel of the food Gaye prepared, for some strange reason I don't feel awkward about sharing a meal with the man who killed my father.

○

There is something about food that blurs barriers, brings a table of unlikely people together, throws guardedness to the wind.

While we wait for the prison lunch to arrive, small talk with the guest in orange flows surprisingly effortlessly.

"So, did you ever go to varsity?" I ask him. "Have you studied anything while in prison?"

"No, no," he laughs, self-deprecatingly. "I am not very academic." Mel and I almost simultaneously disagree. We both believe Waluś is highly intelligent.

He tells us how back in Poland he had difficulty learning as a child, blaming it on his own stupidity. For a moment my heart goes out to the young Waluś who grew up believing that he was lesser than; I know the feeling.

"After I was arrested I was diagnosed with dyslexia."

At that point in the conversation, the food arrives – plates laden with chicken, chips, salad and fizzy drinks. They've clearly made a special effort for our visit. By the look on Waluś's face, this 'five-star' fare is a first in 23 years.

"So, what's prison food like?" Mel asks him.

He smiles mischievously, then quickly glances nervously at the AC, reticent to reveal his true feelings in front of the boss.

"Well, let's just say, we often ask: 'What is this?'"

The room bursts out in laughter. It's a relief to laugh.

Mel has noticed that there are no knives with which to cut the chicken and requests some. When the bluntish metal arrives, she holds one up, jokingly pointing at Waluś, and asks the AC, "Are you sure you can trust us in the same room as him, with these?"

There's more laughter; this meal is feeling almost surreally normal.

Before we eat, the Reverend suggests we say a prayer. We bow our heads together. Waluś closes his eyes.

"Thank you God for giving us this opportunity to sit down together. Bless this food that is before us. Let us all go in peace. Amen."

"Are you a Catholic?" Mel asks Waluś.

"I am, but not a very good one."

"Well, I am loving what your latest pope is doing these days." I'm keen to hear what he has to say about the liberal Pope Francis's much more enlightened attitudes towards the marginalised of our planet. I remember being really impressed when in 2013 he said: "If someone is gay and he searches for the Lord and has good will, who am I to judge?"

Last year the Pope angered anti-abortionists when he opened a special, temporary 'mercy' window to make it easier for women who have abortions and confess, to be re-embraced into the bosom of the church.

Waluś is clearly not in agreement. "I have to say I am not at all impressed with him."

"Well, of course you aren't," I chirp, "because he's doing the right thing. He's washing the feet of immigrants. What do you say, Waluś?"

"You know I am conservative," he pauses, "but I have to be careful what I say here today because any of this can be used against me in a court of law."

Of course. That explains his painstakingly weighed answers over the last few hours. He thinks he's being set up. I can't really blame him.

I survey my carb-laden plate.

With all my Bootcamping and trying to eat Paleo style over the last few months, I offer my chips to the guests at the table. Mel offers hers directly to Waluś. He politely declines. A heap of chips is sent to the guards outside.

"You clearly don't need to watch your weight, Waluś. How have you kept so fit and trim in prison?" I ask.

"I think it's mainly genetics; my whole family looks like this," he's almost blushing. "My grandfather was 74 years old when he was showing younger boys in the mountain stream how to swim against the current. I do a lot of physical exercise in prison, sit-ups and also other things like karate to stay in shape."

We've covered religion and diet in five minutes, so Mel decides to introduce love.

"So, have there been any admiring women in the last 20 years, writing you love letters and wanting to marry you? "

"There has been a woman who was wanting to marry me since, I think, 1994, but after 11 years the prison stopped it. I told her she should not wait for me." He seems wistfully sad all of a sudden.

"How did you meet her? Did you read about you and then start visiting you?" I am curious about this woman.

"It was her and a group of her friends who were supporting me. They started to write letters."

"Was she beautiful?" I ask. Waluś pauses.

"She is still beautiful," he says.

"Was she blonde and blue eyed?" Now I'm clearly being provocative.

"She had brown hair and eyes something between brown and green."

"I only ask because maybe Waluś wants to keep the Aryan race going?" I say, half playfully.

He comes back at me quickly. "Nothing wrong by trying," he says amidst more laughter at the table.

I keep on getting flashes of how absurd this situation could look to the outside world, me sharing a meal, making small talk, cracking jokes about the Aryan race and the Pope with my father's killer. But somehow it doesn't feel wrong.

Sometimes it feels like Mel can read my mind. She feels it too. "It's good that we didn't eat at the beginning of this. Food makes people far too nice to each other; we all become bonded in some way."

For a split second we are all lost in this little human moment.

"So, is this supper for you, Waluś?" I break the moment with a question. It's almost 3pm.

"He was supposed to have had supper already," says the AC.

"Jeez, what time do you eat?" asks Mel.

"Well, our dinner is usually served at 2:30pm," Waluś responds drily.

"So what time is lunch, 11am?" We all laugh.

"And what time is lights out?" says Mel. "Six pm?"

"Well, actually," says Waluś, "there is never a lights out in prison unless the Eskom fails."

"So, the lights stay on all the time?" Images of prisoners tortured by 24-hour light abound.

"No, no," he explains, "you can put your own lights out, but otherwise they stay on."

"So don't you get hungry during the night? I mean, the last time you eat is at 2:30pm?" I am genuinely finding prison meal times mindboggling.

"You do get hungry, but then you just think about something else." He answers in his usual matter-of-fact, resigned-to-his-fate, East European way.

"Now," says Mel, "without telling any fibs, what is the prison food like? Is it any good?"

There is raucous laughter around the table. Waluś is laughing loudest.

"I would prefer to say: no comment."

The AC is laughing hard, "Why? Are you afraid of me?"

"Let me put it this way," says Waluś, "today I am shocked to see this chicken we are eating because there is no blood near the bones. The chicken we get is usually covered in blood. Chicken is always rare, like a steak, underdone."

"Maybe I should visit you every day so you can get cooked chicken," I laugh. "What else do you get to eat, say, for breakfast? Do you get eggs or porridge?"

"Usually porridge," he says. "Eggs we get for supper. Two eggs." Just in case we think they are starving him.

"We sometimes get hamburger patties and sausages," he adds, and then, not missing a beat, "I like to call this 'divine' food. You know why I call it divine? Because God only knows what it is."

He is actually hilarious. I laugh with the man who killed my father. It's surreal.

By the end of lunch, plans are set in place to meet again.

CHAPTER 28

Second time around

On 28 April 2016, the day after Freedom Day, we arrive at the gates of Kgosi Mampuru II for our second visit with Janusz Waluś. It's 28 degrees in Pretoria, a clear, blue-skied day welcomes us.

I've called in Mel's rental's number plate along the way. This time we're waved through by smiling guards without a boot check. It almost feels as though we are regulars now.

Exactly 21 days have passed since our first visit. A lot can happen in three weeks. Things have taken a downward turn for Waluś's parole. After Judge Nicolene Janse van Nieuwenhuizen initially granted him parole and dismissed the government's Justice Minister Michael Masutha's application for leave to appeal her judgment, in a turn around, Masutha was successful in having Janse van Nieuwenhuizen's judgment overturned, which in plain speak means the Justice Minister has been granted leave to appeal. Right now the situation for Waluś means a whole lot more waiting.

I wonder how he's feeling about his bad news. Personally, I'm somewhat relieved – not necessarily because he's still in prison, but since our first visit, I don't feel like I'm quite ready to stop seeing him. Now at least I know where to find him. My greatest concern is that he's deported back to Poland, never to be seen or heard of again.

As we arrive at the area commander's office, the Reverend, this time dressed in neatly pressed prison-issue khakis, comes out to greet us. Once again, I've chosen to go for head-to-toe black.

The organza curtains in the AC's office sway gently in the warm breeze. It still feels like high summer although the calendar tells us that winter is coming.

The AC and Reverend kick off by praising me for the way I conducted our first meeting, the questions I asked Waluś and how I contained myself during such a difficult encounter. They encourage me to ask as many questions as I may have for him today. The area commander now confides that he thinks Waluś is holding back. "I think he was used and manipulated by other people and he's still not telling us everything."

I am not sure whether I agree with this whole conspiracy theory. My face clearly shows my ambivalence.

"But do you feel he is showing any true remorse for what he has done?" asks the area commander.

I think back to our session exactly three weeks ago. It's a hard one: "I think on one level he still ideologically feels he saved the country from some kind of communist disaster, but on a human level I think he is very emotional and regrets the pain he caused me and my family for taking a father and husband and breadwinner away from us. I think his regret is heightened because he can identify with his own pain of not being a father and his child growing up without a father. I do believe he is genuinely sorry for that. I think it's that guilt that makes him able to identify with our loss."

The AC flatly disagrees. "I don't observe him showing real remorse. His thinking is still the same as he was back then." My face must be showing some irritation at the area commander's outburst. "But," he catches himself and rearranges his thoughts, "I did notice that when he spoke about the pain you and your family experienced, I saw him showing some conflict. But that's not what we are here for. It's for you to reflect on these things."

In his usual placating manner, the Reverend interjects. "Let's see today how the story unfolds."

It's 09:45am. Time to call the prisoner in.

Janusz Waluś has been waiting patiently outside. Once again

he walks in, head bowed, and acknowledges each of us by looking up and quickly nodding. I almost feel familiarity seeing him again. This time around my heart does not beat as loudly at the sight of my father's killer.

Coffee is offered. Waluś refuses. The AC laughs and says Waluś is not a coffee person; he'd much rather prefer an Amstel. A small grin creeps onto his face. "I wouldn't mind one." Once again, I notice Mel fiddle with her phone recorder.

The Reverend again leads the session in prayer.

"Thank you, Lord, for the gift of life; thank you for creating us in your own image. Thank you that you brought us together again as a family so that we can sit down together and talk and listen, as you speak through us. Help us, oh Lord, so that whatever we are trying to achieve may bring understanding to our lives. We pray for the Hani family, particularly Lindi Hani; bless her and give her wisdom so she will remain in you because you are in us."

The Reverend welcomes Waluś and the rest of us in the room. "Let us continue where we left off."

I immediately look the prisoner straight in the eye. "Hello, Waluś, how are you? How has this week been for you?" I am clearly referring to his failed parole appeal. "I don't know whether to say I am sorry or whether I am glad." Halfway through I stop myself. "No, I am actually not glad—"

In all honesty, even though I probably should have, I did not revel in joy when I heard the successful outcome of the government's appeal.

"I was actually quite sorry it didn't work out for you."

Waluś shrugs. "It's just one of those things; I am so used to it. One more thing doesn't matter."

"You didn't let yourself get hopeful?" I ask him.

"You see, I think the best definition of 'hope' is one by the author Tom Clancy, where he says hope is the feeling when you have got the feeling that the feelings which you really have got is not permanent."

The room does a collective *phew!* Everyone's a little stunned.

"So, you don't let yourself get hopeful?" I ask again.

"It's like this. You must be hopeful, but you must always be prepared for the blow all the time. If I hadn't been hopeful, then I would not have taken any action. I am not saying it's not a bit depressing, but you can't allow it to overcome you. But I thank you for asking."

"Did you go to court?" I ask him.

"No, I didn't," he replies.

I suddenly notice purple ink stains on his thumbs.

"What's on your thumbs?"

"That's just my identity."

Mel quips in, "Don't they know who you are by now?"

Waluś is quick as lightning. "I think it's to check I didn't change in 23 years."

The room laughs. The atmosphere is easing.

"Waluś, after meeting you I went and did some research about a few things regarding Daddy's death. I think it was four to six months before you shot my dad, there was another attempt on his life. Were you part of that at all?"

"No. I don't even know what you are talking about. The one in Lesotho?"

"No," I explain, "it was the one when we were in South Africa, a few weeks before he died, the one in town, in Marshall Street."

"No, I knew nothing about that."

"So, you or your organisation were never part of that?"

"No, we weren't."

"Okay, so I would like to talk to you about Gaye. It's about The List – the one with the different leaders' names on it, like Madiba, my dad and Joe Slovo. Gaye says this list was part of research for a story that she was writing for *Die Patriot*, and she says you came to the house in Krugersdorp where you found this list lying on a table and you saw it and took it. And that's how the list landed up with you. Is this what happened for you?"

Waluś pauses. It is clear he is on high alert. "It wasn't exactly like that, but maybe this is the way she remembers it. I think it was taken by Clive."

"Oh, so you didn't take it directly?" I ask.

"I didn't even know she was the one who composed it. I just got the list from Clive."

"So, you got it from Clive, and what was the purpose of it?" I pursue. Today I have all my ducks in a row, like a legal eagle on *Ally McBeal*.

"You see the only purpose of the list with your late father's name on it was that there were addresses on it. Some names on the list, I did not even know. It was just your father we discussed."

"So, was Gaye ever around when you discussed this?"

"No, she was never around. She knew nothing about our plans. We made it very clear that we would not involve her." The basic version of Derby-Lewis and Waluś stays intact. I can't help wondering whether this is the truth or they are just very well rehearsed when it comes to their story.

"So, was Gaye ever around when my dad's name came up, when you were having discussions?"

"No, it was always just Clive and I."

"And you never discussed this plan with any of your CP comrades?"

"No," he says, "never."

Then Mel drops a bombshell.

"Okay, so when we spoke to Clive and Gaye, I got the distinct feeling that Clive was covering up for Gaye, like sometimes he would be saying something and she would interrupt and say, 'Let me talk now'—"

Mel stops herself and glances at me in a panic. At this point we have not revealed that we have met with Gaye and Clive. Damn Mel. I am mad enough to spit. We agreed not to reveal this information. We had discussed at length keeping this a secret. I feel completely betrayed. I can't look at her.

Having dug herself in, Mel continues. "Do you really think that a couple as politically compatible as the Derby-Lewises would never have discussed such an important thing as the plan to kill Chris Hani? When they were alone in bed together, surely you would talk to your spouse? I find it hard to believe that a couple that close would never have mentioned this plan, especially as this list was actually composed by Gaye?"

Waluś seems genuinely perplexed. "Look, I don't know these things. I can't say he didn't or he did say something to her as I wasn't in the room with them. I don't know of any such talk that they had; I never heard from him that he discussed this with his wife. I was also in a relationship with a lady at the time who was very supportive of CP policies, but I never spoke a word about this plan to her."

Now the area commander jumps in. "Do you think Clive was doing this as an individual or on behalf of the organisation?"

"I think he acted in the interest of the CP, but in my opinion I think he was completely working alone," says Waluś, "that it was him who had come up with this idea. That is just my opinion."

Then it's the Reverend's turn.

"When you interact with Clive, how is he feeling about these meetings that you are having with Lindiwe?"

Well, now that Clive is out the bag, we may as well all have a free for all.

"After our first meeting, I have not met Clive," says Waluś.

"Has Clive told you about our meeting with him?" asks Mel. I'm watching the room ask their questions, and I want to drown the lot of them. This is exactly why I wanted to meet Waluś alone.

"I never even knew you had met Clive," says Waluś. "I am phoning Clive perhaps once a month because of the limitations on the phone here in prison."

I fight back my fury and take back some control.

"How often did you used to go to the Derby-Lewis's home in Krugersdorp?"

"It was not that often, maybe once a week."

"I want to ask you now about a friend of yours, a friend who you did martial arts with, I think his name was Alex? There've been stories that he was spotted in Dawn Park on the day that Daddy was shot. There are also stories about two cars, that you came in one car, the red Ford Laser, and left in another?"

Waluś smiles, as though he is familiar with this story.

"It is sheer fantasy," he says. "I only had one car and – concerning

223

Alex, he only learned about these things after it happened. I would never have discussed this plan with him."

"But," I ask, "was he *capable* of helping you? Did he have a background with firearms?"

"He was very competent with firearms and I think probably, if I had asked him, he would have helped me," says Waluś, "but I would never ask him. He was a friend, in the same club; we shared some conversations, but he was not part of the CP."

I find this Alex character intriguing. "So, what kind of world did he move in?"

Waluś tries to find the right words. "You see, he was like a typical Greek. He had business here, he had business there, with some money from here, some money from there, not holding any steady work. But he was not involved in dishonest things, not stealing. Just a typical Greek who didn't work for anybody but himself."

"How do you know he was competent with firearms?"

"We went to the shooting range together sometimes."

"So, you were good friends?"

He shrugs his shoulders in his typical way, as though the concept of 'friends' is something of a foreign one. "Yes, we were good friends."

"So, is he still around?"

"I don't know what has happened to him. Last time he came to visit me I was still in Maximum Security – that was over 12 years ago. Since then I have not heard from him. I am not sure if he is even in the country any more, otherwise I am sure I would have heard from him."

I decide that it's time to try to get some answers about Waluś's former employer Peter Jackson, a so-called 'chemicals and glassware transporter'. I have read that Jackson was a suspected arms carrier and that Waluś may have transported military equipment to UNITA in southern Angola.

After Daddy was killed, for a short time Peter Jackson was a person of interest to the Brixton Murder and Robbery Squad. The Dutch journalist, Evelyn de Groenink, who Mel and I met one afternoon in Pretoria, personally saw a SAP file with a handwritten instruction in Afrikaans: "Inligting oor Peter Jackson sal nie opgevolg word nie." ("Information on Peter Jackson will not be followed up.")

When I bring up Jackson's name, Waluś is enthusiastic in his characteristically downplayed Polish way.

"He was a very rich man, but a very decent man. He tried to help our business when I was involved in the glass business with my father, but he lost some money trying to help us because the business was beyond help. After that my father went back to Poland. Peter Jackson then went on to employ me as a truck driver."

"Did he also employ your brother?" I ask.

"My brother was in his own business."

Waluś's brother, Witold, came to South Africa with his father in the 1970s and established a glass business in QwaQwa. In 1993, when Waluś was sentenced to death for my father's murder, Witold made an impassioned plea in mitigation of sentence, citing as his brother's motives the family's experience of communism in Poland and the fear of it infiltrating South Africa. The court ignored his plea and the death sentence was upheld.

Witold went on to become a successful Pretoria-based business-man in the military truck business. Throughout Waluś's time in prison, Witold has been his main source of support.

I return to Jackson.

"Do you feel like you owed a debt to Peter Jackson?" I watch Waluś carefully.

"In a way, yes, I did, because I know he lost quite a lot of money trying to help our business – it was like throwing good money after bad money. Whatever he invested into our business, nothing would make it come right."

"And what business was he in?"

"He was in a lot of businesses, but the one that I know of was the one where he was involved in the making of plastic containers."

"Was he a very well-connected man?" I ask.

"I only knew him as an employer and as a friend, but I didn't know of any of his connections."

Waluś's answers are straightforward. They sound honest to me;

225

however, it doesn't feel like we are getting anywhere deeper with Peter Jackson. I decide to change my line of questioning.

"Can I ask you why you didn't get rid of the gun immediately?"

Waluś smiles.

"That is a most wise question and my decision on the day was very stupid. Unfortunately, I was always a person who was following orders – I was told by Clive to bring the gun back. So that is what I did."

"Did you never ask him why you should do that? I mean, why would he need a used gun?"

"No, I am not asking him," says Waluś.

"You didn't use gloves when you shot my father, so there would have been your fingerprints?"

"No," Waluś interrupts, "I did use gloves."

"So were these gloves also found in the car?" I ask.

"Yes, they were."

Waluś sits in his orange overalls, his face clouded by regret. His naivety is striking.

I have, surprisingly, been able to ask Waluś questions uninterrupted. Now Mel decides to take it right to the moment before he shot Daddy.

Waluś breathes deeply and, slowly, begins to describe how he went out that morning to do a recce of our Boksburg home. "I saw your father get into his car. He was wearing a tracksuit and I followed him to the shops where it looked like he bought a newspaper. I was very surprised that he was alone, without guards. I decided to seize this opportunity. When he got out of his car, I got out of mine. I called his name. I did not want to shoot him in the back. He turned to me and I shot him. He fell down and I went closer and shot him again, twice in the head."

There. He had said it. The moment that changed everything in my 12-year-old world. The point of no return, the one that would change things forever.

The room is silent for a very long time. I blink my tears away. I swallow back my scream, maintain my composure. I deliberately keep eye contact with Waluś.

"Not today, Satan, not today," I hear the voice in my head.

Finally, Mel, who's clearly emotional, asks: "After you shot Chris, please describe in detail exactly what you did: go back to the moment when you see this man, your target, who's shot and bleeding, lying on the ground – what happened next?"

"I turned around and went straight to my car and started it."

"But how were you feeling?" she probes.

"When you are involved in a thing like this, you shut out all feelings."

"So you had absolutely no feelings?"

"There was a feeling that this was bad, but it was done." Waluś looks down.

"So where did you drive to?"

"I began to drive through Boksburg, home to Pretoria."

"And what was going through your head during the drive?"

"I have not got time for recollections because everything was happening very fast. You see, the first thing I could think of was to get away."

"Was your heart beating fast during all of this?" Mel is really trying to get him to go to a place that he clearly finds hard to access.

"I did not check if my heart was beating fast, but I am sure it was. Everything happened very quickly. I was apprehended maybe five minutes after I drove away."

"So, what happened then? How did you get arrested?"

I am watching the details unfold; I feel completely detached.

"Listen, it was very strange ... There was a police car that drove past me. As I sat in the traffic, I passed them; I went in front of them. I did not think they were after me. But then suddenly they drove in front of me and pulled me over."

My anger is rising again. I need to take back control. It feels like Mel has become Christiane Amanpour and this is not CNN. I find my voice and take Waluś back to our house, in the moments before he gets away. I ask him where he parked his car.

"I am not now sure if I parked the car behind your father's car or if I parked it a couple of metres off the street."

"Do you remember which way you drove out? Do you recall that it was a cul de sac?"

"Yes, I remember that."

"So, let's talk about Mrs Harmse, who saw you—"

"I think she saw me before I stopped ..."

"Apparently, there were reports that you may have driven in front of her – do you recall that at all?"

"No, I really don't think she was behind me; she stopped on the spot."

"Okay, explain to me – so she drove directly towards our house, and then what happened?"

"She stopped."

"She stopped her car in the middle of the road? So she saw what you were doing?"

"Yes," he says.

"And then she drove away?"

"Yes, she drove away."

"Did you ever think of shooting her? I mean, she had seen you—" Christiane again.

"I was thinking if someone has to get out of the car and start to shoot at me, then I will have to do something, but I did not think of shooting her because she had seen me. That had always been made clear by Clive that no bystander would be hurt."

And, of course, like an obedient soldier, Waluś obeyed everything Clive told him to do.

I change the line of questioning now and ask Waluś about the reports that cigarette butts and beverage cans were found next door to our house. "Have you ever heard of that?"

"Yes, I heard there was some speculation that there were cigarette butts and cans of cool drink next door. I have heard that some people think somebody may have watched me from behind the fence – maybe they did, but I couldn't see anything. I never saw anybody there. As I see it, I don't see any reason for somebody to be standing there and watching me."

"Do you believe in coincidence?" I ask him.

"Yes, I do believe there are coincidences."

"Now, tell me, have you ever heard the story that the previous government planted undercover cops around Dawn Park?"

"There were so many stories after it happened. Maybe I heard something like that, but at a certain point I stopped to read the news because there were so many reports like that ... One was more ridiculous than the other."

Now I ask him something I have been wondering about for a very long time.

"Do you think it's possible that there were two parallel plans to murder my father? Please just keep an open mind and hear me out ... On one hand, there's you and Clive, and then there's the unknown 'other', possibly from within some disgruntled ANC quarters, with a parallel plot, planning Dad's assassination – but you guys get there first. Do you think that is possible?"

Waluś listens carefully.

"As I said before, we can't rule these things out – it can be possible."

"Do you think it's possibly the reason why you guys have been continuously accused of non-disclosure, of not telling the truth, because there appears to be all this evidence of some kind of conspiracy, with so many things unexplained? You guys are in the middle of it all; you keep saying you have nothing to do with it. And maybe you are telling the truth, but you guys just happen to be the fall guys for the other plan as well?"

"As I said, you can't rule it out," says Waluś. "It could have been someone else who was also planning your father's death; it can be, because of all these stories. The thing is this – when something big and important happens, people love to talk, to have their stories and theories. To think, 'I am the person who knows something.'"

"But," I interject, "if I was sitting in prison, being accused of something I wasn't part of, and you and Clive have been saying consistently for 23 years that you know nothing about a bigger conspiracy – you have always said it was just Clive and you – have you never thought of doing your own private investigation? Asking someone out of prison to try to investigate? Because the only reason you guys have been kept in prison for so long is because you have been accused of non-disclosure – every time there's been a chance of amnesty or parole, it's always been refused on this basis. As far as I can see, your story over the last 23 years has always been the same – you haven't deviated once from your version of events. But at the same time, there's always been this other thing hanging over you, saying you are not disclosing – so have you never wanted to get to grips with what else might have happened, just so that you could get to the bottom of it? Even if you never get out of prison – just for your own peace of mind?"

Waluś has been listening intensely.

"The thing is, what kind of possibility for an investigation do I have? When you don't have money, when you are in prison, how can you pay for that? And on top of that, what guarantee do I have that the person who investigates will even tell the truth?"

"What about your friend Peter Jackson – could he not have helped you?" I ask.

"Peter Jackson is such a busy man, I wouldn't even think of asking him. I have never thought of investigating any of this because, as I said, everything is such a big smokescreen – how do you even get to the truth? Everything is so mixed up – and twisted. I know what I know and I am not deviating from it because I know it's the truth. That's all I know and even if, like the very important point you have made – even if there was a parallel plot to kill your father – what can I do to change that now?"

His words strike true. What chance does he really have?

"Tell me," I say, "when you and Clive were together in prison, when these conspiracy ideas came up, did you try to put your heads together? See if there was a loophole somewhere?"

"When all these things came up, we always just said to each other that we could see it was total nonsense – we denied knowing anything else because we did not know anything else."

"There was this one source," I suggest, "who said she phoned Gaye and told her there was a possibility that her husband wasn't the only one planning this murder and that he could get exonerated because there was another group, but apparently Gaye dismissed it. I was just curious, because if I had a husband who was sitting in prison and there was a possibility of him being freed, I would jump at the opportunity. Did she ever bring that idea to Clive?"

"I never heard anything like that," says Waluś.

Mel now brings up the bodyguard theory – that my father always had bodyguards around him, but on the day of his assassination, he had given his bodyguards time off. "Did you know that on that day there would be no body guards?"

"I had no idea of that," says Waluś. "When I saw on that day he was alone, I took my chances."

"Did you phone Clive straight after you had shot Chris Hani?" Mel asks again.

"As I have said, I was arrested almost straight after I had done it – I didn't have any time."

Mel's on a roll again. She goes back to Waluś's arrest. "So, the police stop you five minutes after you shoot Chris, and then what happens? "

"They search the car."

"And they find the gun?" asks Mel.

"Yes."

"So, what did they say the reason for stopping you was?" I interject.

"They didn't give any reason. One of them got out of the car. The traffic had stopped and they told me to get out. They said they wanted to search the car."

"Where was the gun?" I ask.

"It was under the left passenger seat."

"Was it wrapped in anything?"

"I think it was in a plastic packet, I am not even sure of it," says Waluś.

Now I move forward in time. "Tell me about the trial. How were you feeling during this time? Do you feel you were treated fairly by your lawyer?"

"I can't complain about the lawyer. The legal team was quite all right. The case was actually lost from the outset. I knew what the sentence would be."

Waluś and Clive were sentenced to death by Judge CF Eloff on 15 October 1993, six months after Daddy's murder. Ironically, their lives were later saved by 'the enemy' when, in 1995, the sentence was commuted to life in prison because the ANC opposed the death penalty.

"And were you prepared to die?" I ask him.

"It was the sentence; it was not a case of if I was prepared or not. I accepted the court's decision," says Waluś.

"No, but what did you think would be the outcome?" I probe. "Did you think life or death sentence? Remember, this was before the death penalty was abolished?"

"I was sure I would get death penalty for the reason ... because of the high-profile nature of the case."

"Do you remember how you felt back then?"

"What could you do but accept it?" says Waluś with typical Polish resignation.

"Yes, but that's your logic," I probe. "I am talking about your emotions – how did you feel?"

He takes a deep sigh. Suddenly he looks very tired.

"The thing is, I am not very emotional person – you can't get emotional. I have had to go through many things in this life."

I want to know more. "Tell me about them," I ask him.

"I was couple of times in a car accidents where nobody who saw the car could believe that I could come out of there alive. I was a racing driver for about six years, in Poland. I was involved in some street fights; these things can all put you in a kind of a shell, where you don't feel easily."

"I don't know about that," I interrupt him. I really want to probe deeper. "Because these things you are describing are all physical things. Things that have happened outside of you. When you close off emotionally, you are of course protecting yourself from things that have happened in the past; I mean, car accidents and street fights – you recover physically from them. But when you say you are not an emotional person maybe something happened to you before all that, something in your life when you had to protect yourself by putting a shell around your emotions."

What I tell him now surprises me – I have not planned to do this:

"For example, due to me losing a father so early and my sister's death, I am very hesitant to open up to people. I have all the diagnosed 'daddy issues', so in romantic relationships I am very hesitant because I don't know what it means to have a man in my life. That's why I am the way I am, because of the emotional trauma of death. So, what I am asking is: what was your emotional trauma?"

I am not sure why I am opening myself up to him like this. Laying my own emotional baggage before him. Maybe if I share a part of myself, he may tell me something about his soul, a secret I am looking for. I don't think too much about why right now; somehow it just feels right.

"I really don't know," he says. "Maybe I was simply born like that."

"Was your whole family like that? Unemotional?"

"No, my father was emotional; my mother, I would say, was more impulsive than emotional. Now you are making me think of these things and, with me, I really don't know why. I mean I do have feelings … maybe I have got emotions, but I don't let them overcome me."

"Have you always been like that? From since you were a young boy?" I ask. I am desperate for an answer that will help me understand this man who killed my father.

"From maybe the age of 12 or 13 I stopped showing emotion. You start to protect yourself from feeling."

Strange that – my emotional growth was also stunted when I was 12. *Look for the similarities* … But on this front, for now, it seems he can tell me no more.

The Reverend, who's been listening intently, asks, "Janusz, how did you feel when you heard you could attend your mother's funeral in 2005?"

"I was very grateful to the Correctional Services. I did not expect that I would be allowed to attend my mother's funeral. It was, of course, not a happy event, but I was very happy to be able to attend."

I ask him whether he's spoken to any of his family since we last met.

"I have spoken to my brother and to my daughter."

"Have you told them about our meeting?"

"I told them," he looks nervous, as though he may have done something wrong, "but I told them we don't want anyone else like the media to know."

" No, no," I interrupt him, "I don't mean that – I mean, what was their reaction to the news of you meeting me?"

"They were very glad as, I must say, I have been very glad to meet you, Lindiwe."

I feel a pang of emotion. A strange soreness in my heart.

"What did your daughter say?"

"She was very happy to hear I had met you. She knew it was good meeting, not easy – as I am sure it wasn't for you an easy thing to meet me ... But it was good. I was – I am – really very appreciative, Lindiwe."

My heart aches a little deeper.

"How did you feel after that day, when you left the meeting with Lindi?" asks Mel.

"I felt very exhausted, but on the other side, I felt happy."

"Happy?" I ask him. I am surprised. He immediately tries to excuse his feeling.

"No, no," I correct him, needing to explain myself, "I am not questioning you. I just remember you saying you never felt here or there when it came to happiness in prison. So I am surprised to hear you say so."

In all honesty, I feel a strange little glow inside. I know how weird that is, feeling joy because my father's killer felt a tinge of happiness after meeting me.

"Yes, I remember saying that," he says, "but after our meeting, it happened. I did feel happy."

"You look happier," I say. It's true, he does. The greyish, sunken-eyed look he had when we first met has changed. He seems lighter.

"I can only thank you and all you people in this room for that."

"Do you feel lighter?"

"Certainly," he says.

We've been speaking for over two hours. The area commander suggests lunch. As in our first encounter, Waluś gets up to leave; he is a man who has become used to expecting nothing, cocooned in self-preservation when it comes to hope. The AC stops him, tells him he should stay. An unguarded smile lights up his face.

○

The serious atmosphere from the morning session soon dissipates as food is brought out. This time it's beef, vegetables and fizzy drinks. As usual, Waluś prefers water.

Mel immediately introduces a touch of frivolity and asks him, "So what music do you like?"

"Mainly classical. Mozart, Strauss, Brahms, Beethoven."

"Anything more contemporary?"

"Any type of European folk music, some Spanish music," says Waluś.

"How 'bout Kanye West and Beyoncé?" Mel teases, an impish grin on her face.

Waluś clearly has never heard of *Yeezus* or Queen Bee.

"Were you upset when Prince died?" I ask. "You know, Prince the musician?" It's the week after Mr Purple Rain passed away. I mean, surely he's heard of Prince?

"The one who was killed by his girlfriend?" Waluś is clearly confused.

"Nooo!" we laugh. "I think you're talking about some musician from the seventies."

His eyes twinkle. He doesn't seem to mind being teased.

"Are you watching the news here? Do you get the newspaper?" I ask.

"Only when I get it from someone else. I used to get from Clive. But I'm mainly listening to the radio. I am not completely out of touch," he half grins.

"Did you ever watch that programme on eTV, the one that was made about you: *Behind Waluś the Killer*?" I ask. "The one

235

where they travelled to Poland to try to find your family; I think your brother, Witold, refused to speak to them. But I remember the journalist found some neighbour in Poland to talk to, where people referred to you by your nickname – Kuba."

"I heard about the programme, but I never saw it." Waluś is politely trying to stop himself from tucking into the beef stew while answering our questions. He has clearly not seen such good food in a long while.

"Have any journos tried to interview you while you were in prison?" I ask.

"There was one Dutch interview that was only supposed to be shown in Holland, but the next thing it was all over South Africa. I am very careful when it comes to journalists."

Mel looks down. I begin eating. We both feel the elephant in the room. We are here with the intention of writing a book, and Mel is a writer and a journo.

"I am a car journalist, that's why I find it interesting that you were a rally driver," Mel tries to distract. It's not a lie – she is a motoring scribe. "How long was your racing career?"

He begins to calculate. "Altogether it was from 1974 to about 1981, about seven years long."

"You are very modest," I say. "You are always saying how you can't do this, you can't do that – did people know you as a racing driver in Poland?"

"In around 1977 I was, say, number 10 in Poland," he says, always the picture of downplay.

I ask him now if his brother ever goes to Poland to check in with his daughter Eva. From Waluś's response, it's clear that things aren't rosy between his two relatives.

"I have tried to get to the bottom of their problem with each other, but I don't really understand it. I just know they don't talk to each other."

Then, quite out of the blue, he cryptically quotes Oscar Wilde: "When I was young I thought that money was the most important thing in life; now that I am old I know that it is."

I'm curious why he would use this quote. "Is their fight

something to do with money?"

"I think that has something to do with it." He isn't saying more. "I was in jail already."

There's a long silence. We all focus on our plates. Food is a wonderful distraction.

"You mention you buy cigarettes, but you don't smoke, do you?" I finally break the silence. "Do you use them to trade?"

"Now you are going to get me in trouble," he looks sheepishly at the area commander. "I don't smoke, but I do smuggle."

Everyone bursts out laughing. Waluś the Smuggler.

"The thing is," he tries to explain, "you see, I never have enough food. People who aren't exercising and don't need as much food sometimes trade food. Like a piece of meat can be traded for two cigarettes. So I am not stealing from the kitchen, I am only exchanging."

"Yes, but smuggling is the same as stealing," says the AC, half sternly half playfully.

"But can't you just buy cigarettes in jail?" I ask. I have clearly missed the point.

"I am not buying from the kitchen, I am buying from those who don't want their meat," he explains.

"But," says the Reverend, "how safe is it – buying food from someone you don't know?"

"Won't someone maybe poison him?" I ask the AC, concerned. "And how old is the food you are buying?" Waluś seems to be thriving amid all this attention. "Can you not buy food from a shop here?"

"No, we are not selling food," explains the AC. "Not cooked food."

"The food I am buying is like tinned tuna or chakalaka, but the shop is very expensive."

"So, what do you most need in prison?" asks Mel.

"Food and clothing," says Waluś.

"So today you have extra food, Waluś, and you have meat," says Mel.

"And it's good meat," he responds with a full-faced grin. "I just forgot how to eat, using a knife and fork," he says playfully. Right now he looks happy, almost like a small child. I am not sure why, but it pleases me to see him like this.

"So who is your actual lawyer? Is it Advocate Du Plessis or is it Julian Knight?" I enquire.

"The one is the lawyer – that's Knight – and the other is the attorney," he explains.

"I am very curious about this lawyer Knight and why he is taking your case," I say. "Satisfy my curiosity, Waluś, and go find out."

"If you learn anything from Lindiwe, Waluś, it's to become more curious," Mel interjects. "The only reason we are here today is because of Lindi's curiosity."

"You see," I say, "if you had been more curious, you would have asked yourself, why does Clive want me to keep the gun? You might have thought, let me throw it away. You might not have been caught with the weapon and, at best, they would have had only circumstantial evidence."

"You are 100 per cent right, Lindiwe," Waluś concedes. One senses he has berated himself many times for his mistake. "The problem is, a person just can't go and change himself."

"But haven't you grown over these last two decades? Aren't there some changes in you?" I ask.

"There are some changes," he admits. "But not so much in regard to curiosity and asking questions. There is this quote by Admiral Nelson, I can't remember exactly the words, but it says that very often the order you disobey makes you promoted."

For a moment we chew on his most recent quote. I am not sure if any of us really understand the reference, but it sounds profound.

"So, Lindi," the Reverend changes the subject, "when your father was killed, your sister was in the house. What was her reaction?"

"By the time we arrived home from Lesotho, we found her completely devastated because after she heard the first gunshot, she ran out and the second gunshot passed her ear, nearly hitting her. She saw Daddy lying there and started screaming and screaming. She ran to the home of the SABC journalist, Noxolo Grootboom, who was our neighbour, and Noxolo came running over to find my dad lying in the driveway."

"And he had already left?" asks the Reverend. Oddly, he now refers to Waluś in the third person. It is almost incongruous that we are all sitting happily together, breaking bread with the man who did this to my father.

"Yes, he was gone by then."

Waluś watches as we speak about the day. Perhaps it as surreal to him as it is to me.

Lunch is over. Waluś's plate is almost as clean as it was before the food was dished up. Just before he leaves the table, I reach behind me.

I nervously bring out a thick book. It's *Fall of Giants*, the first in The Century Trilogy by Ken Follett. Sometime during our first visit, Waluś revealed that he reads a lot in prison, books on history and philosophy, and writes a lot of letters to pass time.

The size of this book suggests it can be used as a doorstopper or a serious weapon to scare off an intruder. "I am not sure if this is politically correct, or whether it's in fact allowed, but I remember last time you mentioned that you liked reading so I thought you might like to read this. I'm also a bookworm, so I know how it feels to have a book to look forward to reading. It's a trilogy. It's very thick; it will take some of your time up. So, if you enjoy it let me know, I can lend you the second one."

"Thank you, Lindiwe, I would like to read this very much," he says, taking the book as if it is some precious treasure. He is clearly taken aback by my gesture.

The guards have been summoned to take Janusz Waluś back to his cell. He slips out of the room, the Ken Follett tucked under his arm.

I feel a weird sadness for him. It's strange. The deep ache that held all the anger, the hate I used to feel, the terror- and sweat-filled Bogeyman dreams in which I thought I would drown seem to have left with the silver-haired man. Almost like a ghost, he has vacated the space, with no traces of himself left behind.

I know leaving my book with him means I might see him again.

Afterword

Meeting my father's killers had always been something I'd both dreamed of and dreaded doing; it just happened a lot sooner than I thought.

It felt as though, unless I sat face to face with the two men who orchestrated Daddy's death and shot him at point blank range – looked into their eyes, saw how their minds and hearts of darkness worked – there would always be something missing. In active addiction, I was far too obsessed with scoring the next gram to pursue this desire but once I achieved the unfathomable and got clean and sober I found the courage to face my demons.

However, instead of feeling instant clarity – as I'd hoped – in the days and weeks that followed my meeting with Waluś, I felt more conflicted than ever. I was torn between hating him and huge swells of empathy for him. I went to my weekly relapse prevention groups where I tried to make sense of my internal dichotomy: unable to deny that I found myself inexplicably liking the man who killed my father while desperately wanting to be repelled by him.

Over this past year, I have slowly come to understand that perhaps the reason I was and am still so drawn to Janusz Waluś is because from the moment he murdered my father, our lives became forever linked. There was no escaping him. I had to accept that this deep and aching intersection had left a gaping hole inside me.

Meeting him opened up that wound of long-buried pain, which left me wanting something more from him. Not his apologies or his explanations, nor all the details around Daddy's death, but – almost unbelievably – a connection. He was one of the last living links to my father; he saw him at the very end.

When I sat in front of Waluś in prison, knowing that he murdered my father in cold blood, I had nowhere to run. My life had always been about running and hiding from that pain – that's why I used drugs – but having him right there, and having to deal with my feelings, allowed the searing pain to dissipate.

As I got to know him and hear his story, I saw Janusz Waluś clearly: not as Satan's spawn, as I'd imagined him, but as a man who had committed an evil act, serving out his prison time with quiet resolve and dignity. I found myself having unexpected respect for his stoic attitude.

Perhaps above everything, I learned about deep parts within myself. I discovered that I had a huge propensity to accept things I could not change and be kind in the most difficult situations. I am not sure whether I have forgiven him for murdering the man I loved so deeply, but I do know that I have accepted and let go of the putrid anger and hatred that once engulfed me. I hope I left him with a sense of relief, a sprig of hope and the feeling that somewhere in there in his grey world behind bars, there is some warmth and human kindness from unexpected quarters.

Those few individuals who know about my meetings with my father's killers have asked if today I feel a release, a relief, whether the encounter proved to be a catharsis. I am not sure if the answer is that simple, that black or white. I guess it's like jumping into the unknown, the fire of what you fear most, and then experiencing the gift of release where Fear no longer holds you hostage. Ironically, after meeting with me, I think both Clive Derby-Lewis and Janusz Waluś were left with much more.

○

By dealing with my demons, resentments and anger, my relationship with my beloved daughter Khaya has blossomed in ways I never thought possible when I was blacked out or high in active addiction. Today I am present and involved; I'm able to see her for the amazing human being she is. The more I like myself the better a parent I become.

On telling Khaya that uncomfortable things would be revealed in the writing of this book, she astounded me with her wisdom when she calmly said, "At least everything will be out." She damn near brought me to tears with her, "You know, Mummy, everybody has something" ... What a champ. I am constantly awed by her love and capacity to forgive. I started my sobriety journey for myself but, Lord knows, I continue with a ferocious fight because there is no way I am going to steal any more of my baby's time.

Sometimes, of course, progress doesn't feel like it's happening fast enough, but on days when I am not regretting my past wrongs or panicking about my future, about who I am and what I have or haven't done, I experience true moments of serenity.

My rebirth – as I choose to look at my life now – is often filled with amazing surprises. I never thought there would be a time when I would experience a sense of peace with my mother, but over the last two years an unexpected healing has taken place between us. I can sense that me living my best life clearly fills her with pride. I like to think of us as a work in progress, which is the beauty of relationships, right?

Although I always believed I had a great relationship with my sister Momo, it couldn't have been that strong because it was riddled with my lies and deception. Today our foundation is rock solid. My sister is still my loudest cheerleader and best friend.

When it comes to my beloved Khwezi, I have a deep sense that as I get stronger in my recovery, the more at peace my sister grows in the other realm.

But perhaps the place I feel my changes most deeply is my perception of *myself* in terms of what being Chris Hani's daughter means to me. From the moment Daddy was shot, I had my guard up about being my father's daughter because that fateful Sunday morning was the last time I was just Lindiwe. It especially upset me when I was introduced, not as myself but as "Chris Hani's daughter" – usually in the most inappropriate settings. High on coke and trashed on booze at a party or a club, the last thing I wanted to be associated with or acknowledged for was being "Chris Hani's daughter". Of course, my father Chris Hani was always my hero. Coming to terms with the fact that he was the whole country's hero was an extremely difficult process for me.

While I was immensely proud of him, of what he stood for and of what he achieved in his lifetime, his hugeness only made me more achingly aware of how little I had done in my life, how I was nothing – a fraud, a fake and an addict – and that I could never come anywhere close to reaching the realms of my father's life, so why bother even trying? I mean, one of the reasons I used drugs and booze was to block out being reminded of my link to my father, to kill the painful awareness of what an immense disappointment I must be to him.

Usually, once people found out who my father was, they would immediately proceed to tell me where they were and what they were doing on the day of his death. They would extrapolate on their theories about who had conspired to kill him, while I was left listening, just a vessel, expected to witness their pain, silently nodding while being torn apart by my own hurt. It was as though I disappeared, as though they forgot that he was *my* father, murdered in our driveway, that I had lost my dad. I was torn between pride and the pure selfishness of wanting to keep him to myself.

Today I am learning to accept that people need to remember my father, pay their respects to him, and by telling me their stories, they are healing from their pain, just like I am healing by telling mine. And as I get better, my heart opens in ways I didn't think possible; it's no longer so much about poor me, and slowly I am able to receive others.

Living one day at a time and filling each of these days with presence and commitment has made me feel less and less as though I have wasted my life. There is something so exhilarating about being able to say, "I am a recovering addict". Besides raising my daughter, getting clean and sober is the most successful thing I have ever done. It is a badge I wear with pride.

When I think of Daddy I am no longer filled with this terrible shame about the life I wasted for so long. I think all the blessings I am inundated with in my new, clean life are his stamp of approval, it's as though he's cheering me on, like he used to when I won my races all those years ago in Maseru.

There is not a day that passes where I don't experience at least one true moment of joy. The more I live in my truth, the more life opens up, presenting endless possibilities. Today when I look in the mirror I am beginning to like what I see, and have started to accept myself, flaws and all.

They say an addict hurts at least 40 people while abusing substances. But I guess the person I hurt most in my years of using was *myself*. So by staying clean and sober "just for today", I make amends to myself and so the circle of healing grows.

Acknowledgements

I would really like to mention my higher power for consistently protecting me from harm and always being a presence I can turn to.

I have been incredibly blessed to have experienced intense and powerful love this far, and I've had the best teachers who have gone on to be my guardian angels. I would be nowhere without my father, Thembisile Martin Hani. Thank you for teaching me unconditional love, love for reading, exercise, theatre and being the epitome of a gentleman and a soldier.

To my sister Nomakhwezi Lerato, the pain of missing you has not lessened through the years and I don't think it will. However, through writing this, I have let go of that searing white anger I was consumed by after you left me. I now truly understand that you are in a better place and I see so much of you in Khaya. Thank you for always telling me how amazing I was even when I didn't believe you. You always thought I was destined for greater things and this small step is a tribute to you. I love you forever and a day.

Sikhulule, my first love. There were so many days I felt that I would not make it without you, where I felt my heart would literally break onto a million pieces. I thank you for always allowing me to be myself and teaching me love.

My grandfather, Ntatemoholo Sekamane you were so tough and loving, thank you for raising the Sekamane brood and extending yourself to your grandchildren.

Makhulu, thank you for Daddy. Thank you for your kindness and unconditional love.

Mama there are no words to completely convey my gratitude and love. You made what had to be incredibly hard seamless to me. My childhood was filled with so much joy and unbridled freedom, which would not have been possible without your determination that it should be so. As an adult, facing my own challenges, I have come to understand and accept what life gives one, and how one has to work hard to persevere. Thank you for being the most amazing grandmother to Khaya and for being the best mother you could to me. I love you.

Ausi Neo aka Momo, you are my rock, my cheerleader, my best friend, my boss, my children's mother, Khaya's other mother and my beloved sister. I have tears forming as I think of all you have done and all that you are to me. There is no way I would have been able to get clean and write this book if you were not in my life. Since I can remember you have always been my protector. I am in awe of you and when I grow up I want to be like my big sister. I love you to the ends of this earth.

Siviwe my amazing Sbals, I have always wanted a brother and Momo made the wisest choice by marrying you. Thank you for your unconditional support and love. I don't know many men who would take on what you do, including me, but I am forever grateful that you are one of them. You are such an incredible Khulu to Khaya and we love you to pieces. Thank you my Sbals.

My gorgeous children – Lukhanyo, Zukolwethu and Nantombi. You bring me so much joy and I love you to the moon and back. Thank you for being kind, loving, hilarious and supportive children who just make your aunt want to be better all the time.

Sammy, your prayers have not gone unnoticed. Thank you for always keeping me in your prayers and being Nkhono to me and great Nkhono to Khaya although you will forever be our Sammy. I love you.

Pali, you have always supported me and even came all the way to Joburg to help with Khaya when she was born. You are an amazing sister and your strength and fighting nature is inspirational to me. I love you.

Tsitso, my darling B. Ours didn't start smoothly, with you usurping my role as youngest. Your consistent belief in me and your support is so overwhelming. I love and take pride in the man that you are becoming and am so happy that you are in my life. I love you so much.

Malome Mophete, thank you so much for always being supportive and understanding. Love you.

Malome Tjaoane and Mabasotho thank you for being constants in our lives, and just for your love and support. Love you.

Ausi Tlalane, thank you for being an amazing older sister and just listening without any judgement. I love you.

Carsten, Chilli and Milla – I love you and you have my heart.

Selloane, I love the woman you are becoming and your never-ending love and support. I love you and thank you for my gorgeous Silva.

Aunty Faz, you took a broken young girl into your heart and there is no way I can thank you for that. I was blessed to have you as a mother while navigating through the rough teenage years, up until today. Uncle Sam, thank you for opening your home, heart and being there for me. I love you both.

Darling Aunty Foz, thank you for not only being my mother but an amazing friend and a true testament of courage and kindness but most especially teaching me what forgiveness looks like. I am in awe of you as you continue to fight to live your best life. I love you.

My cousins, Luigi, Alessia, Tsepo and Arif, without you guys my life would be that much less. I love you guys, and thank you for always standing by my side no matter how hard I made it.

The Surtie family, thank you for all your love and support.

To the following families that made my childhood incredible growing up in Maseru: Baffoe, Tsotsi, Maieane, Mofolo, Monyane, Pokane, Mccarthy. I have so much love for you.

The Dongwana family, thank you for all your love and support.

The Mhlanga family, thank you for opening your home during

my childhood and always making me feel like one of the family. I love you.

To Uncle Ronnie, Tandy, Samuel and the Watson family – I love you and thank you for all your love and continued prayers.

Nomathemba, our 31-year-old connection transcends friendship – you are my sister. You will never know how much your love and support has meant to me and of course that occasional kick up my rear. You, my friend, make my heart sing.

To Ausi Kay and Alex Sexwale, I love you and thank you for always being there.

Zani, thank you for my incredible gift.

Gogo Tomato, thank you for always being there for me and Khaya. Your support and love means the world to me. We love you very much.

I would like to thank Saheti and the larger Greek community for your constant support during my time there and now while Khaya is there. Kpia Soula, your support towards me and my family is so appreciated.

The wonderful and loving Constantinides family for everything you did for me. You made what was the worst moment of my life that much more bearable and I will forever be grateful.

Houghton House, you saved my life. I would like to thank all the counsellors who helped me and continue to help me today. Alex, Nikki, Lauren, Sascha, Lindsey, Zarina, Franke and Miriam – thank you for your support during my time there.

My amazing counsellor Etienne, words are not enough. Thank you for pushing me and believing that I can do it.

Thank you to Elli and my outstanding relapse prevention group. You guys have been incredibly helpful throughout this entire journey.

To all the amazing friends I have met in recovery, thank you so much for all your support.

To all my friends who have stood by me – Keabetsoe, Cherie, Vuyo and Mathahle – I love you guys.

It takes a village to raise my Khaya and without the support of the following people it would be that much harder: Uncle Bones, thank you for all you do for us, for your kindness and support. To the women who have helped me and continue to help me raise Khaya – Matlou, Dolly, Matumelo and Zempilo – you have my eternal gratitude. Kea Leboha.

To the Sekamane and Molisane families, thank you.

To Chris, your constant and continuous support and love means the world. Thank you.

To Ntate Ngatane, thank you for always being there for our family.

To Janusz – it feels weird to express my gratitude to you. But, there was something magical that began to happen to me during our meetings, which felt like healing and acceptance. Thank you for giving me that space and being willing.

To my Mel, without you none of this would have happened so quickly. You saw something in me while I was in active addiction and I believe that was when the wheels started turning. Thank you so much for treating me with such kindness and love, for respecting my story and for your endless patience. This journey has been so meaningful and I have grown so much largely due to your constant encouragement. I love you.

Finally, my reason for breathing. I always knew I would have a daughter but never in my wildest dreams could I have dreamed of an amazing child like my Khaya. You are everything I prayed for and more. I love your courage and wisdom beyond your years. Thank you for choosing me, thank you for having faith in me and thank you for being incredibly loving and just all round brilliant. I am incredibly blessed to have you. I love you to the moon and back my Kiki.

To every single person who has always supported and believed in me, I have not forgotten. I have a place in my heart for you.

And finally to the South African people who have always kept our family in your hearts and prayers – thank you.

– Lindiwe Hani

☽

Lindiwe Hani, we have walked a long, long journey together. From the moment our paths crossed I had a gut feeling about you and this story. I would like to thank you for trusting me with your deepest pain and secrets. It was a hard one to navigate – and there were times when I know I drove you mad with my demands and 4am WhatsApp reminders. I was often torn between being a fellow recovering addict, the co-writer, a friend and also the publisher. Sometimes I got it all mixed up. But we made it. You are an amazing woman, a real courageous champ. I learned so much this last year, about both you and recovery – but most of all, I learned a lot about myself and you were the one who taught me. Thank you. I am so damn proud of you. I love you deeply.

Thank you my darling Mat for being my beautiful anchor and trusted love. You are the sun and moon in my life. I love you forever.

James and Dan – my two amazing sons – you have grown to understand your mother is a writer and crazy woman – you give me so much space to be me. I adore you both. Lili and Nic, my other two special ones, and Juliane Birling my new sister – I love you all.

To my siblings Jennifer, Gillian and Neil – I send you much love.

My friends Martine Margoles, Pumla Dineo Gqola, Val Wiggett, Megan Furniss, Peta Frysh, Darryl Tuchman, Candice Etberg, Monica Cromhout – thanks for years of love and support.

To Bridget Impey – my friend and mentor – you will never know how much you teach me about publishing and how much your unswerving support means to me.

Thank you to Maggie Davey, Nadia Goetham, Shawn Paikin, Palesa Motsomi, Megan Mance, Patience B Tshuma, Janine Daniel, Leigh-Anne Harris and Shay Heydenrych and all the other staff at Jacana who tirelessly work to make my MFBooks come to life.

Thank you Sean Fraser for your insights and sensitive editing.

Thank you to the prison authorities at Kgosi Mampuru Prison for organising and allowing us to interview Janusz Waluś. Janusz, thank you for the courage to pitch up.

Thank you to all the lovely souls who attend my writing

workshops who inspire me to keep learning.

Thank you Chris Hani for leaving behind such a gigantic legacy and a beautiful daughter. Your life inspires us.

Thank you Andrew Nkadimeng and the National Arts Council for supporting this work.

I would especially like to thank Anton Harber and the Taco Kuiper Fund for Investigative Journalism, administered by Wits Journalism, whose invaluable assistance helped make this work possible.

Much thanks to Luli Callinicos, for the use of excerpts from your interview with Chris Hani, weeks before he died in 1993.

Lastly, I need to thank Lucy the Stray cat who kept me and my iPad great company on dark winter mornings when words were struggling to be delivered.

– Melinda Ferguson